THE
1960S

THE
1960S

Edward J. Rielly

American Popular Culture Through History
Ray B. Browne, Series Editor

GREENWOOD PRESS
Westport, Connecticut • London

Library of Congress Cataloging-in-Publication Data

Rielly, Edward J.
    The 1960s / Edward J. Rielly.
        p.   cm.—(American popular culture through history)
    Includes bibliographical references and index.
    ISBN 0-313-31261-3 (alk. paper)
        1. United States—Civilization—1945–.   2. Popular culture—United States—
History—
    20th century.   3. Nineteen sixties.   I. Title.   II. Series.
E169.12.R53   2003
973.923—dc21   2002066888

British Library Cataloguing in Publication Data is available.

Library of Congress Catalog Card Number: 2002066888
ISBN: 0-313-31261-3

First published in 2003

Greenwood Press, 88 Post Road West, Westport, CT 06881
An imprint of Greenwood Publishing Group, Inc.
www.greenwood.com

Printed in the United States of America

The paper used in this book complies with the
Permanent Paper Standard issued by the National
Information Standards Organization (Z39.48-1984).

10 9 8 7 6 5 4 3 2 1

Contents

Contents

Series Foreword

Popular culture is the system of attitudes, behavior, beliefs, customs, and tastes that define the people of any society. It is the entertainments, diversions, icons, rituals, and actions that shape the everyday world. It is what we do while we are awake and what we dream about while we are sleep. It is the way of life we inherit, practice, change, and then pass on to our descendants.

Popular culture is an extension of folk culture, the culture of the people. With the rise of electronic media and the increase in communication in American culture, folk culture expanded into popular culture—the daily way of life as shaped by the *popular majority* of society. Especially in a democracy like the United States, popular culture has become both the voice of the people and the force that shapes the nation. In 1782, the French commentator Hector St. Jean de Crèvecœur asked in his *Letters from an American Farmer*, "What is an American?" He answered that such a person is the creation of America and is in turn the creator of the country's culture. Indeed, notions of the American Dream have been long grounded in the dream of democracy—that is, government by the people, or popular rule. Thus, popular culture is tied fundamentally to America and the dreams of its people.

Historically, culture analysts have tried to fine-tune culture into two categories: "elite"—the elements of culture (fine art, literature, classical music, gourmet food, etc.) that supposedly define the best of society—and "popular"—the elements of culture (comic strips, best-sellers, pop music, fast food, etc.) that appeal to society's lowest common denominator. The so-called educated person approved of elite culture and scoffed at popular culture. This schism first began to develop in western Europe in the fifteenth century when the privileged classes tried to discover and develop differences in societies based on class, money, privilege, and lifestyles. Like many aspects of European society, the debate between elite and popular cultures came to the United States. The upper class in America, for example, supported museums and galleries that would exhibit "the finer things in life," that would "elevate" people. As the twenty-first century emerges, however, the distinctions between popular culture and elitist culture have blurred. The blues songs (once denigrated as "race music") of Robert Johnson are now revered by musicologists; architectural students study buildings in Las Vegas as examples of what Robert Venturi called the "kitsch of high capitalism"; sportswriter Gay Talese and heavyweight boxing champ Floyd Patterson were co-panelists at a 1992 SUNY–New Paltz symposium on Literature and Sport. The examples go on and on, but the one commonality that emerges is the role of popular culture as a model for the American Dream, the dream to pursue happiness and a better, more interesting life.

To trace the numerous ways in which popular culture has evolved throughout American history, we have divided the volumes in this series into chronological periods—historical eras until the twentieth century, decades between 1900 and 2000. In each volume, the author explores the specific details of popular culture that reflect and inform the general undercurrents of the time. Our purpose is to present historical and analytical panoramas that reach both backward into America's past and forward to her collective future. In viewing these panoramas, we can trace a very fundamental part of American society. The "American Popular Culture Through History" series presents the multifaceted parts of a popular culture in a nation that is both grown and still growing.

Ray B. Browne
Secretary-Treasurer
Popular Culture Association
American Culture Association

Introduction

The decade of the 1960s was a time of great change in American culture. The winds of change, sometimes more like a tornado, swept across the cultural landscape, uprooting the old and depositing the new. These changes were exciting, troubling, horrifying, energizing, depending on one's individual attitudes toward past traditions and beliefs. Every historical period brings some transformations, but the 1960s seemed to replace an old world with a new one. Even those Americans who wanted to remain faithful to past practices could not totally resist what was happening around them.

If change was like a powerful tornado in the 1960s, the decade began instead with a light breeze, significant but generally welcome. Modernization was in the air. For the first time, the country would have a president born in the twentieth century, regardless of the outcome of the 1960 election. That choice was aided by a new force in politics—television. The first televised presidential debates occurred, and the electronic medium gave its blessing to Senator John F. Kennedy over Vice President Richard Nixon. The Massachusetts Democrat was handsome, charming, and self-confident; the camera liked him, and so did the voters. On Inaugural Day, the former war hero, Dwight Eisenhower, in his seventies, turned the White House over to the forty-three-year-old Kennedy, the youngest man ever elected president, and to his beautiful wife, Jacqueline, and their young children, Caroline and John. The decade was off and running.

The country quite literally was running, as the new President pushed a program to get America more physically fit while the First Lady set the style in women's fashions. Dark clouds occasionally blew by, first a failed invasion of Cuban exiles with U.S. support at the Bay of Pigs in Cuba, and then a confrontation with the Soviet Union over Russian missiles in Cuba.

The former led President Kennedy to advocate construction of fallout shelters, and the latter brought the possibility of nuclear war home to Americans who, despite their fears, did not fully understand how close they had actually come to war. Yet these events failed to dampen the optimism most Americans felt in a nation enjoying economic prosperity and continued status as the greatest of the world's superpowers.

Women were flocking to stores and poring over Sears catalogs to find a pillbox hat like the kind that Jackie wore. At home, they were trying new recipes that Julia Child demonstrated on public television and giving some thought to a new type of kitchen appliance called the microwave, still too expensive for most families. Fathers and mothers, if they had not already done so, were thinking of moving their families to suburbs and considering adding a second car, possibly the cute and economical Volkswagen Beetle. Shopping was more convenient with the spread of shopping malls where consumers could find lots of shops grouped close together and plenty of parking space. A McDonald's probably stood nearby, offering a quick hamburger, fries, and soft drink. Life was good for most Americans.

Literature and the arts moved farther away from established traditions, sometimes building on changes that had started in the previous decade, such as the birth of rock and roll, most prominently displayed in the late 1950s by Elvis Presley. New directions in literature were ushered in by the Beats, including the 1950s Bibles of the Beat generation, *Howl*, a poem by Allen Ginsberg decrying the dullness of the Eisenhower years and heralding the coming of a vibrant counterculture, and the autobiographical novel *On the Road* by Jack Kerouac. As the 1950s turned into the 1960s, Andy Warhol switched from commercial art to serious, realistic depictions of objects and people from popular culture. Images of soup cans and Coca-Cola bottles became art, and pop art became the artistic rage of the decade, forever mangling the old distinction between high and low art. Before long, Roy Lichtenstein was borrowing comic-strip techniques for his canvases.

Much of the nation's confidence and optimism were derailed when on November 22, 1963, an assassin's bullet shattered the nation's innocence. The Kennedy years, known as Camelot after the idealistic reign of king Arthur portrayed in the popular musical of the early 1960s, ended with the death of the young president, and change, which had seemed so benign, increasingly grew more complex, mixing good with bad, celebrations of human creativity with violence, dissent, and divisiveness.

Other assassinations would follow: Civil Rights leader Martin Luther King, and the dead president's brother, then running for that position himself, Robert Kennedy. The longest war in American history, the Vietnam War, heated up steadily during the second half of the decade and generated such powerful antiwar sentiment that the country was ripped apart over the conflict as millions of young men and women began seriously to question (often demonstrating against) not only their national government but anything that smacked of traditional authority. By the late 1960s, millions of adults had joined the young in opposing the war, but they were less likely to share the younger generation's interests in drug use, including LSD and marijuana. Nor did the older generation much like the new, freer sexual attitudes. "Make love, not war" was a common slogan that fused two paths of resistance to inherited norms regarding sexuality and patriotism.

A young rock group calling themselves the Beatles landed on American shores in 1964, starting a revolution that swept through music and fashion. When they performed on *The Ed Sullivan Show*, the result was "Beatlemania," a kind of crazed frenzy that resulted in massive record sales, new hairstyles for young men (imitating the long mop-top style of the group), and fascination with anything British. A multitude of other British groups followed the Beatles' path to America, bringing with them also the "peacock" look, with textured vests, paisley shirts, and very wide ties. The miniskirt, soon omnipresent on young and not-so-young women, also was a British export, principally the work of British designer Mary Quant. Much more would happen in fashion as in music before the end of the decade.

Not a little of what transpired in music did so at concerts, some of them folk concerts, others rock, as rock gradually assumed from folk the musical mantle of the counterculture. Among all of the 1960s concerts, Woodstock, in 1969, stood out, quickly becoming one of the defining events of the decade. Although rock became the most prominent form of music in the 1960s, folk staged a strong comeback, country spread its popularity into urban areas, soul music conveyed the dreams and pains of African Americans, pop and classical retained adherents, and jazz expressed, albeit for a smaller number of listeners than rock, perhaps the greatest degree of innovation. For future generations of Americans, the music of the 1960s would come largely to define the decade, along with the Vietnam War and political assassinations.

Not too far behind the music in popularity, though, was dance. The ultimate dance of the 1960s was the twist, popularized by Chubby Checker. A variety of other youthful dances with such strange names as the frug, the jerk, and the mashed potato attracted practitioners, not all of them young. Millions of teens learned new dances by watching their peers dance on Dick Clark's *American Bandstand* show, which also helped many singers reach stardom. Ballet also earned headlines during the 1960s, especially when the great Russian dancer Rudolf Nureyev defected to the United States in 1961.

The counterculture steadily increased in influence and visibility. Hippies in long hair, beads, and psychedelic clothing celebrated the Summer of Love in San Francisco in 1967, bringing the section of the city known as

Haight-Ashbury forever into the nation's geographical consciousness. Young people experimented with communal living, free love, and alternate types of spirituality. Masses of young people turned out for antiwar demonstrations, most publicly at the Democratic National Convention in Chicago during the summer of 1968, in the aftermath of the King and Robert Kennedy assassinations. In opposition, President Nixon established his political success largely by appealing to what he labeled the "Silent Majority," those Americans, primarily older, who longed for a return to the way things had been, even as the world was inexorably changing.

The 1960s also experienced revolutions in sports. Vince Lombardi took his Packers from small-town Green Bay to the first Super Bowl, in 1967, winning sports immortality for himself and his team while helping to inaugurate the Super Bowl as an American institution. In 1961, Babe Ruth's unbreakable single-season home run record of sixty was broken by another Yankee, Roger Maris. A young former Olympic gold medalist, Cassius Clay, won the heavyweight boxing championship from Sonny Liston in 1964. Within three years, the champion had joined the Nation of Islam, renamed himself Muhammad Ali, refused induction into the Armed Services, and for that refusal was stripped of his title and convicted of draft evasion. His refusal to serve highlighted growing opposition by African Americans to fighting for a country that appeared at home to deny them true equality.

Americans changed their travel habits during the 1960s. Cars were used more than ever, as family members had to drive to get to work and go shopping from their homes in the suburbs. More families went on extensive vacations by car on the improved highways that were replacing the old Route 66 and other suddenly antiquated roads, stopping along the way at motels and appreciating the ongoing beautification of the highways inaugurated by the Johnson administration. They had to share the highways, however, with large trucks that were hauling much of the freight that a few years before would have snaked across the land on railroads. Railroads declined in importance, especially for carrying passengers, and airplanes attracted new travelers as improved planes and greater wealth allowed more Americans to fly. The sky seemed more welcoming with the successful space flights beckoning Americans ever higher, despite a rash of skyjackings.

Throughout the 1960s, much else happened in popular culture, a great deal of it radically new. The growing medium of television, which started to broadcast in color, proved especially useful to advertisers, and advertising reciprocated with an unparalleled explosion of its creative imagination. New buildings soared skyward, seemingly denying gravity itself, as architects and engineers discovered new ways to combat wind and weight. Moviegoers enjoyed a diverse menu of films that exhibited a high level of artistry while also reflecting changing attitudes and lifestyles in the country. *In the Heat of the Night, Midnight Cowboy, The Graduate, Easy Rider,*

Bonnie and Clyde, and *Rosemary's Baby* were only a few of the films that staked out new filmic territory in racism, sexuality, drugs, violence, and the supernatural. Television, a common guest in families' living rooms, therefore remained more conservative. Nonetheless, some of the 1960s series, such as *The Twilight Zone, The Fugitive,* and *Gunsmoke,* earned lasting critical acclaim and an equally long life through reruns. *Rowan and Martin's Laugh-In* and *The Smothers Brothers Comedy Hour* were two of the most overtly 1960s shows in their irreverence and social satire.

In all of these ways and more, the 1960s changed the popular culture of the United States dramatically and permanently. The decade was a wild and heady ride, sometimes agonizingly sad, on occasion simply foolish, but seldom boring. Above all, it was a time to be young. Almost anyone who was anybody in those days was young, or so it seemed.

Timeline of the 1960s

1960

- The Winter Olympics are held in Squaw Valley, California, featuring the American hockey team upsetting the heavily favored Russian team and winning the gold medal (February 18–28).
- Elvis Presley is discharged from the U.S. Army (March 5).

  Joan Baez and Pete Seeger play at the Newport Folk Festival (May).
- The Summer Olympics take place in Rome, Italy, with Cassius Clay, the future Muhammad Ali, winning the gold medal in light heavyweight boxing; other major U.S. winners are Wilma Rudolph, Rafer Johnson, and the basketball team (August 26–September 11).
- John Kennedy and Richard Nixon engage in the first of their televised presidential debates (September 26).

  Martin Milner and George Maharis take their first ride in their Corvette on the television series *Route 66* (October 7).

1961

Bob Dylan begins to perform in Greenwich Village clubs (January).

- Jacqueline Kennedy wears a pillbox hat to the presidential Inauguration, setting off a pillbox craze among American women (January 20).

  Poet Robert Frost recites his poem "The Gift Outright" at the Kennedy Inaugural (January 20).

  The first Hardee's fast-food restaurant opens, specializing in charcoal-broiled hamburgers and cheeseburgers (May 5).

  Newton Minow labels television a "vast wasteland" before a gathering of the National Association of Broadcasters (May 9).

  Russian ballet star Rudolf Nureyev defects to the United States (June 16).

  Ernest Hemingway kills himself with a shotgun in his Ketchum, Idaho, home (July 2).

Roger Maris of the New York Yankees breaks Babe Ruth's single-season home-run record by hitting his 61st of the year (October 1).

Wilma Rudolph is named female athlete of the year by the Associated Press (December 18).

1962

John Glenn becomes the first American to orbit Earth (February 20).

Wilt Chamberlain scores one hundred points in a game, a National Basketball Association (NBA) record (March 2).

Jack Paar concludes his run as host of *The Tonight Show* (actually called *The Jack Paar Show* during his tenure); substitute hosts preside until Johnny Carson takes over on October 1 (March 20).

Students for a Democratic Society (SDS) releases its Port Huron Statement (June 12).

Ray Charles' album *Modern Sounds in Country & Western Music* goes gold (July 19).

Actress Marilyn Monroe dies after apparently taking a drug overdose (July 22).

Sonny Liston becomes heavyweight boxing champion by knocking out Floyd Patterson (September 25).

The Beverly Hillbillies strike oil on television as one of the most popular television series ever (September 26).

Federal legislation is approved declaring LSD a hallucinogenic drug that must be regulated by law (October).

James Brown records *The James Brown Show Live at the Apollo*, one of the most famous live albums of all time (October 14).

1963

Schlitz sells beer in new tab-opening aluminum cans (February).

Julia Child demonstrates on television how to prepare *bœuf bourguignon*, beginning a series of cooking lessons on educational television stations (February 11).

Sylvia Plath, author of *The Bell Jar*, commits suicide (February 11).

Wilt Chamberlain sets a National Basketball Association (NBA) field goal percentage record of .528 (March 19).

Timothy Leary, the LSD guru, is dismissed from the faculty of Harvard University (May).

Joan Baez, Pete Seeger, and other artists perform at the first nonprofit Newport Folk Festival (July).

Little Stevie Wonder becomes the first performer simultaneously to top the American pop singles, pop albums, and rhythm and blues singles charts (August 24).

Dr. Martin Luther King, Jr., delivers his "I Have a Dream" speech at the Lincoln Memorial in Washington, DC (August 28).

Millions of people remain in front of their television sets by the hour to watch events relating to the death and funeral of President John F. Kennedy, with regular programming returning on November 26 (November 22–25).

1964

Los Angeles Dodger pitcher Sandy Koufax is named athlete of the year (January 20).

The Beatles perform on *The Ed Sullivan Show* (February 9).

Cassius Clay (later Muhammad Ali) becomes heavyweight boxing champion by knocking out Sonny Liston (February 25).

Kitty Genovese is murdered outside her apartment building in New York City while neighbors ignore her calls for help (March 13).

Twelve Beatles records are on the top one hundred list (April).

Jim Ryun, a high school student, runs the mile in less than four minutes (June 5).

A San Francisco bar features topless go-go girls (June 19).

The first Arby's fast-food restaurant opens, specializing in roast beef sandwiches (July 23).

Students initiate the Free Speech Movement at the University of California, Berkeley (October).

At the Summer Olympics in Tokyo, the United States wins ninety medals, the Soviet Union ninety-six (October).

ABC, CBS, and NBC simultaneously broadcast in color for the first time (December 20).

1965

Disc jockey Alan Freed, rock-and-roll pioneer caught up in the "payola" scandals, dies in poverty at Palm Springs, California (January 20).

Singer Nat "King" Cole dies of lung cancer (February 15).

A teach-in to oppose the Vietnam War occurs at the University of Michigan, beginning a new antiwar tactic (March 2).

The restaurant T.G.I. Friday's opens in New York City, catering to young singles (March 15).

The Astrodome, an indoor domed sports facility, opens in Houston (April 9).

In a rematch, Muhammad Ali knocks out Sonny Liston in the first round with the famous "phantom punch" (May 25).

Bob Dylan switches to an electric guitar at the Newport Folk Festival and is roundly booed (July 25).

The Highway Beautification Act is enacted to improve the appearance of the nation's highways (October 22).

Vatican II ends in Rome; church officials later issue new guidelines that modernize Catholic ritual and church architecture (December 5).

1966

From this date forward cigarette packages contain a warning that "Cigarette smoking may be hazardous to your health" (January 1).

Simon and Garfunkel's "The Sounds of Silence" is Number One in *Billboard* for the week of January 1 (January 1).

Truman Capote's novel *In Cold Blood* is published (January 17).

Barry Sadler's "Ballad of the Green Berets" begins a thirteen-week reign atop the charts (March 6).

The U.S. Supreme Court rules that Ernesto Miranda's rights were violated during questioning after his arrest, leading to promulgation of the Miranda rights in law and on countless television crime shows (June 13).

Singing legend Frank Sinatra and young actress Mia Farrow marry (July 19).

Radio station WOR-FM in New York City switches its programming to rock as FM stations begin their association with the counterculture (July 31).

Starship *USS Enterprise* makes its first flight as *Star Trek* launches on NBC (September 8).

Betty Friedan and other advocates for women's rights create the National Organization for Women (NOW) (October 29).

Physician Sam Sheppard, model for the lead character on the television series *The Fugitive*, is found not guilty of murdering his wife (November 16).

1967

The Rolling Stones perform the song "Let's Spend the Night Together" on *The Ed Sullivan Show* (January).

The Green Bay Packers defeat the Kansas City Chiefs 35–21 in the first Super Bowl (January 15).

Johnny Carson wears a Nehru jacket on *The Tonight Show*, creating an instant fashion craze (February).

The Smothers Brothers Comedy Hour premieres on CBS (February 5).

Random House publishes the supernatural thriller *Rosemary's Baby* by Ira Levin (April 13).

Muhammad Ali refuses induction into the Armed Services and subsequently is stripped of his championship and convicted of violating Selective Service laws (April 28).

The Beatles' album *Sgt. Pepper's Lonely Hearts Club Band* is available for sale in the United States (June 2).

The Monterey International Pop Festival occurs in Monterey, California, beginning the Summer of Love (June 16–18).

William Styron's *The Confessions of Nat Turner* is published by Random House and engenders controversy over its depiction of Turner (September 9).

The rock-musical *Hair* opens on Broadway (December 2).

Three days after recording "(Sittin' On) the Dock of the Bay," Otis Redding dies in a plane crash (December 10).

1968

Abbie Hoffman and Jerry Rubin found the Youth International Party, a radical group better known as the Yippies (January 16).

The New York Times runs an article entitled "An Arrangement: Living Together for Convenience, Security, Sex," which publicizes the growing practice of college students living together outside marriage (March 4).

Students for a Democratic Society (SDS) members occupy buildings at Columbia University to protest the Vietnam War (April).

The science-fiction film *2001: A Space Odyssey* opens in New York City (April 3).

Dr. Benjamin Spock, author of *Baby and Child Care*, and four other antiwar protestors are tried for conspiring to aid draft resisters; Spock and three others are convicted, but the verdict is later overturned (May 20–June 14).

The documentary *Hunger in America* airs on CBS (May 21).

Valerie Solanas shoots and seriously wounds pop artist Andy Warhol (June 3).

The encyclical *Humanae Vitae*, by Pope Paul VI, is published, reaffirming opposition by the Catholic Church to artificial means of birth control (July 29).

Tom Wolfe's *The Electric Kool-Aid Acid Test* appears from Farrar, Straus and Giroux, describing the 1964 LSD trip across the country by Ken Kesey and his Merry Pranksters (August 19).

Jeannie C. Riley achieves a gold record with her single "Harper Valley PTA" (August 26).

Television viewers watch massive antiwar demonstrations at the Democratic National Convention in Chicago (August 26–29).

Tommie Smith and John Carlos protest U.S. racial injustice and South African apartheid with a black-glove salute after winning medals at the Olympic Games in Mexico City (October 16).

Jackie Kennedy marries Greek shipping tycoon Aristotle Onassis (October 19).

Elvis Presley returns to concert performances from films with a televised performance popularly known as "The 68 Comeback" (December 3).

1969

The New York Jets deliver on quarterback Joe Namath's promise of victory by defeating the favored Baltimore Colts in Super Bowl III, 16–7 (January 12).

The first commercial Boeing 747 flight lands successfully (February 8).

The Doors' Jim Morrison is arrested and charged with obscene actions while performing in Miami (March 1).

The *Concorde* supersonic airliner makes its first flight (March 2).

Beatle John Lennon and Yoko Ono marry (March 20).

Delacorte Press publishes Kurt Vonnegut's novel *Slaughterhouse-Five* (March 31).

Bandleader Duke Ellington celebrates his seventieth birthday at a White House party hosted by President Richard Nixon (April 29).

The film *Midnight Cowboy* opens (May 25).

The play *Oh, Calcutta!*, featuring total nudity, opens Off-Broadway (June 17).

Police raid the Stonewall Inn, a gay bar in Greenwich Village, precipitating the "Stonewall Riots" and the beginning of the gay liberation movement (June 27).

Harper Lee's novel of southern racism, *To Kill a Mockingbird*, is published (July 11).

The film *Easy Rider*, starring Peter Fonda and Dennis Hopper, opens (July 14).

Neil Armstrong walks on the moon (July 20).

Members of Charles Manson's "family" commit multiple murders, including the murder of actress Sharon Tate (August 9).

Almost one-half million people watch many of the country's most famous singers and musicians perform at Woodstock, New York (August 15–17).

The Arlo Guthrie film *Alice's Restaurant* opens (August 24).

The "Amazin' Mets" complete their World Series triumph over the heavily favored Baltimore Orioles (October 16).

Jack Kerouac, author of *On the Road*, dies of alcoholism (October 21).

The Rolling Stones perform at the Altamont Music Festival, with one person dying in a confrontation with members of the Hell's Angels motorcycle gang (December 6).

Tiny Tim, falsetto singer of "Tiptoe Through the Tulips," and Miss Vicky (Victoria May Budinger) marry on Johnny Carson's *The Tonight Show* (December 17).

PART ONE

LIFE AND YOUTH DURING THE 1960S

THE 1960S

1

Everyday America

Everyday life in the United States brought both increased comfort and growing social challenges during the 1960s. The economy, increasingly urban rather than rural centered, proved healthy, improving the quality of life of the majority of Americans. Salaries, corporate profits, increased use of credit and installment buying, and a strong stock market characterized the economic life of the decade.

Developments in health care, including invention of the pacemaker and new surgical procedures, held out the promise of a longer and more pleasant life, while Medicare and Medicaid made health care more accessible to millions of Americans. Smoking was recognized as a dangerous habit, and efforts to reduce smoking accelerated. Parents continued to receive guidance from Dr. Benjamin Spock, the "baby doctor."

The 1960s initially seemed to most Americans like a new world, younger and more energetic. President John F. Kennedy and his family brought glamor, charm, and enthusiasm to the political scene, but that spirit soon dissolved in assassinations as the president, his brother, and prominent civil rights leaders were gunned down.

Americans felt the tide changing after November 22, 1963. Although democratic ideals spread through the Civil Rights and feminist movements, changes were often accompanied by social upheaval, including massive demonstrations and even urban riots. Crime came increasingly to be felt as a deeply ingrained threat to everyday peace and security, and the Vietnam War, generally supported by Americans early in the decade, became a catalyst for powerful social protest. After the Tet Offensive of 1968, the nation largely turned against the war effort in the face of rising casualties and the perception that the nation was engaged in an effort it seemingly could not win.

THE ECONOMY AND HEALTH CARE

Increasing numbers of Americans during the 1960s continued to move from farms and small towns into cities or suburbs, while many others already in cities opted to move out into the surrounding suburban communities. The farm population during the decade consequently decreased from 8.7% of the total population in 1960 to 5.1% in 1969, continuing the steady decline that had been occurring throughout the century.[1]

The majority of Americans benefited from the continuing economic expansion as the country shifted from an industrial economy to a postindustrial business and service economy less reliant on heavy industrial manufacturing. The gross national product almost doubled during the 1960s, surpassing $930 billion in 1969.[2] Salaries tended to rise, with per capita income close to $4,000 by 1970, almost double what it had been ten years before, and the government during the mid-1960s provided a tax cut for corporations and for individuals in the top tax rate to stimulate continued growth. Several oil companies established their headquarters in the South, for example, Mesa Petroleum and Tenneco in Texas; or in the West, such as the Los Angeles-based Getty, Occidental, and Union. This geographical shift of the oil industry from the Northeast to Sunbelt states signaled a larger shift along the same geographical path for a range of American industries.

Wherever Americans were working, they were able to invest some of their additional earnings in a stock market that remained bullish for much of the decade. Three-fourths of Americans in this robust economy owned their homes, most of them financing the purchase with a mortgage, typically paying 20% down and financing the rest over a period of twenty or more years through a bank or savings and loan institution. The list price of the home rose from an average of about $16,000 at the beginning of the decade to approximately $23,000 by the end, while interest rates rose from 6% to almost 8%. The average construction cost of a new home increased from $12,625 to $15,550.[3]

The home mortgage was only one source of indebtedness for most American families. In a more affluent environment, Americans were less likely to worry about buying appliances, cars, and other large-ticket items on credit. Both household installment buying and car loans more than doubled during the decade, and the credit card became a common means of purchasing items large and small. San Francisco's Bank of America introduced its Bankamericard early in the decade, and later in the decade MasterCard and Master Charge appeared. Bank of America sold its credit card business to a banking consortium, and the card became the VISA card; Master Charge and MasterCard merged, the latter name surviving. By the end of the decade, some fifty million bank cards were in consumers' billfolds and pocketbooks. Short- and intermediate-term consumer credit (e.g., car loans, installment credit, small personal loans, and credit-card debt) climbed from about $56 billion in 1960 to over $122 billion in 1970.[4]

Despite the relatively rosy economic picture facing Americans in the 1960s, shoppers liked a bargain. Discount stores buying directly from manufacturers and featuring high-volume sales, self-service, and low prices began to push aside traditional department stores. In 1962 alone, four major discount chains—Wal-Mart, Kmart, Target, and Woolco—opened.

As the decade approached its end, the economic boom began to subside. With the Vietnam War overstimulating the economy, prices and interest rates began to rise, depressing the housing market, real earnings, and business profits, while increasing unemployment.

American workers were less likely to belong to unions as the decade advanced, and the power of unions, although still considerable, began to lessen. Approximately 31% of nonfarm workers were union members in 1960; by the end of the decade the figure was down to about 27%.[5] The merged American Federation of Labor and Congress of Industrial Equality (AFL-CIO), headed by George Meany; the United Automobile Workers (UAW), with Walter Reuther as president; and the United Steelworkers of America (USWA), led by I.W. Abel, used their strong political clout to gain good wages and benefits for their members and elect candidates of their choice, including Presidents Kennedy and Johnson. However, the legal troubles of Jimmy Hoffa of the Teamsters, who was accused of ties to organized crime and convicted of jury bribing, cast a partial cloud over unionization; and at the end of the decade Meany and Reuther clashed over the Vietnam War, Meany supporting the war effort and Reuther opposing it. The election of Republican Richard Nixon as president in 1968 further weakened organized labor's influence.

A combination of prosperity for the majority and expanded social programs for the poor created real advances in medical care that improved the quality of life for millions. The pacemaker was developed in 1960 by William Chardack, permitting many people with diseased hearts to live reasonably normal lives. Eye surgery proved easier and safer with laser surgery, first used by Dr. Charles Campbell in 1962. In the same year, Valium became available as a muscle relaxant, helping to ease both physical and emotional pain. Another boost to eye care (and to people's concern about personal appearance) occurred in 1965 with the invention of soft contact lenses. Dr. Michael De Bakey invented an artificial heart in 1963 to keep pumping blood while the patient underwent heart surgery. Four years later came the first successful heart transplant, as Dr. Christiaan Barnard, a South African, placed a new heart in a grocer named Louis Washkansky. The patient lived for eighteen days, suggesting longer-term survival possibilities for future heart recipients. By 1969, a Houston surgeon, Denton A. Cooley, was able to implant an artificial heart in a patient.

The line between life and death became a bit clearer in 1968 when the American Medical Association adopted a new definition of death. The determining factor became brain death, or the absence of brain waves. The new standard was especially important for surgeons trying to determine when an organ could ethically and legally be removed for transplant from a patient on life-support systems, and for families of terminally ill patients trying to make the hard decision whether to stop treatment.

The dangers of cigarette smoking became more evident during the 1960s. In 1964, the Surgeon General's Report linked smoking to lung cancer and a number of other illnesses, including heart attacks. National legislation followed in 1965 requiring a warning label on tobacco products: "Caution: Cigarette smoking may be hazardous to your health." Many Americans as a result tried to stop smoking, and the customary association of smoking with glamor slowly began to fade.

Millions of parents looked to the "baby doctor," Benjamin Spock, for assistance, as parents had been doing since 1946, when his *The Common Sense Book of Baby and Child Care* first appeared. By the 1960s, the renamed *Baby and Child Care* was still supplying helpful information about infant nutrition and illnesses while reassuring parents fearful of their new parental responsibilities. During the 1960s, though, some Americans would accuse Dr. Spock, who became a prominent antiwar activist, of fostering rebellion by encouraging permissive child-rearing practices.

Health care became more available to Americans in 1966 when Medicare and Medicaid programs went into effect. Approved by Congress and President Johnson in 1965 as amendments to the Social Security Act of 1935, Medicare provided compulsory health insurance for all U.S. citizens sixty-five or older who were eligible for Social Security or Railroad Retirement benefits. Medicaid provided medical assistance to low-income Americans who were aged, disabled, or pregnant; and to members of families with dependent children, along with certain other categories of people with special needs and limited resources. Medicare also made available hospital insurance and, for a monthly premium, an optional medical insurance plan to cover physician and outpatient services.

POLITICS AND POLITICAL LEADERS

Americans elected John F. Kennedy as president in 1960 by a razor-thin margin over Richard Nixon. The youthful Kennedy, at forty-three the youngest man ever elected president and the first president born in the twentieth century, seemed to epitomize a nation that finally had left the post–World War II years behind. His beautiful and stylish wife Jacqueline (almost universally referred to familiarly as Jackie) and their young children, John and Caroline, brought vigor and exuberance to the White House.

President Kennedy, aided by his brother Robert, who served as Attorney General, hailed a New Frontier in space, promised that the United States would put a man on the moon before the end of the decade, encouraged physical fitness, and embraced the Civil Rights movement.

As television use increased during the 1960s, the telegenic Kennedy and his beautiful wife used the new medium successfully. Kennedy performed

President John Kennedy and First Lady Jacqueline Kennedy ride to The
White House on Inauguration Day in 1961. Many Americans felt the
Kennedys brought a sense of style and vigor to the White House.
Source: Photofest, Inc.

calmly and confidently during the first-ever televised presidential debates
to establish himself as a legitimate presidential candidate against the better
known Richard Nixon. Later, Americans followed the First Lady on a televised tour of the White House. She also appeared regularly at cultural events
and set fashion trends with her bouffant hairstyle and pillbox hat. Meanwhile millions of Americans followed closely the lives of the Kennedy children and were charmed by photographs of the president playing with them
or taking his family boating. The same Americans grieved with the First
Family when their son Patrick died shortly after his birth in August 1963.

On November 22, 1963, President Kennedy was assassinated while riding in an open limousine in Dallas, Texas. The event was all the more trau-
matic for Americans because the First Family had become so much a part
of their own lives through television and the print media. Kennedy's funeral was covered live on television and ushered in a period of national
mourning. Many Americans felt that a special time of youth, excitement,
and promise had been snuffed out almost before it began. In the national
dialogue, the term assigned to this brief moment was Camelot, the

legendary home of King Arthur and the Knights of the Round Table and the subject of the musical *Camelot*, which was a favorite of the Kennedys.

President Kennedy's apparent assassin, Lee Harvey Oswald, was quickly apprehended. Two days after his arrest, Oswald was being transferred to another facility when Jack Ruby, a Dallas nightclub owner, walked up to Oswald and shot him. Oswald's death, and the subsequent death of Ruby from cancer in 1967, left open the still debated conspiracy theory regarding the president's death—that others, including Cuban dictator Fidel Castro, organized crime figures, and perhaps even government agents, might have been involved in the assassination.

Lyndon Baines Johnson succeeded Kennedy as president and inaugurated a series of Great Society programs, including his War on Poverty, especially after scoring a landslide reelection victory over Republican Barry Goldwater in 1964. The ambitious Great Society that Johnson envisioned was modeled after the New Deal of Franklin Roosevelt. Johnson sought to extend economic opportunity and justice under the law to all. Among his efforts that had considerable impact on Americans were the Food Stamp Act to help low-income families afford nutritional food; the Economic Opportunity Act, which established the Job Corps and VISTA (a domestic version of the Peace Corps created under President Kennedy to assist underdeveloped nations); the Housing and Urban Development Acts to provide additional public housing and assist both renters and home owners to afford adequate housing; and the previously mentioned Medicare and Medicaid programs.

Few Presidential campaigns have shocked and divided the public as much as the 1968 race for the White House. The campaign was marked by a strong showing in the Democratic primaries by Senator Eugene McCarthy, who attracted vehement support from young voters, especially those who opposed continuation of the Vietnam War; the assassination of Robert F. Kennedy, at the time a U.S. Senator from New York, after his June victory in the California primary; widespread antiwar demonstrations at the Democratic Convention in Chicago; and a strong showing on the part of segregationist George Wallace, Governor of Alabama, who carried five southern states in the general election. Americans split not only along party affiliation, but by age, race, views on women's rights, and whether the United States' foreign policy was directed toward trying to save or conquer. For the rest of the decade, the generation gap and other manifestations of national divisiveness would haunt the nation. In addition, a third Kennedy brother, Massachusetts Senator Edward "Ted" Kennedy, accidentally drove off a bridge on Chappaquiddick Island off the coast of Massachusetts in July 1969. Mary Jo Kopechne, who was in the car, drowned. The accident contributed to the growing sense of tragedy associated with the Kennedy family and the national questioning of whether the family labored under some sort of curse. The accident helped bring to a turbulent political end what had become an increasingly violent and turbulent decade.

CIVIL RIGHTS AND THE FEMINIST MOVEMENT

Americans were coming to see both African Americans and women differently in the 1960s, as both groups struggled to achieve equal opportunity in basic areas of daily life. Throughout the history of the United States, African Americans had resisted bigotry in many forms, including slavery, southern Jim Crow laws, and discrimination in such areas as housing, employment, and education. The modern Civil Rights Movement began in the 1950s and accelerated in the 1960s.

Although many men and women were deeply involved in the movement, the most widely recognized leader was Dr. Martin Luther King, Jr. King was a Baptist minister and head of the Southern Christian Leadership Conference. He preached nonviolent resistance patterned after the Indian leader Mahatma Gandhi and employed a wide range of nonviolent strategies, including boycotts, sit-ins, and marches. His efforts included demonstrations in Birmingham, Alabama, in 1963, that were met by brutal police repression and were widely reported on television news, leading to expanded popular support for the Civil Rights Movement; and the March on Washington in the same year, during which Dr. King gave his famous "I Have a Dream Speech" before the Lincoln Memorial, presenting his vision of a society in which all people would be judged by their character rather than their skin color. The speech quickly became one of the most famous documents in the history of the country, taking its place with President Kennedy's Inaugural Speech as two 1960s documents that countless Americans would revere, and schoolchildren would study, even memorizing selected passages.

On April 3, 1968, King gave his final speech, "I've Been to the Mountaintop," in which he described both his vision of the future and his belief that he would not live to see it. That prophecy came true the following day when he was shot and killed in Memphis, Tennessee.

The assassination of Dr. King by James Earl Ray, who was arrested and convicted of the murder, sparked riots in several cities that disrupted life for millions and further divided the nation. Earlier race riots had occurred in Harlem in New York in 1964 and 1967, in the Watts section of Los Angeles in 1965, and in Detroit during the summer of 1967.

The struggle for equal rights was never easy during the decade, as organizations such as the Ku Klux Klan as well as a variety of individuals and state governments fought back, sometimes violently. Segregationists understood that the church was often the center of life in African American communities, including the center of civil rights planning. Consequently there was a wave of church bombings, especially in Arkansas and Alabama. The most deadly attack was directed against the Sixteenth Street Baptist

Martin Luther King, Jr. provided moral and political leadership to the
Civil Rights Movement before being assassinated in 1968.
Source: Photofest, Inc.

Church in Birmingham, Alabama, on September 15, 1963. Four girls, aged
ten to fourteen, died in their Sunday School classrooms. In 1964, three civil
rights workers—Michael Schwerner and Andrew Goodman, both white,
and James Chaney, an African American working with the National Association of Colored People (NAACP)—were murdered in Mississippi by Ku

Klux Klan members. These and other deaths contributed to both a clearer understanding for Americans of the dangers involved in the Civil Rights Movement and wider support for ending racial injustice.

Death came by assassination also to other leaders of the Civil Rights Movement. Medgar Evers, a prominent NAACP activist, was gunned down outside his home in Jackson, Mississippi, in 1963. Malcolm X (born Malcolm Little), a charismatic speaker who in 1964 left the black separatist organization the Nation of Islam (headed by Elijah Muhammad), was murdered in 1965, in his case by three African Americans having some ties to the Nation of Islam, although it was never proved that they were acting on behalf of the organization.

Malcolm X had become a rival of Dr. King's for the mantle of most influential black leader in America. Increasingly during the 1960s, segments of the African American community had become more militant, often carrying out their struggle for justice under the Black Power slogan. A broad concept with an assortment of economic, educational, political, and social associations, Black Power often included a militant commitment to black nationalism, that is, African American advancement without reliance on white assistance and without much interest in integration. It was very much a self-help attitude because, as some militant proponents argued, blacks could rely on and trust only other blacks.

The Black Panthers, inspired by Malcolm X, rejected the nonviolent, integrationist approach of Dr. King. Huey Newton and Bobby Seale founded the Black Panthers in North Oakland, California, in 1966, naming the organization after an animal that combined blackness with a reputation for fighting fiercely. The Black Panthers focused simultaneously on community service through such social programs as free breakfasts for school children and a paramilitary style of clothing and demeanor. Committed to black nationalism, the organization grew more confrontational, becoming involved in a well-publicized shootout with Oakland police in 1967. A police officer was killed, and Newton, who was wounded, was convicted of manslaughter but later saw his conviction overturned.

Despite the skepticism felt by many African Americans toward government action, the federal government did take many strong stands in favor of equal rights during the 1960s. Important legislation included the Civil Rights Act of 1964, which outlawed racial segregation in public facilities and banned gender discrimination; ratification of the Twenty-Fourth Amendment to the U.S. Constitution in 1964, prohibiting poll and other voting taxes; the Voting Rights Act of 1965, making literacy tests for voting illegal and authorizing federal examiners to register voters in federal and state elections; and the Civil Rights Act of 1968, which included several provisions to ensure fair housing practices. These developments helped increasing numbers of African Americans to improve their living conditions and participate in the democratic process.

African Americans were not alone, though, in seeking redress of conditions they considered illegal and unjust. The American Indian Movement (AIM) tried to focus the nation's attention on treaty violations. Founded in 1968 in Minneapolis, Minnesota, the organization pushed for a stronger self-governing role on Indian lands and for the U.S. government to uphold treaty agreements. To dramatize their demands, members of the organization and supporters temporarily occupied Alcatraz Island, site of the former prison, in 1969. A Sioux treaty, they claimed, required that unused federal land revert to Indian ownership.

On the whole, the American Indian civil rights efforts were much smaller in scope than efforts waged by African Americans. The federal government, however, did enact the American Indian Civil Rights Act of 1968 in an attempt to ensure that Native Americans living under tribal governments would possess the same civil right protections enjoyed by other Americans. In addition, the Civil Rights Act of 1968 is sometimes called the "Indian Bill of Rights" as it explicitly extended the federal Bill of Rights and other civil rights laws to Native Americans residing on reservations. Throughout American society, old stereotypes involving Native Americans began to lessen during the 1960s. Television programming grew more sensitive to their depiction, and in a society more open to diversity, many Americans learned more about the sufferings and accomplishments of Native Americans.

GENDER ISSUES

Gender joined race as a focus of civil rights struggles. Women increasingly looked at themselves and concluded that a variety of forces had kept them from realizing their potential. The resulting growth in the feminist movement brought about major changes in American society.

Betty Friedan, a graduate of Smith College and a middle-class housewife, began to feel in the 1950s that despite her marriage, children, and comfortable home, she was missing something in life. Wondering whether other women had similar feelings, she mailed a questionnaire to Smith graduates. The results of her survey and further research convinced her that the root of the problem lay in the feminine mystique, that is, the generally accepted view of the ideal woman as a person defined by marriage and motherhood. The result was her book entitled *The Feminine Mystique* (1963), which argues that women lose their own self-identity within such a definition and stop growing intellectually and emotionally.

Friedan's book propelled her into the vanguard of the feminist movement. In 1966, she formed the National Organization for Women (NOW) with the help of other like-minded women and served as its initial president. The organization spread rapidly, forming chapters throughout the country, and advocated for changes in a number of common practices, such as opposing help-wanted ads that stipulated hiring of men only and the practice of airlines firing stewardesses (later called flight attendants) if they married or reached the age of thirty-two. NOW published a bill of rights for women, argued for the right of women to decide whether to have an abortion, and pushed the concept of equal pay for equal work regardless of the gender of the worker.

Many significant changes occurred during the 1960s, at least partly in response to the feminist movement. Title VII of the 1964 Civil Rights Act outlawed sex discrimination in businesses employing twenty-five or more people, the Equal Employment Opportunity Commission (EEOC) banned males-only (and females-only) advertisements in newspapers, women were permitted to rise in the military beyond the rank of colonel, laws against abortion began to ease, and the word "sexism" moved permanently into the English lexicon to denote a pattern of ingrained discrimination against women.

During the 1960s, women's career paths became more varied. Previously acceptable choices such as teaching, nursing, and secretarial work (seen as extensions of the woman's traditional nurturing role) were joined by expanding opportunities in business and the military. Pay disparities on the basis of gender were serious obstacles for women, especially for those increasing numbers who were single heads of households. The federal government attempted to address the problem with passage of the Equal Pay Act in 1963. The percentage of the workforce made up of women rose during the decade from approximately 32% to over 36%.[6]

The popular media continued to portray women in traditional roles, for example, on the television series *The Adventures of Ozzie and Harriet* and *Leave It to Beaver*. Readers of such popular women's magazines as *McCall's* and *Ladies' Home Journal* would have seen little evidence of a feminist movement. Nonetheless, changes were occurring, and not only in the workplace. Women were furthering their education in greater numbers, with bachelor's degrees conferred on women increasing between 1960 and 1970 from about 136,000 to 343,000, and master's degrees rising from approximately 26,000 to 83,000.[7] The advances in education would lay the groundwork for subsequent gains by women throughout American society in the 1970s and beyond.

CRIME

Despite general prosperity and improvement in the quality of life in many facets of society, not all was well in the United States during the 1960s. In addition to assassinations and social conflict over civil rights and feminism, crime and war negatively impacted society at home and abroad.

The Kitty Genovese case seemed to symbolize to many Americans a growing impersonality of modern urban society. In the early morning of March 13, 1964, Kitty Genovese was attacked and murdered outside her

New York City apartment building. Her calls for help lasted for thirty-five minutes and were ignored by other residents. The incident struck Americans as indicative of a society that had turned away from the concept of neighbors helping neighbors to a world in which individuals lived in fear and isolation, neither responding to others' troubles nor able to expect assistance for their own.

Increasingly, Americans, especially the elderly or others living alone in large cities, had come to view their apartments or houses as something akin to forts. Multiple door locks, window locks, and drawn window shades replaced open windows and evenings spent sitting on the front porch. One effect of the Genovese murder was to alert Americans to the isolation in which many people lived and call forth a greater commitment to interacting with neighbors.

The decade also witnessed a number of horrific serial and mass killings that engendered widespread fear in those locales where the killings occurred, but also throughout the country. Albert DeSalvo, known as the "Boston Strangler," raped and killed women from 1962 to 1964 in eastern Massachusetts, his victims numbering thirteen. The crimes received national media coverage, although DeSalvo was actually convicted only of robbery and rape, not of murder. Whether he committed the murders attributed to him remains questionable. Charles Whitman in 1966 murdered his mother and wife and then climbed to the top of a clock tower at the University of Texas in Austin, from which perch he gunned down anyone he could see. Counting his wife and mother, he killed fifteen during his rampage and wounded thirty-one before being shot to death by police.

Richard Speck, also in 1966, entered a dormitory in Chicago one night and gathered eight student nurses in a bedroom, assuring them that he wanted only money and would not harm them. One by one he took the young women into another room and either stabbed or strangled each one. A ninth potential victim survived by hiding under a bed. Arrested and sentenced to die in the electric chair, Speck saw his punishment changed to eight terms in prison of from fifty to 150 years each after the U.S. Supreme Court ruled that opponents of the death penalty had been improperly excluded from the jury.

In 1969, Americans were shocked by the brutal and bizarre murders carried out by Charles Manson and his followers in California, the victims including actress Sharon Tate, wife of film director Roman Polanski. The murderers left behind expressions such as "DEATH TO PIGS" and "HEALTER SKELTER" (sic) in blood on walls and a refrigerator. Fortunately, the murderers were apprehended and sentenced to prison terms before they could continue their attacks. The horrific nature of these crimes, the fact that they occurred throughout the United States rather than in one area, and the massive media attention given them ended for millions of Americans the old feeling that "it couldn't happen here."

Amid the public perception that criminal violence was endangering the safety of average Americans, the Supreme Court issued a controversial decision affirming the rights of the accused, specifically the right against self-incrimination. The decision was based on the case of Ernesto Miranda, a twenty-three-year-old man arrested on suspicion of kidnapping and rape. After being subjected to two hours of questioning by police, Miranda confessed and ultimately was convicted. He appealed the verdict all the way to the Supreme Court, which ruled that the rights to remain silent and have an attorney present during questioning are fundamental to preserving the Fifth Amendment protection against self-incrimination. The decision was by a razor-thin five to four majority vote of the Court. Henceforth, police were obliged to "Mirandize" a suspect before questioning. That is, they had to inform the individual of the basic rights to remain silent, have an attorney present, and be provided with an attorney if the suspect cannot afford one, along with the caution that anything that the suspect says may be used against the individual in court. This Miranda warning would become well known to most Americans through police shows on television. Meanwhile, many Americans felt that the warnings went too far in protecting criminals rather than victims of crimes.

If Americans often felt more in danger of criminal violence during the 1960s than in the past, statistics seemed to give some credence to that impression. The rate of violent crimes, in fact, ascended sharply. In 1960, rates of aggravated assault, rape, and murder or manslaughter were 85, 10, and 5 per 100,000 people; ten years later the rates per 100,000 for the same three categories of crimes were 163, 19, and 8. In addition, the rate for robberies increased from 60 to 171.[8]

Crime, however, was increasingly perceived by Americans not only as actions by individuals or small groups of people against isolated victims and businesses, but as an evil embedded in the fabric of society. The extent to which organized crime had become rooted in the United States became visible to Americans when Joe Valachi, a member of the Genovese crime family, testified before a Senate committee. He described how the Mafia, also known as the Cosa Nostra, was organized in crime families throughout the country and carried out its gambling, extortion, and other illegal activities through legitimate companies and with the assistance of corrupt politicians and government figures. Valachi died of cancer in 1969, the same year his memoirs, *The Valachi Papers*, were published.

Americans, though, felt much more frightened of street crime and random violence than of organized crime. The average American worried about walking down a city street alone at night or of an intruder in the house more than of organized crime, which remained largely hidden to most Americans. If they intellectually knew that organized crime was a major problem, they felt, all too strongly, the potential for violent crime personally striking them.

WAR IN SOUTHEAST ASIA

Americans were increasingly aware of the danger of crime in their society, but it would be warfare that would come closer to ripping the country apart. At the beginning of the decade, few Americans knew much about Southeast Asia and the countries North Vietnam, South Vietnam, Laos, and Cambodia. Indeed, if they gave much thought to the region, it was more likely to be in relation to exotic vacation spots, or on a geography test in school.

At the beginning of the 1960s, fewer than 800 U.S. military personnel were in Vietnam to carry out America's advisory role.[9] Military advisors, most famously the Special Forces (popularly known as the Green Berets), counseled the Vietnamese in a wide span of areas, from military strategy to ways to improve the country's agriculture, health care, and finances. Americans also helped to train Vietnamese forces and instructed them in communications, intelligence gathering, and use of weapons. The goal was to help South Vietnam develop the ability to retain its independence from communist North Vietnam. The other countries in the former Indochina, Laos and Cambodia, also faced communist threats.

Few Americans, though, paid much attention during the early years of the decade. At the time of President Kennedy's assassination, the number of American military in Vietnam had risen only to 16,000. However, civil unrest in South Vietnam began to make the evening news back home in the United States, and some of the pictures were deeply disturbing. On June 11, 1963, Buddhist demonstrations against the regime of President Ngo Dinh Diem reached a horrifying climax when the much respected seventy-three-year-old Buddhist monk Thich Quang Duc sat down on a Saigon street, remained motionless as another monk poured gasoline over him, and then lit a match, burning himself to death to protest the Diem government. In November, a political coup toppled Diem, who was killed, apparently by members of his own military.

Although Americans were horrified by some of the scenes that saw on television, most still largely supported the war effort, which they believed would contain the spread of communism and which was not yet costing large numbers of American lives (about 300 American deaths by August 1964). Thus, there was little opposition to President Lyndon Johnson's appeal for congressional support in early August of 1964 when two American destroyers apparently came under attack by North Vietnamese torpedo boats in the Gulf of Tonkin. Although the precise extent of the attack would remain highly uncertain, the U.S. Congress, with just two senators and no congressmen in opposition, passed the Tonkin Gulf Resolution on August 7. The resolution granted Johnson the authority to "take all necessary measures to repel an armed attack against the forces of the United States and to prevent further aggression." The open-ended wording permitted Johnson to carry out an undeclared war largely as he saw fit. However, the al-

The Vietnam War was the longest and most protested war in U.S. history, taking the lives of approximately 58,000 Americans. While U.S. soldiers were fighting overseas, Americans staged protests and sit-ins on college campuses nationwide. Source: Photofest, Inc.

most unanimous vote for the Tonkin Gulf Resolution clearly demonstrated that most Americans supported their nation's involvement in the war. Supporting their president and nation in time of war had been the traditionally patriotic approach, and that remained the case through the middle of the decade.

Between 1964 and 1968, the United States steadily moved from an advisory role to spearheading the military action against North Vietnam and the guerrilla forces in the South known as the Viet Cong. As 1968 began, close to half a million U.S. military personnel were in Vietnam, and over 16,000 Americans had been killed in the conflict. Yet there was cause for optimism, as the Viet Cong proclaimed a cease-fire in conjunction with the annual three-day Vietnamese holiday known as Tet, scheduled to begin on January 30.

Instead of at least a peaceful interlude, if not a step toward lasting peace, Tet became the largest military action of the war up to that point. Viet Cong infiltrated into cities and towns across South Vietnam and launched waves of attacks; North Vietnamese units joined the Tet Offensive in selected cities, such as the ancient imperial capital of Hue not far from the demilitarized zone separating North and South Vietnam. In Saigon, Viet Cong even entered the U.S. Embassy compound.

The communist assaults were repelled, in some cases with great loss of American lives, and the Viet Cong (unknown to Americans at the time) were largely destroyed as a coherent military force, resulting in the North Vietnamese forces having to take over prosecution of most of the war from then on. Although a military defeat for the communist forces, the Tet Offensive proved a psychological and public relations victory for them. Back home in the United States, viewers of the evening news and readers of the nation's newspapers, who had been assured that victory was forthcoming, saw what seemed to be just the opposite. Millions of Americans concluded that rather than victory, American forces were not able to secure even the largest cities of South Vietnam. The assault on the embassy seemed to suggest that no place in the country could be made truly safe. Images like the one by AP photographer Eddie Adams of General Nguyen Ngoc Loan executing a Viet Cong suspect with a pistol shot pointblank at his head further aroused opposition to the war. Many people began to question whether the Vietnamese government that the United States was supporting deserved support.

For the rest of the decade, domestic opposition to the war increased. Mothers and fathers joined the college students and other youthful antiwar activists who earlier had provided most of the opposition to the war. President Richard Nixon, elected in 1968, responded to the growing loss of public support for American involvement by beginning a process of demilitarization, gradually turning over primary responsibility for carrying out combat actions to the South Vietnamese.

In 1969, Americans at home learned that U.S. soldiers under Lieutenant William L. Calley had massacred large numbers of Vietnamese civilians at a village called My Lai during the previous year. The number of victims ranged in various accounts from two hundred to five hundred. While large numbers of Americans were angered by the incident at My Lai, they also were greatly disturbed by rising death tolls. In the spring of 1969, the number of U.S. military personnel peaked at close to 550,000. Nixon's Vietnamization plan reduced that total to about 475,000 by the end of the year, at which point over 40,000 Americans had been killed in the conflict.

Back home, there was a growing demand to end the war. Attitudes toward patriotism and supporting the nation in wartime were changing. A more critical attitude spread among Americans of all ages, including parents who had lost sons to the war. Their country was no longer to be supported, "right or wrong," but only when it was morally right. The soldier, traditionally a hero to Americans, fell in stature. Many Americans blamed all soldiers for what some had done, as at My Lai, labeling them "baby killers." Others associated soldiers with drugs, and returning veterans often were treated with great disrespect, with many accounts of soldiers being spat at. Many veterans of the Vietnam War found it difficult to find a job because employers were concerned about drug use, worried about a veteran's emotional stability, or simply transferred feelings about the war to the returning soldiers.

About the time of the Tet Offensive, on January 23, 1968, the USS *Pueblo* was intercepted off the North Korean coast by North Korean ships. One crewmember was killed, several others were wounded, and Lieutenant Commander Lloyd Bucher surrendered. Korean vessels towed the *Pueblo* to shore and held the prisoners for almost a year, releasing the crew on December 23 after the United States issued a formal apology for spying. Many Americans believed that the ship should have continued fighting until sunk, while others viewed the apology as a national embarrassment. Coming shortly before the Tet Offensive in the Vietnam War, the lingering incident contributed to a growing sense of futility on the part of many people regarding American foreign policy and use of the nation's supposed military might.

THE CUBAN MISSILE CRISIS

The Vietnam War dominated America's news programs and front pages as the 1960s advanced, but it was not the only international crisis that directly affected the people of the United States during the decade. Shortly after taking office in 1961, President Kennedy was faced with a plan developed by the previous administration for overthrowing Cuban dictator Fidel Castro. Kennedy gave his approval, and on April 17, 1961, an invasion force of Cuban exiles went ashore at the Bag of Pigs. Quickly defeated, the invasion marked an embarrassing beginning in foreign affairs for the new president.

In the aftermath of the Bay of Pigs incident, President Kennedy urged Americans to take steps to protect themselves in case of attack, including construction of fallout shelters. Many companies, some of them selling their products by catalog, offered underground shelters in various sizes and designs. At the Texas State Fair in 1961, the fallout-shelter display drew huge crowds. Styles of shelters ranged from simple concrete block constructions to elaborate facilities that could comfortably house a whole family behind termite-proof walls and twelve-gauge corrugated metal doors. Top-of-the-line shelters included not only expensive furniture and appliances but pool tables, wine cellars, shelves of books, extensive inventories of food and drink, and other conveniences of home. While waiting to put their shelters into official use during an atomic war, many families utilized the rooms as children's clubhouses or family recreation rooms.

By October 1962, Cuba was even more on the minds of Americans as a nuclear war with the Soviet Union seemed a distinct possibility. Premier

Nikita Khrushchev of the Soviet Union deployed two dozen nuclear-armed ballistic missiles in Cuba. On October 22, President Kennedy announced a quarantine of the island, with American ships ready to confront any vessels carrying offensive weapons.

With Soviet ships en route to Cuba and a confrontation looming, Americans feared nuclear war. Many prayed, churches held prayer services, and families stockpiled food and supplies, in their fallout shelters if they had heeded the President's earlier advice, in their kitchens and basements if not. As the U.S. government sought a solution over an agonizing six-day period, citizens prepared for war. Finally, Khrushchev blinked, as the expression went, and agreed to dismantle the missiles. The United States gave a collective sigh of relief, having come perhaps closer to a nuclear war than at any other time in its history.

THE FAMILY, RELIGION, AND TRADITIONAL VALUES

The various "movements" involving the Vietnam War and the rights of women and minorities, the political turmoil that accompanied the presidential election of 1968, and a variety of changes discussed in later chapters, among them changing sexual standards, increased drug use, and radically different styles in clothes, put great strain not only on the country as a whole but also on individual families. Although many families came through the 1960s unscathed and as united as ever, others split apart, at least temporarily, typically along generational lines.

Moral and religious issues, played out in a variety of behavioral patterns, were often at the heart of family conflicts. Sexual freedom, including premarital sex, multiple sexual relationships, and unmarried couples living together, proved difficult for many parents to tolerate, let alone accept. Drug use by sons and daughters also was a cause of much family dissension.

Established religions lost much of their hold on young people, although searching for spiritual insights remained important to the young, who often traveled different paths for spiritual enlightenment, into drugs and religious cults, for instance. The young were not alone, though, in practicing religion differently. Efforts were made by both church institutions and worshippers to bring about fundamental changes in organized religions. A narrowing of the gap between this world and the next occurred as religions began to view themselves as more closely linked to this life, and sharp divisions between clergy and laity began to weaken.

Roman Catholics watched with great interest deliberations in Rome during the Second Vatican Council called by Pope John XXIII in 1962. By the time that the council had concluded its deliberations in 1965, there was a new pope, Paul VI, and the Catholic Church would never be the same. Lay people began to play a greater role in the church, the traditional practice of going to confession declined, the altar was turned around so that the priest faced parishioners, and Catholics were able to eat meat on Fridays. One of the most difficult issues for Catholics in the 1960s involved birth control. Although the Catholic Church continued to prohibit artificial means of birth control, including condoms and the pill, large numbers of Catholic women of childbearing age, many observers claiming an overwhelming majority of them, chose to practice birth control during at least part of their married life.

While Catholics were modernizing their religion, many Protestant groups were doing likewise. They were less inclined to interpret the Bible literally, more inclined to engage in ecumenical functions with Catholics, and more involved in the Social Gospel, focusing on the poor and those deprived of basic human rights. African American churches especially were in the forefront of the Civil Rights Movement, with some of the most famous clergymen of the decade, such as Martin Luther King, Jr., coming from the Southern Baptist tradition. Many churches in the Catholic and Protestant traditions began to offer social services to the poor in their communities, providing food and clothes for those in need.

Jewish Americans, while practicing Judaism in different ways depending on whether they saw themselves as Conservative, Orthodox, Reformed, or Reconstructionist, also became more involved in modern movements, especially Civil Rights. The Six-Day War between Israel and some of its primarily Moslem neighbors boosted Jewish Americans' sense of Jewish identity.

The social consciousness of the religions kept some young people involved in the established religions, but many older Americans sharply disagreed with the modernizing trends and what they saw as a shift from spiritual to political and social concerns. Religion grew ever more complex as the decade progressed. Tied closely to sexual practices, social concerns, and attitudes toward traditional authority, the nation's religions were caught up in the swirl of change occurring in the United States during the 1960s.

With so many changes in American society, families found it increasingly difficult to function as before. The family at the beginning of the 1960s was likely to join together around the dining room or kitchen table, attend religious services together, go shopping together, and vacation together. Some families continued that pattern, but a great many did not. Children and parents found themselves in disagreement in many areas of everyday life. Even when family members were not at odds, they were apt to go their separate ways much of the time because mothers were more likely to work outside the home, multiple cars allowed children to drive to school or play, and fathers often worked at a greater distance from home.

2

World of Youth

The decade of the 1960s can be considered, with at least reasonable justification, the decade of youth, as Americans came of age in record numbers. The number of Americans between the ages of fifteen and twenty-four increased from approximately 24,500,000 to about 36,000,000 during the decade.[1] In 1966, *Time* magazine named the "Twenty-Five and Under Generation" its Man of the Year. During the 1960s, the first wave of baby boomers, usually identified as individuals born between 1946 and 1964, became old enough to attend college, serve in the military, and assume the general responsibilities of adulthood.

This first installment of the nation's baby boomers entered a world more prosperous than the one their parents had experienced during the Great Depression of the 1930s and the World War II belt-tightening of the first half of the 1940s. This combination of increased numbers and greater prosperity made the young men and women of the 1960s a force to be reckoned with. Their impact on American society was great in several areas discussed in other chapters in this book, including music, clothing fashions, advertising, travel, and the performing arts. Such was their effect that the term "revolution" is often associated with this young generation. That there was a youth revolution during the decade is certain.

Also certain, though, is the reality that one can overstate the impact of youth on American society and the degree to which all (or even most) youth shared the same values and goals. While large numbers of young people were marching against the Vietnam War, working on behalf of civil rights for the nation's minority citizens, experimenting with drugs, and dropping out of mainstream society to live in communes, large numbers of other young men and women were doing what their parents had done (or at least aspired to do): get a good education, find a job, buy a house, raise a family, support the government, and attend church regularly.

Richard Nixon, after all, was twice elected president of the United States, once in 1968 and again in 1972, by appealing to what he called the "silent majority," those men and women, by no means all from the older generation, who remained generally conservative and traditional in their beliefs and lifestyles. This caution against overstatement is not meant to deny the very real and powerful influence of the young during the 1960s but to avoid overgeneralizing their behavior.

EDUCATIONAL OPPORTUNITIES

The 1960s offered significant advances in educational opportunities for the growing number of young men and women of college age, with the total number of students in higher-education degree programs increasing throughout the decade from 3,583,000 to 7,920,000.[2] A consequence of this expanding college population was that the campus became the center for a large portion of the youth revolution. It is reasonable to surmise that much of the civil rights and antiwar activity of the decade might not have occurred without the growing strength of this college population. Also of great importance were educational changes affecting younger students, for these, too, impacted American society, both during the 1960s and long afterward.

As the 1960s opened, schools throughout the South remained routinely segregated, despite the 1954 Supreme Court ruling known as *Brown v. Board of Education of Topeka, Kansas,* overturning the doctrine of "separate but equal" in American education. The Supreme Court had found that separate schools are by their nature unequal, but the court did not provide the legal or financial muscle necessary to implement its decision. Consequently, the South continued to impose a dual school system on its students of all ages. In the North, there also was much segregated schooling, the de facto result of differences in economic levels and residential patterns rather than through Jim Crow laws.

A decade after *Brown v. Board of Education,* the federal government finally supplied the muscle needed to transform segregated educational systems. The tool was Title VI of the 1964 Civil Rights Act, which denied federal funds to school districts that refused to desegregate. At the same time, large numbers of Americans, including college students, entered the civil rights movement. In the educational realm, highly publicized events, such as James Meredith's struggle to attend the University of Mississippi, which he accomplished in 1962 with the aid of federal troops, excited greater interest in the struggle for racial justice in education. Change did not come easily, but it came fairly fast. Aided by additional Supreme Court directives, such as its demand in *Green v. County School Board* (1968) for affirmative action plans by local school boards to bring about immediate integration, about 80% of African American students in the South were learning in integrated schools by the end of the decade. Approximately 44% of African American students in the South by then were in majority white schools. Only a few years before, in 1964 and 1966 respectively, just 2.3% and 12.5% were in integrated schools.[3]

Federal support for educational access across the entire age spectrum had a dramatic impact throughout the decade. The National Science Foundation, initially spurred into action by Russia's launching of *Sputnik* in 1957, continued to provide grants that led to improvements in the science and mathematics curricula of America's schools. The Higher Education Facilities Act of 1963 helped colleges and universities erect much-needed buildings. The Higher Education Act of 1965 established the financial aid triad of grants, loans, and work-study that enabled financially needy students, including many minority students, to attend college. It also provided support for improving teacher preparation and created the National Teacher Corps to bring educational opportunities to impoverished areas of the nation. The Elementary and Secondary Education Act of 1965 supplied funds and encouraged compensatory programs to help disadvantaged youth expand their academic horizons. These efforts expanded the number of students able to attend college and improved the quality of education at all grade levels.

It would be difficult to argue that any of these changes was of greater or more permanent importance than the establishment of Head Start in 1965. Part of President Lyndon B. Johnson's War on Poverty, the program provided an academic head start for boys and girls from low-income families to develop their academic potential. In addition to working on cognitive skills, this preschool program also provided medical, dental, and dietary assistance, and sought to involve parents in the educational process. Recognizing that a child's health and daily diet, as well as parental support, directly impact his or her educational performance was itself a revolutionary insight at the time.

Creative, pioneering educational theories played important roles in the creation of Head Start and in many other educational changes. Books such as A.S. Neill's *Summerhill* (1960) and Jonathan Kozol's *Death at an Early Age* (1967) helped Americans to understand the importance of focusing on the type of start that children received in school and what schools might do to foster or hinder a child's total development.

Across the age spectrum, change came to the country's schools: a more student-centered approach to teaching, open classrooms to foster community, team teaching to help students make connections across the disciplines, bilingual education to enhance learning for immigrants, active minority recruitment, and changes in college core curricula and the addition of new electives to make the curriculum more relevant. Educational change in the 1960s raised both possibilities and expectations from preschool through college. It also encouraged greater student participation in the social and political life of the country.

POLITICAL AND SOCIAL ACTIVISM

The college campus was the locus for a great deal of the political and social activism of the 1960s. College students brought their idealism to the
civil rights movement and later extended their efforts into other arenas. Especially reflective of the idealism that marked youth culture at its best was
the Peace Corps. President John F. Kennedy established the Peace Corps in
1961 and appointed his brother-in-law, R. Sargent Shriver, to direct it. Most
participants were college graduates who volunteered to serve in Third
World countries where, as goodwill ambassadors for the United States, they
worked to improve their hosts' quality of life. Much of their effort was directed toward child care, sanitation, and rural development. Later in the
decade, as growing numbers of young adults came to view the United
States as imperialistic and government work as collaborationist, interest in
the Peace Corps declined, although it never died out.

Students who had worked to extend the rights of minorities and the poor
soon began to look at their own situation. An event that focused national
attention on student rights occurred at the University of California at Berkeley in 1964 when the university sought to stop students from raising funds
and recruiting members for the Congress of Racial Equality (CORE) and
the Student Nonviolent Coordinating Committee (SNCC), organizations
dedicated to overcoming segregation and racial discrimination. When student Jack Weinberg was arrested for soliciting for CORE, another student
activist, Mario Savio, began what became known as the Free Speech Movement. Arguing that students' constitutional right to express themselves was
being violated, the students engaged in rallies and sit-ins, even occupying
the administration building. A student strike and strong support from the
faculty induced the administration to give in on the issue and permit student groups to recruit on campus.

Throughout the 1960s, student rights remained an important cause as
students demanded free expression, smaller classes, relevant curricula, and
a role in campus governance. Having tested their muscle in the Free Speech
Movement, students applied similar tactics to other causes, including the
antiwar effort. The Free Speech Movement was an important transitional
step between civil rights activism and coordinated opposition to the war.

One of many important student political groups was Students for a Democratic Society (SDS). Created as the Student League for Industrial Democracy in the 1930s, the organization adopted its more inclusive name in
1962 and in the same year, after its convention at Port Huron, Michigan,
expressed its commitment to participatory democracy in a document called
the "Port Huron Statement." Members often lived in economically disadvantaged communities, helping to organize rent strikes and offering other
assistance to residents. Chapters were only loosely tied to the parent organization, a structure that encouraged creativity, but also led to problems

with coordinated action. SDS became increasingly radical during the decade and shifted its primary focus to antiwar activities such as teach-ins, marches, and efforts to remove the Reserve Officers' Training Core (ROTC) from campuses. In 1968, SDS members took over buildings at Columbia University in a widely publicized campaign against the war and what they saw as an unholy alliance between military imperialists and the university. By the late 1960s, the diffuse organization was breaking apart. One of the best known splinter groups was the Weathermen, who during their self-declared "Days of Rage" in 1969 blew up a monument to policemen in Chicago's Haymarket Square.

Possibly the most watched example of political activism during the 1960s was the large-scale series of antiwar demonstrations that rocked Chicago and the Democratic National Convention during 1968, and which millions of Americans viewed on television. The protests by primarily youthful demonstrators resulted in forceful, some claimed brutal, police responses (CBS anchor Walter Cronkite even referring on the air to the police as thugs) and led to the famous Chicago Seven Trial. Seven protest leaders were indicted. Abbie Hoffman, Jerry Rubin, and Lee Weiner were Yippies, that is, members of the Youth International Party, an antiwar organization that Hoffman and Rubin created expressly for action at the convention. The other defendants were Rennie Davis, John Froines, David Dellinger, and Tom Hayden, the latter going on to a career in California politics. Judge Julius Hoffman proved controversial in his own right for his theatrical and confrontational style. Ultimately, five were found guilty of crossing states lines to incite to riot, but the U.S. Court of Appeals for the Seventh Circuit overturned the convictions in 1972 and chastised Hoffman, who to some observers had appeared biased against the defendants, for not conducting a fair trial.

Students continued to provide much of the leadership in antiwar activities throughout the decade, although the antiwar effort did not have a great impact on public policy until other forces joined the effort, including Civil Rights leaders, among them Martin Luther King, and certain political leaders. The Tet Offensive of late January 1968 made it clear that the United States was still far from winning the war, and mounting casualties brought larger numbers of mothers and fathers into opposition to the war. When Senator Eugene McCarthy of Minnesota, a strong opponent of the war, embarked on his 1968 presidential campaign, college students provided much of his volunteer force of campaign workers, leading his campaign to be dubbed the "children's crusade."

SEXUAL REVOLUTION

As in many areas of life in the 1970s, the young were not alone in carrying out the sexual revolution, but on the whole they were the most conspicuous segment of that movement. Considerable credit (or blame) for the revolution must be shared by a variety of forces and groups. The growing commercialism of American society created a consumer mentality abetted by greater prosperity than the Great Depression and World War II generations had known. Sex increasingly became part of that consumer society through magazines like *Playboy* (begun in 1953), birth control devices (especially the Pill), and a growing separation of sexual pleasure from marriage, with sexual relationships often viewed as temporary, consumable encounters.

Prior to the 1960s, many people, of course, engaged in premarital sex, but they continued to give public allegiance to permanent and monogamous relationships sanctioned by marriage while confining premarital encounters to their private, secret lives. Sex was not spoken of much in public, and if nice young men and women engaged in sexual relations, they (especially the women) did not broadcast that fact to others. Young men might view sex as part of their rite of passage to manhood, but usually with women they did not intend to marry. In such cases there was a clear dichotomy in their minds between nice girls that one might introduce to one's parents and the girls with whom it was all right to dally. Nice young women were expected to retain their virginity until marriage or, if they had premarital sex with their future husbands, to keep it a secret. Various factors conspired to break down those old standards, bring sex increasingly into the spotlight, and lead to public pronouncements in favor of recreational sex and nonmatrimonial sexual relationships.

The young pushed hard against traditional sexual mores in two major ways. First, many couples maintained a commitment to monogamous relationships but without marriage. Living together became increasingly common, with college students providing the most publicized examples. A prominent case involved a Barnard College student, Linda LeClair, who faced the Barnard Judiciary Council in 1968 charged with lying about her living conditions while sharing an apartment with her boyfriend. The relationship first came to light through a *New York Times* article about new living arrangements. LeClair did not apologize for her behavior or express shame, but defended herself by arguing that the college was violating her civil rights. The case was especially important because it moved beyond sexual morality into the arena of sexual politics and claimed publicly the right to engage in a relationship that included sex apart from marriage. The Judiciary Council found LeClair guilty of breaking college rules and imposed the penalty, if one can call it that, of forbidding her to eat in the college cafeteria. The decision was hardly a victory for the college because the council also recommended that the housing rules be liberalized.

The second major way in which youth rebelled against traditional sexual standards was through various versions of what was called "Free Love." Here the ideal was not the long-term committed relationship (with or without marriage) but acceptance of sex as a means of temporary pleasure and sexual partners as individuals mutually giving and receiving pleasure with no commitment strings attached. The concept of "sex in the streets" was a major attraction of the heavily advertised Summer of Love in San Francisco in 1967, as well as one of the attractions of the big music festivals such as the 1969 gathering at Woodstock.

Meanwhile, free love also became a political issue and tactic. John Sinclair of the rock group MC5, writing in 1968 in an underground Detroit newspaper, the *Sun*, called for an attack on U.S. culture and offered drugs, rock and roll, and public sex as his three main weapons. When the Yippies planned their assault on the Democratic Convention, they actively used sex as a lure to attract demonstrators, continuing to transform sexual activity into an antiestablishment weapon.

Technical advances in birth control and changing sexual mores permitted young Americans to engage in sexual activity freed from worries of pregnancy. The "Pill," an oral contraceptive, had been developed in the 1950s by Gregory Pincus and Howard Rock. By 1960, it had been sufficiently improved so that, aided by not only more liberal attitudes toward sex but also fear of global overpopulation, it received approval from the Food and Drug Administration for commercial distribution. The approved version, Enovid, manufactured by the G.D. Searle Company, initially was prescribed only to married women. Although the Intrauterine Device (IUD) also was improved and became more widespread during the 1960s, and condoms continued to be used, by the middle of the decade the pill had become the primary means of contraception. Its status was helped by legal cases such as *Griswold v. Connecticut* in 1965, in which the U.S. Supreme Court stated that decisions on contraception use fall within married people's constitutional right to privacy. The pill proved popular as well with college students as availability quickly spread to unmarried women.

The right to privacy issue also impacted the abortion debate during the 1960s. At the beginning of the decade, abortion was illegal in the United States, but that began to change as twelve states relaxed their antiabortion laws in the late 1960s. New York state even eliminated its residency requirement, making it possible for large numbers of women from other states to travel there for abortions. Unmarried women could choose the abortion option without interrupting their education or career to carry a pregnancy to term. Opponents of abortion argued that in addition to destroying human life, abortion encouraged premarital sex among the young.

Young women coming of age in the 1960s found Helen Gurley Brown's *Sex and the Single Girl* (1962) a strong influence, as she argued that they should not hesitate to accept sex as recreational and seek their own sexual fulfillment. Marriage could come later if one wanted it then, but a woman should devote the best years of her life to her own pleasure. Traditional morality had little if anything to do with sexual behavior in the new world according to Brown.

Helen Gurley Brown's *Sex and the Single Girl* urged young women to take advantage of the new sexual freedoms. Source: Photofest, Inc.

By the end of the decade, many young Americans had a view of sex radically different from what had prevailed ten years before, although their views were certainly not uniform. For some, sex was part of the antiestablishment lifestyle, even a political strategy for combating an imperialistic power structure. For others, sex was a means of pleasure, part of the consumer society, to be enjoyed by men and women without guilt and minus the responsibilities inherent in permanent, committed relationships. For others, it was a source of pleasure to be enjoyed within marriage, but with more freedom and spontaneity than previously. Yet others passed through the decade without any great alteration in their view of sex from how their parents' generation had generally seen it. That changes in birth control, abortion, and ways of viewing sex were having a demonstrable effect is demonstrated by the drop in the birth rate in the United States. At the beginning of the 1960s, U.S. women ages fifteen to forty-four were giving birth at a rate of 118 per 1,000 population; the rate in 1969 was 86.5.[4]

TURNING ON AND DROPPING OUT

Drug use in the United States immediately after World War II was largely confined to members of the artistic community, including musicians, artists, and film personalities, and to residents of urban inner-city communities, where drugs were seen as a tool to help alleviate the pain of poverty. So long as drugs were largely confined to these sectors of society, most Americans knew and cared little about the issue. Most young Americans who wanted to get high used alcoholic beverages, especially beer.

Beginning in the 1950s, though, and accelerating in the 1960s, drug use spread throughout American society, especially among the young. During the 1960s, the two most common substances so employed were marijuana and LSD (lysergic acid diethylamide). Marijuana, derived from the hemp plant (cannabis sativa) and containing a hallucinogenic agent called tetrahydrocannabinol, proved popular with hippies and other members of the counterculture during the 1960s because it was easily obtained, inexpensive, and readily usable rolled in cigarette form. A marijuana cigarette was called a "joint," and passing joints around from person to person was a common element in countercultural community relaxation. Other names for marijuana included grass, pot, reefer, and weed.

Marijuana often relaxed its users, making them, as the expression went, more mellow. As a relatively mild hallucinogenic drug when used in small quantities, it also could induce euphoria without completely incapacitating the user. Illegal since 1937, marijuana also became an antiestablishment weapon, a symbol of the counterculture's rejection of the older generation's forms of behavior, including their means of relaxation and escape from everyday pressures. It therefore increasingly became associated with members of the antiwar movement as users politicized the drug, making it part of a larger rejection of traditional beliefs and norms. Many users found laws permitting alcohol but outlawing marijuana hypocritical and arbitrary. Consequently, efforts to legalize marijuana began during the 1960s; by 1966, an organization dedicated to legalization, LeMar (for Legalize Marijuana) had established several chapters throughout the country. Proponents of maintaining marijuana's illegal status, including law enforcement agencies and most parents and politicians, claimed that marijuana use led to more dangerous drugs such as heroin.

By the middle of the decade, marijuana use had become common on college campuses. Its use was hard to police because, to most adults, a joint looked much like a normal cigarette, and the odor, although distinctive, could be masked by other odors to fool people unfamiliar with marijuana use. Hence, it was fairly easy for students to enjoy marijuana surreptitiously.

While marijuana had been in existence for thousands of years, its use recorded as far back as the third millennium B.C.E. in China, LSD was a new invention. It was created by Albert Hoffman, a research chemist, in Switzerland in 1943 and initially was used to treat schizophrenia, depression, and other mental illnesses. The U.S. military experimented with LSD as a truth serum and military intelligence weapon, but found the drug's effects too difficult to control.

The person most responsible for popularizing LSD use was Timothy Leary, an academic turned counterculture guru. Something of a rebel throughout his life, Leary was expelled from his high school, West Point, and the University of Alabama. He later earned a doctorate in psychology from the University of California, Berkeley, and joined the Harvard faculty in 1959. At Harvard, Leary directed the Psychedelic Research Project, which included research on LSD and other psychedelic drugs, the term "psychedelic" referring to substances that alter perception and in some cases induce hallucinations.

On a trip to Mexico in 1960, Leary ate hallucinogenic mushrooms, which precipitated what he considered a profound religious experience. From then on, he became an ardent apostle of mind-altering substances, especially LSD. After being fired by Harvard in 1963, Leary continued his proselytizing through many public appearances, especially on college campuses; a research center in Middlebrook, New York; the journal *Psychedelic Review*; and the League of Spiritual Discovery, a Leary-invented religion that called on believers to "turn on, tune in, drop out." This famous three-part call to drug use and a counterculture life referred to, first, turning on to drugs, second, tuning in to one's inner self (also interpreted by many as a summons to rock and roll music), and, finally, dropping out of mainstream society.

Many young people listened to that call, as LSD use burgeoned in college settings and throughout the antiestablishment world of America's young. The drug, also known widely as "acid," actually was legal until 1966. It was common at music concerts and festivals, and wherever large numbers of antiestablishment young people gathered. LSD, along with marijuana, was a popular ingredient of counterculture communities, including hippie communes and nontraditional religious communities.

Communes were viewed by adherents as a replacement for traditional American society. Communes typically included relatively unstructured

Timothy Leary, one-time Harvard professor, became the guru of LSD experimentation. His favorite phrase, "turn on, tune in, drop out," was a call to drug use and a counterculture life adopted by many American college students. Source: Photofest, Inc.

living with members sharing the domestic roles, a close-to-nature philosophy, and rejection of authoritarianism. This lack of structure, however,
made it difficult to sustain most communes, which tended to be short-lived
as members moved on to other experiences. Many members of the counterculture, including hippies, a group that originated in the Haight-Ashbury
district of San Francisco in the mid-1960s, preferred urban life, and found
communes, especially rural ones, a bit too out of the way for their long-term
taste. Hippies, generally peace-loving youths who favored long hair, love
beads, Day-Glo colors, and flowers in their hair, liked to frequent so-called
head shops, businesses that sold drug equipment, incense, and psychedelic
posters and pins. They also liked to use LSD.

Another avenue to dropping out in the 1960s was the new religion or
cult, many of them Eastern in origin or inspiration. Not least among the attractions of the Maharishi Mahesh Yogi, whose transcendental meditation
(TM) was presented as compatible with all religions, and hence not actually a religion itself, were the visits to the Maharishi by the Beatles. The
International Society for Krishna Consciousness (ISKCON), a Hindu sect
better known as Hare Krishnas, actively sought young people as members, especially targeting young men and women from white middle-class
homes, and was attacked by some people as a dangerous cult. The Reverend Sun Myung Moon established his Holy Spirit Association for the Unification of World Christianity in the 1950s, and the organization, more often
known as the Unification Church or Moonies, enjoyed considerable growth
during the 1960s. Many other groups offering spiritual alternatives also
sought out young people, especially college students, during the decade.
Most of these cults or religions shared a communal approach and were led
by a charismatic figure able to appeal to young people seeking some type
of personal enlightenment. The motivation for this spiritual search therefore was often the same motivation that led many young people to experiment with mind-altering drugs.

Drugs, liberated sexual behavior, communes, and alternative religions
all struck many adults and other authority figures as dangerous, a perception strengthened by the actions of Charles Manson and his youthful followers, who committed possibly the most bizarre and sensational murders
of the 1960s. Manson, a thirty-three-year-old ex-convict, led a cultlike group
called "The Family" (primarily young women) that engaged in sex orgies
and heavy use of drugs, including LSD. Manson had originally gathered
his group in Haight-Ashbury, and the members considered Manson not
only their leader but the Messiah.

On the consecutive nights of August 8–9, 1969, the Manson family committed widely publicized and horrifying murders. The first set of crimes
was carried out by Manson followers Susan Atkins, Leslie Van Houten, Patricia Krenwinkle, and Charles "Tex" Watson at Manson's direction but
without him present. A fifth family member, Linda Kasabian, accompanied

the group, but remained outside while the crimes were committed. The five murder victims included actress Sharon Tate, who was eight months pregnant and the wife of film director Roman Polanski, and Folger coffee heiress Abigail Folger. On the door to the Polanski–Tate home in Hollywood Hills, in Sharon Tate's blood, one of the murderers printed the word "PIG."

The following night, Manson personally led Krenwinkle, Van Houten, and Watson to the home of Leno and Rosemary LaBianca, where Manson bound the couple and his three followers murdered them. Police found additional writings in blood, this time on walls and the refrigerator: "DEATH," "RISE," and the strange phrase "HEALTER SKELTER" (sic). The phrase later was interpreted to refer to an apocalyptic state after which Manson would be recognized as leader of the world. All participants were arrested several months later and convicted, finally ending the terror engendered by the brutal murders.

Manson's long hair and communal lifestyle led many Americans unfairly to associate him with hippies in general. The murders excited considerable animosity toward counterculture lifestyles and helped lead to major efforts against drugs, including President Nixon's 1970 war on drugs, and to the president's political championing of the "Silent Majority." Although the Manson murders did not end LSD use, they seriously undermined the popular perception of the drug as an avenue to a new and better world of harmony, peace, and spiritual enlightenment.

PART TWO

POPULAR CULTURE OF THE 1960S

3

Advertising

Advertising, for better or worse, came of age in the 1960s. Several social and technological changes, along with a new advertising philosophy, coalesced to make the decade a golden age of advertising and change forever how advertising agencies went about their work of helping companies sell their products. Nor would the consuming public's attitude toward buying remain unchanged.

A new, younger public stood ready, albeit unknowingly, for changes in advertising. By the beginning of the 1960s, about 50% of the American population was under twenty-five years of age,[1] and that population increasingly turned away from their parents' generation in a wide range of areas, including political, moral, and sexual attitudes. They adopted new clothing styles, new hairstyles, and new fashions in entertainment. Many resorted to drugs to get high. They steadily turned against the Vietnam War and threw themselves into the antiwar movement. They prided themselves on being anticonsumer, but that attitude was more wishful thinking than reality. Advertisers, finding in the younger generation a desire for change, cleverly built their marketing strategies on precisely that desire.

While a new generation was emerging, major developments in technology made it possible to market products more effectively. In 1950, fewer than four million households in the United States had televisions. By the middle of the 1960s, the total had risen to well over fifty million,[2] and by the middle of the decade, color television was replacing black and white programming. Color advertising, always more effective than black and white, was now possible on America's television screens as well as in magazines.

The maturation of the 35-millimeter single-lens camera permitted photographers to do location shooting more easily and cheaply than before, freeing them from studio settings. Polaroid cameras allowed photographers to run quick lighting checks. Television crews had more mobile equipment, including hand-held cameras, to permit greater opportunities to go where the action was, or where advertisers could film the most appealing commercials.

Advertising, though, would not have responded as effectively as it did to a changing public or capitalized as thoroughly on new technological changes if it had not been for a major philosophical shift in how advertisements and commercials were created. As the 1960s opened, most advertising agencies still retained their old in-house structural division between art directors and copywriters. And they still drew their employees from traditional sources: the same Eastern schools, the same white Anglo-Saxon ethnic pool.

These traditional approaches began to change in 1949 when Bill Bernbach joined with Ned Doyle and Maxwell Dane to create the new Doyle Dane Bernbach advertising agency. Under Bernbach's leadership, DDB began a revolution in advertising that by the 1960s was sweeping its competitors as well into an agency-wide creative revolution. Bernbach brought art directors and copywriters together into a creative team that permitted text and visual components of an advertisement to complement each other in conveying a persuasive message. Talent was the thing that Bernbach looked for in his people, and he looked not just to the old sources but wherever talent might be found. The new and creative led the way, technology served the creative imagination, and the public bought as never before.

Advertising averaged 2.2% of the nation's gross national product (GNP) during the 1960s, producing $18.8 billion in 1969, a figure that averaged out to more than $300 per household. With the continued spread of television and its transformation from black and white to color, television advertising in the final year of the decade totaled $3.3 billion. Radio advertisers spent about $1 billion.[3] If the 1960s marked a golden age in advertising, that golden age also was very green.

SUPERSTARS OF ADVERTISING: BILL BERNBACH AND MARY WELLS

William Bernbach and Mary Wells were the two most important members of the advertising world during the 1960s. Bernbach, co-founder of Doyle Dane Bernbach, may well have been the most important advertising executive in the industry's history.

Bernbach was born in 1911 in New York City and attended New York University. After college, he was working in the mailroom of Schenley Distillers when he wrote an advertisement and submitted it to the advertising department of the company. The ad eventually was used in *The New York Times*, although the identity of its creator by that time had been lost. When Bernbach saw the ad, he recognized it as his creation, claimed its authorship, and was rewarded with a salary raise and transfer to the advertising department.

It would be a while yet before this advertising genius was in a position to begin a transformation of the industry. Service in the army during World War II lay ahead, after which Bernbach joined Grey Advertising. An outstanding copywriter, he became creative director at one of the more creative and flexible of the large advertising agencies. Grey, for example, broke with most of its competitors by hiring Italians, Jews, and other religious and ethnic minorities. In this relatively open environment, Bernbach cultivated his then radical advertising philosophy, arguing that creativity was more important than technical skill, that making a persuasive ad was more art than science.

In 1949, Bernbach joined with Maxwell Dane and Ned Doyle to form Doyle Dane Bernbach, with Bernbach as president. Changes that he implemented in his own agency, and that soon spread throughout the industry, included consolidating the art and copywriting functions into one department, with the result that a creative team worked together to create an advertisement in which text and visuals complemented each other. With creativity supreme, the writers and artists became the powers within advertising, with corresponding increases in their salaries. The account executive was toppled from his throne as chief decision-maker, and marketing research and media analysis, though still important, became secondary to creativity.

Doyle Dane Bernbach hit it big with its first account, for a bargain department store named Ohrbach's. DDB transformed the store's image into that of a sophisticated store, significantly improving both its clientele and its revenue. Then came Volkswagen and Avis, two of DDB's most famous accounts. The resulting advertising campaigns were enormously successful and securely established the firm's reputation.

The Volkswagen campaign began in the 1950s but hit its peak in the 1960s. While most automobile manufacturers were changing the styling of their makes every year to encourage a perception of obsolescence, DDB emphasized the relative permanence of the Volkswagen. Print advertisements, and later television commercials, paraded the simplicity and uniformity in design of the "Beetle," or "Bug," reassuring consumers that neither mechanical deficiencies nor changes in styling would necessitate changing cars. The advertising campaign acknowledged the plainness, even ugliness, of the car, which made the vehicle all the more endearing. One ad stated, "We finally came up with a beautiful picture of a Volkswagen." The picture was of a snow-covered road and wintry landscape, with tire tracks the only evidence that a Volkswagen had been present. While engaging in self-mockery regarding the aesthetic character of the Beetle, the ad, of course, also highlights the reliability of the little car, even in deep snow. Another ad features an egg with a drawing of a Volkswagen on it,

This 1964 magazine advertisement emphasized the economical and practical nature of the Volkswagen Beetle. Reprinted with permission from Volkswagen of America, Inc.

the background all black, and below the picture the simple declaration that "Some shapes are hard to improve on." These ads reflected a popular approach of Bernbach's—a dominant but simple photograph with a creative textual statement below it.

The Avis campaign took the unusual approach of selling the fact that the rental company was not first in the business, that being second actually was better because, as the advertisements noted, "We try harder." DDB perfected this type of negative campaigning in which defects turn into positives. Some of the headlines on Avis ads proclaimed that "Avis can't afford dirty ashtrays," and that "Avis can't afford unwashed cars." "Are you working like a dog to get to the top?" another ad asked. Then "Shake hands with Avis." Television commercials took a similar line.

DDB had many other important individual advertisements and commercials, as well as advertising campaigns, in the 1960s, such as Levy's ads asserting "You don't have to be Jewish to love Levy's real Jewish Rye" with photographs of people from diverse ethnic backgrounds; print advertisements and television commercials personalizing in lyrical tones the joys of visiting Jamaica; a series of commercials starring actor Jack Gilford's childlike love for Cracker Jack; the commercial for Alka-Seltzer with an actor portraying an Italian diner proclaiming, after many failed attempts to film the spot, "Mama

Mia! That's a spicy meatball." In addition, there was DDB's famous foray into political ads on behalf of the Lyndon Johnson presidential campaign of 1964. In one of the most famous political ads in history, created by DDB's Tony Schwartz, a young girl plucks petals from a flower while counting from one to nine. Then a male voice counts backward with the camera coming up close on the child's right eye and the eye yielding to a picture of a nuclear explosion. The final voiceover warns voters to "Vote for President Johnson on November third. The stakes are too high for you to stay home." Although never mentioning Republican candidate Barry Goldwater by name, the ad powerfully reinforces the sense of the candidate held by many that he was trigger-happy and might get the United States into a nuclear war.

Doyle Dane Bernbach, under the leadership of Bill Bernbach, was enormously successful. By the end of the 1960s, DDB was the sixth largest advertising agency in the United States, the seventh largest in the world. Its billings increased during the 1960s from $25 million annually to $270 million.[4]

This great creative and financial success was the result not only of Bill Bernbach's vision and imagination but also because of his ability to attract the best talent in the advertising business. Many DDB employees made their way into either the Art Directors' Hall of Fame or the Copywriters' Hall of Fame. The latter had only nineteen members by the end of the 1960s, but six of them, including Bernbach himself, were with DDB.[5] Another DDB copywriter in the Hall of Fame is Mary Wells, considered by many to be the second most important advertising figure of the 1960s.

Mary Wells, after serving as fashion advertising manager for Macy's department store, joined the McCann-Erickson advertising agency in 1953. In 1956, she joined Doyle Dane Bernbach, eventually becoming copy chief and a vice president. In 1964, she switched to Jack Tinker and Partners, where she teamed with artist Stewart Greene and copywriter Richard Rich to develop award-winning television commercials that made effective use of humor, a Wells trademark. Major accounts for Wells at Tinker and Partners included Alka-Seltzer and Braniff Airlines. The Alka-Seltzer commercials established another important creative relationship for Wells, with the director Howard Zieff.

Wells, Rich, and Greene formed their own agency in 1966, with Wells as president, and the new firm, Wells, Rich, Greene, Inc., helped to define advertising for the rest of the decade and beyond. The Braniff account moved with WRG, and Braniff's president, Harding Lawrence, soon became Mary Wells's husband. WRG introduced colored planes for Braniff, announcing "The end of the plain plane." One of the most famous commercials that Wells did for Braniff was "Braniff International Presents the Air Strip." In a spot that would have been roundly condemned as sexist if created in later decades, a hostess steadily strips, although the concept and voiceover ("After dinner on those long flights she'll slip into something a little more comfortable") are far more provocative than what the audience actually sees. The hostess remains fully clothed, but sheds one uniform for another as her role changes from greeting to serving dinner to assisting Braniff customers on the remainder of the flight.

As DDB had done earlier, WRG made creative use of self-putdowns for clients' products. Advertisements for Alka-Seltzer included the famous line "I Can't Believe I Ate the Whole Thing." Commercials for Benson and Hedges highlighted in humorous fashion possible disadvantages of an extra-long cigarette and chronicled the search for Mr. Benson. Again here Wells worked with Howard Zieff, a widely acclaimed director of commercials in the 1960s. Zieff also directed for WRG the memorable "Driving School" commercial for American Motors, in which the driving instructor encounters one disastrous student after another; and the "Little Italy" spot for American Motors that starred a young Robert DeNiro. Zieff later turned to full-length theater films, including *House Calls* (1978), with Walter Matthau and Glenda Jackson; and *Private Benjamin* (1980), starring Goldie Hawn.

In a decade notable for its emphasis on love, including the "Make love, not war" antiwar slogan and the famous "LOVE" image from sculptor and painter Robert Indiana, it was not surprising that the concept of love became an important element in Mary Wells's approach to advertising. She adopted the slogan "love power" for her agency and approached the consumer with affectionate regard rather than the manipulative cynicism that characterized some advertisers. So when Menley and James, a pharmaceutical manufacturer, decided to introduce a cosmetics line in 1969, Wells chose the name "Love." Love Cosmetics was packaged and displayed in psychedelic designs, with prominent use of the word "Love" in birds and flowers. Calling to mind the new interest in natural love freed from traditional social and moral restraints, Love Cosmetics were marketed as natural rather than artificial makeup. Simple cylindrical packages replaced the elaborate containers of many cosmetics, and the products, advertising claimed, enhanced rather than concealed one's natural beauty.

Wells, Rich, Greene came into being in 1966, and by the following year was heralded as one of the most exciting and important advertising agencies in the world. Mary Wells' work was especially effective on television. Her humor, creativity, and respect for her audience led viewers to enjoy her commercials so much that they assumed the products also must be good.

THE NEW MARKETS

Advertisers in the 1960s inherited a largely conservative consumer public. Most American buyers tended to look carefully at their purchases. Older buyers especially, their financial conservatism grounded in the Great Depression, required serious demonstration of their need to purchase a particular object. They were likely to stay with brands and styles, although automobile manufacturers had made inroads with their planned obsolescence. Men were especially conservative in clothing and usually wore their clothes until they actually wore out. Young parents inherited children's clothes from relatives and friends and often passed the clothes, which children usually outgrew before outwearing, on to other children. This static approach to buying did not make for a dynamic world of consumers, and it tended toward conformity.

Then along came the new young generation of the 1960s. The change in demographics meant that at the beginning of the decade almost one-half of Americans were twenty-five or younger, with the population continuing to grow younger. It was estimated that this age group had about $13 billion in spending money, with the total at $25 billion if teenagers down to thirteen were included.[6]

This new youth market arose at the same time that a tremendous creative revolution was occurring in advertising, led by Bill Bernbach, Mary Wells, and many others. Developments in technology, especially color television and improved photographic equipment, opened up new possibilities. In addition, America's young were not only increasing in numbers but also changing in attitude, rejecting many social, moral, and political tenants of their parents' generation. Included in the reaction against the establishment was a perception that advertising was essentially fraudulent and manipulative, and that the mass conformity of society resulted from both manipulation and intellectual stagnation. The young saw themselves as anticonsumer and antiadvertising. They believed in change.

That belief in change created interesting opportunities for the advertising industry. Freed from the conservative tendencies of their parents, feeling, in fact, a call actively to rebel against what they saw as a restrictive set of social norms, and determined to assert their individuality, millions of young Americans turned to new styles in clothing, eating, and entertainment. Change became good, static conformity bad. And with a youthful impetuosity sanctioned by multitudes of peers, the young turned toward the new and then the newer. "The Now Generation" was what the advertising world dubbed the young of the 1960s.

Advertisers and manufacturers recognized that the Now Generation provided a major consumer market. The "throwaway" world came in with them, from disposable diapers to clothes discarded because they were out of style rather than worn out. To appeal to the young, agencies took out ads in underground newspapers and magazines. Departing from the earlier minimalism of DDB Volkswagen ads and much of early 1960s advertising, they introduced psychedelic graphics and used models in hip clothing and long hair. Even agency artists and copywriters took to dressing hip. Rock music provided background to commercials. While fostering this new consumerism, advertisers offered their products as anticonsumer, antiestablishment, anticonformity. "New and improved" became an omnipresent slogan.

Advertisements by the J. Walter Thompson agency proclaimed 7-Up the Uncola and trumpeted the drink amid psychedelic butterflies and sunrises, even labeling the drink "Wet and Wild" to place the drink within the sexual revolution. Batten, Barton, Durstine, and Osborn (BBDO) spoke of the "Dodge Rebellion" and in a television commercial pitted the driver of a Dodge Challenger against a fat white policeman speaking with a southern accent. Pontiac ads were even more antiestablishment by imitating the film *Bonnie and Clyde*. Young men and women dressed like the famous outlaws emerged from a bank robbery and made their escape in a 1930s Packard that they quickly exchanged for a new Pontiac Firebird convertible.

The concepts "young," "counterculture," and "creative" became virtually synonymous within advertising agencies in the 1960s. To be creative was to think young. To think young was to identify with the young counterculture, at least superficially and, regarding the efficacy of advertising, strategically. Not everyone could actually be young, but people could adopt a youthful attitude. As the 1960s reached its midpoint, advertisers increasingly were aiming a youthful image more at the nonyoung than the young themselves. After all, the marketing strategy went, those who were young knew they were young, but everyone else could act and think young by buying the right car, the right clothing styles, the right kitchen oven, the right anything. Advertisers well understood the reality, that despite the huge population of young Americans, most of the money still nestled within the pocketbooks of adult America. The key was to get older Americans to loosen up and spend. And what could be a greater inducement that to wave the myth of eternal youth at them? If children did not want to be like their parents, then their parents could be like them.

Hip advertising appeared regularly in such mainstream magazines as *Life, Look*, and even *Ladies Home Journal*. Cars were an obvious way to appeal to people's desire to act and think young. And to act young was to be at least just a little rebellious. In addition to the car advertisements already discussed, with their call to rebellion against authority and traditional attitudes, BBDO invited drivers, most of them well beyond the age of reason, to catch "Dodge Fever." Then there was the Oldsmobile, definitely for the older and more affluent consumer, but nonetheless now billed as the "Youngmobile"; in commercials, buyers were summoned to the music of guitars and tambourines and the invitation to "Escape from the ordinary." The transforming power of the Ford Mustang was much heralded, turning humdrum citizens into exciting men and women of the world. And who would not be enticed by such names as the Rambler's Rogue, the Mercury Comet, and the Plymouth Fury?

Advertising campaigns by Carl Ally, and by Scali, McCabe, Sloves summoned supposedly more discerning consumers who were privy to special insights regarding Volvo and the nature of the consuming and advertising worlds. Most buyers were suckers, the campaigns implied, but purchasers of Volvo understood that advertising was all a scam where major American automakers were concerned. Volvo, though, was a car that would last and not be changing every year. Planned obsolescence was a plot that Volvo drivers understood and rejected. The marketing approach was similar to that waged by BBD for Volkswagen, but with more cynicism about society and less humor.

Think young and reject the blandishments of mass consumer society, men and women were told in advertisements and commercials for almost every conceivable type of product. Collectors of S&H Green Stamps were assured that "With this little square you swing." Dash laundry detergent informed its users that "Somebody had to break the rules." A rider of a Suzuki motorcycle could "Express Yourself." Booth's House of Lords gin was the "nonconformist gin." Tareyton smokers were so determined to assert their individuality that they "would rather fight than switch." Consumers were assured that they were ignoring "the ad man" when they purchased a Fisher stereo.

Despite the infatuation with counterculture on the part of advertising agencies, the women's liberation movement, or feminism as it was commonly called in the 1960s, was not part of marketing strategy until the end of the decade. Then agencies began to target the new woman, often with decidedly traditional products in mind. Hand lotion, for example, something one would have expected to see modern women rejecting, came under the marketing vision of J. Walter Thompson. Pond's lotion was changed from its traditional white to pink, the fact of change more important than the actual color, and its wearers were shown in such nontraditional feminine activities as applying a blowtorch to a sculpture or working on a motorcycle.

Another product marketed to liberated women was the Virginia Slims extra-long cigarette manufactured by Philip Morris. Long and slim, the cigarette was featured in Leo Burnett advertisements and commercials with trim, beautiful women stylishly attired. "You've come a long way, baby, to get where you've got to today," women were told. Presumably, the long way toward liberation included the ability to smoke long cigarettes while remaining essentially a sex object.

Also in the 1960s African Americans began to be recognized as important consumers. Although idealism regarding recognizing all Americans as equals certainly played a role in some marketing strategies reaching out to the African American community, the primary reason for targeting African Americans is expressed in the title of the book *The $30 Billion Negro*, published in 1969. The African American author, D. Parke Gibson, who ran an advertising firm, makes a compelling case for bringing African Americans into the marketing equation. Gibson clarifies the historical separation of African Americans from the mainstream and argues for their recognition not only on the basis of racial justice but also for business reasons.

Gibson pointed out that during the late 1960s, African Americans, then still often referred to as Negroes, were spending over $30 billion on goods and services.[7] The African American community consisted of six million families. Approximately 40% of these families owned their own homes, over 50% owned at least one car, and 75% of the households had one or more television sets. African Americans made up 11% of the total U.S. population and 92% of the nonwhite U.S. population. Further, nonwhites constituted approximately 75% of the global population, so a changed attitude toward attracting nonwhite consumers at home promised the possibility of even larger markets abroad.

Like virtually all ethnic or racial groups, the African American population exhibited certain purchasing patterns that substantiated Gibson's argument regarding the financial benefits to be realized by marketing to that population. Patterns ranged from spending more for food in supermarkets than white consumers to consuming 70% of the Maine sardines and about 50% of all the grape soda sold in the country. In addition, African Americans tended to be concentrated in a relatively small number of urban centers, facilitating targeted advertising.

Initially, most advertising to the African American consumer population occurred in black publications and on black-audience radio stations. *Ebony* magazine was the favorite with advertisers attempting to reach the best educated and most affluent members of the population. By 1967, $7 million annually was being spent on advertising in *Ebony*'s pages. Johnson Publications, publisher of *Ebony*, also produced the news weekly *Jet*, a homemaker's magazine called *Tan*, and *Negro Digest*. All of them provided avenues for advertising, as did *Tuesday*, a monthly magazine supplement for largely white-oriented Sunday newspapers, and other publications.

Advertisements in these African American outlets involved many of the same products and even the same marketing themes found in ads placed in white markets. The major difference lay in use of African American models. Clairol, for example, continued pushing hair coloring with its famous line penned by Shirley Polykoff of Foote, Cone and Belding—"Does she … or doesn't she?" The question originally was suspected of conveying a sexual meaning, although the follow-up sentence quickly clarified the reference, "Hair Color so natural only her hairdresser knows for sure!" Polykoff and her agency nonetheless had to fight hard to retain the question. Not surprisingly, the other famous question in Clairol ads, "Is it true blondes have more fun?" was dropped in black-oriented advertising.

Pepsi-Cola was losing a lot of African American consumers to Coca-Cola in the early 1960s. Pepsi countered that trend in various ways. The company hired Harvey C. Russell as vice-president for special markets in 1962. At that time, Russell was the highest-ranking African American executive in a major U.S. business firm. New marketing strategies for the African American consumer followed. Pepsi advertisements, for example, were among the first to feature a woman with an Afro hairstyle. Recognizing that African Americans averaged ten years younger than the national population, Pepsi increased its sales by emphasizing the theme it also used nationally, "Now It's Pepsi—for Those Who Think Young." Thinking and acting young, discussed earlier in this chapter, became a national advertising mantra during the 1960s.

Reflecting some advertising courage, Greyhound took the image of the bus, a symbol of segregation in the South, and tried to make it an agent for integration as well as a means of financial success for the company. Rosa Parks had refused to move to the back of a bus, setting in motion a major component of the Civil Rights Movement. "Freedom Riders" rode buses south to take up the cause of racial justice. Then, in the 1960s, Greyhound Lines embarked on a major minority hiring plan, bringing in African Americans who included a high-ranking sales executive, salespeople, and drivers. The former Brooklyn Dodgers pitcher, Joe Black, one of the first African Americans to play major league baseball, signed on as a vice-president and special markets representative. By 1964, African American drivers were operating buses in the South. Meanwhile, Greyhound was also a pioneer in integrated advertising in both white and black publications, with ads showing black and white passengers being welcomed aboard by a black driver. Still, despite Greyhound's efforts, integrated advertising moved ahead only in fits and starts during the decade.

Some companies advertised their products in campaigns that used African American history, an important effort at a time when most schoolchildren, black and white, knew little if anything about the important historical contributions of black Americans. Among the companies and campaigns were American Oil's *American Traveler's Guide to Negro History*, National Distillers' (maker of Old Taylor whiskey) *Ingenious Americans*, Pepsi-Cola's *Adventures in Negro History*, and Scott Paper's *Distaff to History*. The Scott Paper Company booklet featured important African American women and proved so popular that it was serialized in newspapers. The Pepsi materials were adopted by more than five hundred school systems. All of these Negro History programs were widely disseminated.

The more cynical observers of American society might argue that the advertising world cared only about getting more money from African Americans. The reality was much more complex. Financial gain was important for manufacturers and advertising agencies, but true equality could not come until all citizens were asked to buy as well as to vote.

THE CREWCUT CROWD
AND OTHER ADVERTISING PHENOMENA

Advertisers took to the counterculture in a big way, using hip attitudes and details of style to market a think-and-act-young mentality to not only the young (who already were acting young) but to more affluent older Americans. Although a large number of young people never bought into the counterculture, most advertisers tended to ignore them. However, there were some exceptions.

When Young and Rubicam took on the Peace Corps as a client in the late 1960s, the agency essentially advertised against the counterculture. One commercial for the Peace Corps uses the song "Age of Aquarius" from the musical *Hair* and an image of a disembodied head of a longhaired man in the stars. The voiceover states, "It's one thing to predict the future; it's another to help make it." The point is that the Peace Core solves real problems in the real world. A radio ad in 1968 featured a mother urging her son to act like everyone else and get out and demonstrate. "Anybody that would join the Peace Corps," she warns her son, "is a troublemaker." In the ad, the counterculture opposition to mass conformity has been turned on its head, and the real individual is the young man or woman who joins the Peace Corps.

Young and Rubicam was one of the most successful advertising agencies of the 1960s, even if it was not quite the trendsetter that Doyle Dane Bernbach was, and perhaps not the equal in imaginative power to Wells, Rich, Greene. In the early 1960s, a young, innovative individual named Stephen O. Frankfurt was appointed president of the firm. His leadership of Young and Rubicam kept the organization consistently near the creative vanguard of the industry. Another of its major accounts was Eastern Airlines. Young and Rubicam popularized the airline's new Boeing 727, the "Whisperjet," through an imaginative commercial mingling the sights and sounds of the jet with sights and sounds of animals, primarily birds, in the Florida Everglades. Later in the decade, the agency embarked on an effective advertising campaign for Eastern called "The Wings of Man."

David Ogilvy ran another major, and certainly unique, advertising agency in the 1960s. Ogilvy paid close attention to market research and rejected humor in his commercials and ads, claiming that no one buys products from a clown. Although he was out of the mainstream with his attitude toward humor, and not much imitated by other agencies, in his own individualistic way he produced a number of creative and effective efforts. Ogilvy's campaigns included a series of ads for Hathaway shirts in which a debonair middle-aged man with a patch over his right eye models Hathaway shirts in a variety of sophisticated settings, and ads and television commercials for Schweppes quinine water starring Commander Edward Whitehead, the Schweppes chief executive. One of Ogilvy's most famous print advertisements was for Rolls Royce. A photograph of the automobile takes up the top half, and a lot of text detailing the many advantages of a Rolls Royce the bottom half. The most memorable portion of the ad, though, is the quotation right below the picture: "At 60 miles an hour the loudest noise in this new Rolls-Royce comes from the electric clock." That statement was intended to convey in one sentence the essence of the car's quality.

Research remained important during the 1960s, although industry increasingly came to agree with Bill Bernbach that good research, while helpful, was less important than creativity. There were some new directions in research. The old determiners of potential buyers were demographics, social class, and psychological characteristics. To this mix were added lifestyle patterns relating to attitudes, feelings, work habits, and leisure activities. Hobbies, vacation patterns, membership in clubs, sports interests, and political and social opinions were just a few of the factors examined to determine how best to push a product and to whom the product should be pushed.

Products had been marketed to children for decades, but in the 1960s researchers took a closer look at how to approach children. Sociologists, psychologists, and market researchers looked especially closely, sometimes at the behest of advertising agencies, in other cases to warn against misleading children (and their parents) into unwise purchases. Strong protests against advertising directed toward children began in the second half of the decade. Market analysts meanwhile were coming to many conclusions about the children's market.

The children most susceptible to advertising, researchers found, were below thirteen years of age; teens had already come to the conclusion that products in advertisements and commercials often turned out to be different from what they were in real life. Advertisers learned that effective approaches included depicting children wanting specific toys or a specific brand of a product rather than generalized products like ice cream. Children responded more strongly toward moving pictures than still pictures, and to action verbs rather than nouns. Making acquisition of a particular toy or other desirable product contingent on purchasing a product (which might include, for example, a required coupon) continued to be common. An image of a child enjoying a product was another successful advertising gambit.[8]

Also during the 1960s, advertisers came under legal scrutiny for misleading advertising. One of the most prominent cases involved Colgate's Rapid Shave. A Ted Bates television commercial showed Rapid Shave making it easy to shave the sand from sandpaper. It turned out that instead of sandpaper, the commercial used a sheet of Plexiglas with loose sand on it. The sand pulled easily down the sheet of Plexiglas, leaving a bare swath. The Federal Trade Commission ruled the commercial misleading and issued a cease-and-desist order on December 29, 1961. Bates and Colgate strongly contested the ruling, claiming that it would preclude all substitute materials in advertising. The First Circuit Court of Appeals upheld the FTC decision on November 20, 1962, although it required a more focused statement from the FTC, and the U.S. Supreme Court ruled in support of the FTC on April 6, 1965.

Yet another shaving cream supplied one of the decade's most enticing commercials, by way of the William Esty agency. The product was Noxzema shaving cream. A beautiful and sexy Swedish actress and model, Gunilla Knudsen, gazed into the camera while a man shaved, with "The Stripper" song playing in the background, and purred, "Take it off. Take it all off." The Noxzema commercial was one of the many imaginative pitches by advertising agencies that made the 1960s a golden, and memorable, age of advertising.

4

Architecture

The 1960s featured enormous variety in architecture, with no single theme or set of principles dominating. Even the spirit of revolution that permeated so much of American life in the decade sometimes gave way to conservative, even reactionary attitudes. As the decade opened, the major influences on architecture were older architects, and as the decade ended there were increasing attempts to incorporate classic architecture into modern buildings and to preserve the great buildings of America's past. Throughout the decade, however, changes that were occurring in how Americans lived, shopped, worked, worshipped, went to school, and sought entertainment affected how architects and builders carried out their design and construction efforts.

Three giants from earlier decades still held sway over much of architectural thought as the 1960s opened—Frank Lloyd Wright, Walter Gropius, and Le Corbusier (Charles–Édouard Jeanneret)—although Wright had died in 1959, Le Corbusier would die in 1965, and Gropius in 1969. Wright, perhaps still the most famous name in American architecture at the beginning of the twenty-first century, followed an organic approach, believing that a building should rise out of its environment and remain part of it. Gropius, founder of the Bauhaus school in Germany after World War I, named after what he called the art school (the Bauhaus, or Building Institute) that he was commissioned to restructure, helped to establish the International Style that featured industrial designs and a steady focus on the building's purpose. Gropius later served on the Harvard University faculty where he influenced large numbers of young architects. Le Corbusier, like Gropius, took a "modern" approach to architecture, thinking of buildings as machines consisting of an interplay of geometric forms. Unlike Wright, Le

Corbusier sought to define buildings as strictly human constructions separated from the natural world.

Mies van der Rohe and Philip Johnson continued the modern international style, the former especially influential because of his position as
director of the Illinois Institute of Technology, as well as designer of several of the school's buildings. Mies, in architectural style, was in a direct
line of descent from Gropius and had considerable influence on Johnson
during the latter's early career. Other important architects in the 1960s included Richard Neutra, whose efforts to integrate houses into their natural environment, especially in California, echoed Wright's philosophy;
Utzon Saarinen, whose symbolic impulse led to such buildings as the John
Deere headquarters in Moline, Illinois, made from a steel that weathered
to a brown reminiscent of rusted farm implements, and a TWA terminal at
New York's Kennedy Airport that seems to many viewers to resemble a
bird ready to take flight; Paul Rudolph, a student of Gropius at Harvard
and best known for his Art and Architecture Building at Yale University
with its rough, corduroy texture; and Charles W. Moore, whose often play-
ful, even flamboyant designs included the Faculty Club at the University
of California, Santa Barbara, where faculty could drink their coffee, smoke
their pipes, and engage in philosophical discussions surrounded by neon
lights and a pedestrian bridge. The two architects probably most reflective
of the spirit of the 1960s were Louis Kahn and Robert Venturi; for that reason they will be discussed in greater depth later in this chapter.

Sometimes with, sometimes without these and other talented architectural figures, much was happening in the 1960s. Urban renewal was raising issues of fair housing for the poor. Changes in transportation, roads,
and inner cities shifted increasing numbers of people into suburbs, and
businesses went with them. Shopping centers grew in numbers and di-
versified in form. With prosperity widespread, but hardly universal, in the
1960s, additional office space was required, and cities continued to look
upward for that space. Renewed emphases on educational opportunity and
the arts led to new schools and museums. Public buildings became increasingly allied with other arts that complemented their architecture. The
Second Vatican Council changed the way that Catholics worshipped, requiring new types of churches that brought parishioners into closer contact with the celebrant. The winds of cultural change were blowing across
the landscape of American life, and architecture was responding, like a garden planted in a striking variety of flowers, but, of course, with some weeds
creeping in as well.

At the same time, it is important to remember that many Americans
went through their daily lives largely unaffected by thoughts of architectural design. They continued to live in their older city homes and farm
houses (or new but similar versions) constructed of traditional materials,
such as wood, brick, or stone, containing familiar rooms (kitchen, bath,
bedrooms) arranged in the old square or rectangular design. The parlor,

however, began to give way to a modernized version known as the living room, which increasingly became the center of family life, which was much more likely in the 1960s to revolve around a television set than a piano, that mainstay of the old parlor. Meanwhile the dining room in many homes dissolved into a combination dining and kitchen area. Many families modernized their homes by adding aluminum siding in the 1960s, eliminating the need to repaint every few years. For most people, if they built a new home (in the suburbs often a ranch style) or added on to the existing one, they employed a builder rather than an architect.

Inside these homes, average Americans led their daily lives with gas or electric kitchen appliances, favored kitchen counters to increase working space, added an automatic washer and dryer to avoid having to visit a laundromat, tended to eat off almost unbreakable dishes that went by such names as Melmac, liked Early American styles in living room couches, rested (especially the father) in a reclining chair, and bought carpets with strong colors or very visible designs (but preferred tile for bathroom floors). Such living could be quite comfortable if not necessarily aesthetic. Aesthetics were left to people like architects.

LEADING FIGURES OF AMERICAN ARCHITECTURE

Louis Kahn and Robert Venturi were the two most important architects of the 1960s because of the buildings they created and their reflection of attitudes manifested throughout American society during the decade. Kahn expressed a serious social conscience and believed that architecture should speak to the people. His belief in his profession as a process of dreaming paralleled the imaginative explorations found as well in many other dimensions of 1960s life. Venturi put into practice his conviction that art should imitate life. His architectural designs embodied an array of ways in which everyday Americans lived, including strip malls, neon signs, even trash cans. Of all the leading architects of the decade, he probably was closest to the pop artists who led painting in new, radical directions.

Louis Kahn (1901–74)

Louis I. Kahn may have been the most important architect in the middle of the twentieth century. His social consciousness, pluralism regarding architectural traditions, combination of theory and practice, and influence on younger architects both reflected the spirit of the 1960s and helped to shape architecture for the rest of the century.

Kahn was born in Estonia in 1901 and moved with his family to the United States in 1905. He studied music and painting before earning a degree in architecture from the University of Pennsylvania, where he studied under Paul Cret, a Beaux-Arts classicist. (The Beaux-Arts, or Second Empire style, usually featured a square plan, classic detail, mansard roof, and considerable use of columns, among other characteristics.) Kahn later traveled in Europe, held a fellowship to the American Academy in Rome, and taught at Yale University and his alma mater, the University of Pennsylvania. Kahn's broad knowledge in the arts, the nondoctrinaire education he received at Pennsylvania, and his travels encouraged an openness to different styles and influences.

Much of Kahn's early work centered on improving public housing, anticipating the broad concern in the 1960s for public housing that would more sensitively respect the occupants' individuality. Along with work within the United States, he was a housing consultant for the government of Israel. Like many teachers, he found that he learned his subject best when he had to teach it, and his teaching led to growing artistic maturity and ultimately to important commissions.

Kahn's theoretical importance had much to do with his view of space. He believed in serving and served functions (that is, spaces) that follow a natural order of importance in a building. His view of a primal, or central, space ordering the surrounding spaces and offering limitless possibilities gave his architectural followers great freedom and fit well the spirit of the 1960s.

Turning away from the modernist International Style that had broken with most of what preceded it, Kahn incorporated past and present, the traditional and contemporary, into his work. He embraced a sense of order but wanted that order to be both rationally and emotionally realized. Architecture, for Kahn, does what nature cannot do, thus differing from the organic architecture of Frank Lloyd Wright; however, a building should invite connections, including human connections inspired by the building. Light was a major interest for Kahn, who believed that humans gravitate toward the light, a concept that has metaphoric as well as structural implications for architecture.

The human dimension remained always important in Kahn's thinking. He believed that architecture should come from the people and speak clearly to the people, an attitude that meshed well with the political and social "power to the people" movements of the 1960s. Viewers, he held, should immediately see the structural nature of a building, for clarity rather than obscurity invites the connections that Kahn hoped to induce.

Kahn returned to the University of Pennsylvania in Philadelphia to create one of his best known buildings, the Richards Medical Research Building. Completed in 1965, its towers seemed to recall the hill towns of Tuscany that Kahn had visited in the late 1920s. He created a beautiful building whose connections among its parts are clearly evident, but unfortunately he lost sight of the research functions to be performed there. As a research building, its functionality yielded to aesthetics. That would not be the case with what is perhaps Kahn's masterpiece, the Salk Institute at La Jolla, California, completed in 1968.

Kahn worked with Jonas Salk, famous for developing an effective polio vaccine in the 1950s, in designing a complex that utilizes structural originality and beauty to serve the research needs of scientists. More than just spacious facilities, the Salk Institute is designed to foster an intellectual community, in practical and symbolic ways contributing to the quest for truth.

The Institute recalls both Roman ruins and medieval monasteries. It includes two rows of four-story towers that house private studies for the researchers. Laboratories along the perimeter of the complex are linked by bridges and staircases to the towers. Between the rows of towers is a central canal with a small stream flowing toward the Pacific Ocean, symbolizing humanity's eternal and infinite search for knowledge. The Institute has been compared to Thomas Jefferson's design for the University of Virginia campus, what Jefferson called an "academical village." In Jefferson's plan, the central green flowed toward the West, symbolizing, like Kahn's stream, the great possibilities of the human mind.

In the late 1960s, Kahn began a project that would be a showcase for his use of space and light. The library at Philips-Exeter Academy, Exeter, New Hampshire, was completed in 1972. Reminiscent of Roman ruins, its outer walls of brick (also reflecting the mills that remain an important part of the New England heritage) remain disconnected at the corners, as if time had eroded them. The box-within-a-box structure moves outward from a central atrium (the primal space) illuminated by a large skylight. The bookstacks surround the atrium, as do the study carrels, lounge areas, and balconies. The Roman influence is also present in the atrium, in classical Rome a central open area popular in the homes of the wealthy.

Louis Kahn continued to teach and design until his death in 1974. His students viewed him as something of a guru, almost Confucian in his instruction. Fond of aphorisms not always readily comprehensible, Kahn gave his students much to ponder. He expressed his respect for the building and its materials with questions that personified the building, such as wondering what the building might want to be.

Kahn's comments caught the dreaming of an America ready to seek after new frontiers, on earth and in space. "Feeling and dream has no measure, has no language, and everyone's dream is singular," he said. Yet he was perceptive enough to realize that dreams have an impossibility about them, something Americans by the end of the 1960s readily understood in the aftermath of too many assassinations and so much social upheaval, and with continuing thoughts of "what might have been." "When I place the first line on paper to capture the dream," Kahn said, "the dream becomes less."[1]

Robert Venturi (b.1925)

Robert Venturi, born in Philadelphia in 1925, attended Princeton University, where he earned a B.A. degree and a M.F.A. As a student, he followed a pattern similar to Kahn's, studying under another architect inclined toward the Beaux-Arts style but who encouraged wide study in art history, even in archaeology—in this case, Jean Labatut, director of the graduate program in architecture at Princeton. Like Kahn, Venturi absorbed European influences, spending the mid-1950s as a fellow at the American Academy in Rome, although his interests were more in the Renaissance Mannerists than in classical Rome. Venturi later worked for Kahn as a junior designer in his firm and as a teaching assistant at the University of Pennsylvania.

Even more than Kahn, Venturi came to reject high-tech modernism and championed an inclusive, common-people focus in his architecture that stamped him as the quintessential architect of the 1960s. He made extensive use of pop art in his designs and, more than any of his predecessors, welded mass culture to high culture. Art was to be for the people, so Venturi looked to see what the people were doing. What he saw included highway strips, housing subdivisions, billboards, neon signs, gas stations, fast-food restaurants, and shopping centers. All of this was the stuff of art for Venturi, and he incorporated it into his designs, much to the chagrin of many of his architectural contemporaries.

Venturi published a book entitled *Complexity and Contradiction in Architecture* in 1966, written with the assistance of Denise Scott Brown, a faculty colleague at Pennsylvania who later became his wife. The book had an enormous impact, more even than his buildings, on the younger generation of architects and on architecture for the remainder of the century.

Espousing a wide-ranging inclusiveness and eschewing absolutes, Venturi readily grasped the contradictions in modern life. No summary can equal his own words:

Architects can no longer afford to be intimidated by the puritanically moral language of orthodox Modern architecture. I like elements which are hybrid rather than "pure," compromising rather than "clean," distorted rather than "straightforward," ambiguous rather than "articulated," perverse as well as impersonal, boring as well as "interesting," conventional rather than "designed".... I include the non sequitur and proclaim the duality.

I am for richness of meaning rather than clarity of meaning.... I prefer "both-and" to "either-or".... A valid architecture evokes many levels of meaning and combinations of focus: its space and its elements become readable and workable in several ways at once.[2]

Venturi forthrightly accepted symbolism, arguing that what he called the pure architecture of modernism, while rejecting symbolism and ornament, actually produced buildings that were thoroughly symbolic, but of a complex of exclusionary attitudes that Venturi found unacceptable. He would later write at length on architecture as symbol in *Learning from Las Vegas*, first published in 1972.

Two of Venturi's best known buildings are the Guild House in Philadelphia (1963) and the Vanna Venturi House in Chestnut Hill, Pennsylvania (1964). The Guild House is an apartment building for elderly residents sponsored by the Society of Friends. Designed to resemble Philadelphia row houses, it exhibits traits borrowed from a medley of sources: a central arch from classical architecture, a large marquee sign reading "Guild House" imitative of pop art, double-hung windows borrowed from housing projects, a white-glazed brick facade on part of the front that echoes Renaissance palaces, and a fake antenna on top of the building to symbolize how the elderly spend much time watching television. The totality achieves a result Venturi desired in his buildings—an apparently common building at first sight, with complexities and contradictions in design continuing to appear the longer one looks.

Venturi designed the Chestnut Hill house for his mother. As he writes in *Complexity and Contradiction*, "This building recognizes complexities and contradictions: it is both complex and simple, open and closed, big and little."[3] Careful observation shows an essentially symmetrical structure distorted by unbalanced placement of windows and a vertical slot above the off-center door. Internal contradictions include a staircase that leads nowhere, and a constant tension results from two vertical structures (a fireplace-chimney and another stair) that compete for primacy of place and visually distort each other.

A design for Copley Square in Boston shows Venturi's unorthodox use of space. Believing that Americans are uncomfortable with large, undefined space, where they feel that they should be working at the office or watching television in the living room with their families, Venturi defined the space by filling it. Keeping with his artistic acceptance of ordinary items from everyday life, he used not only trees, bushes, and benches, but trash cans, drains, and lampposts in his design.

Venturi returns to this subject of enclosed space in *Learning from Las Vegas*, where he contrasts the piazza model with the highway strip, specifically a stretch of road running through Las Vegas. Learning from the physical landscape and borrowing from folk art, for Venturi, are two characteristics of being revolutionary in architecture. Traditional architects, he argues, favor the enclosed space of the piazza to the sprawl of a sign-laden highway because they have been trained to take the easiest approach to space. Venturi, however, finds considerable beauty in the highway strip, even in billboards.

HOMES, STORES, AND OFFICES

One of the major demographic changes in the United States during the 1960s was the movement to the suburbs. This led to huge changes in lifestyle as families became wedded to the automobile, with the family car multiplying to cars to accommodate increased driving distances and the growing number of wives who worked. As suburban housing divisions proliferated, cementing a permanent relationship between real estate developer and builder, most Americans who chose suburban life found themselves living in homes similar in appearance to their neighbors' residences. Most suburbanites thought in terms of a builder rather than architect, unable to afford the individually planned house that stood in sharp contrast to the largely homogeneous buildings constructed with cost control in mind. These "little boxes" might be criticized as conformity by many observers, but others looked at the same houses and saw a strong community bond with neighbors socializing at backyard barbecues.

Those Americans who had the financial wherewithal to seek individuality in homes found plenty of architects and ideas available. Many wealthy Americans opted for second homes, a practice that mushroomed during the 1960s as a means of getting away from the pressures of daily life. Especially in second homes, usually in rustic settings, owners wanted buildings that meshed with the environment. The father of this union of home and nature was Frank Lloyd Wright, whose Spring Green, Wisconsin, house, Taliesin (1911, part of it rebuilt after a 1914 fire), and Kaufmann House, also known as Fallingwater (1937), at Bear Run, Pennsylvania, remain classics of the organic movement.

Halfway across the country from Wisconsin, the California style was based on the organic theory of architecture, with the climate and vegetation of large portions of the state conducive to this approach. These houses, popular in the 1960s, typically were low, with unpainted wood, gently pitched roof, and lots of glass to afford appealing views of the outdoors. Interior space, as in the Hunt House, Oakland, by Hunt and Company (1960), usually is quite open, with only partial, freestanding barriers separating kitchen, living room, and dining room. A large terrace or deck helps to dissolve the distinction between outside and indoors. In many areas, second homes adopted regional characteristics. Shingles, for example, added to the authenticity of houses along the shore or in rural areas, whether in California, along the East Coast, or anywhere in between.

Charles Moore, a follower of Louis Kahn, was one of the foremost home architects during the 1960s, especially in California. Learning from his master to use space in creative ways, Moore planned homes such as the Karas House in Monterey (1965), which includes bridges and lofts to create rooms in this three-story house that reject the traditional laying of one story on another. The living room, for example, rises to three stories, lighted by a large window and an outside reflector.

Stylistically, some homes from this time were abstract, favoring simple solutions to use of space and light for comfort and beauty; others were expressionistic, with the owner wanting to express personal emotion and create a dominant mood. An abstract construction could permit majestic views of the surrounding nature, but organic houses—that is, those designed to be one with nature—were by definition expressionistic. Most Americans, of course, had to find more economical ways to stamp their individuality on their suburban homes. For them, interior decorating and outside gardening might have to suffice. Yet large numbers of Americans lacked even this modest way to seek an individualized living space.

The words "house" and "home" usually are positive expressions; "housing" normally is not. Those who have sufficient money have their own house; those who have a lot of money hire an architect; those who have little money live in public housing.

A great deal of public housing was constructed in the 1960s, some necessitated by demolition of housing—often rundown tenements—during urban renewal efforts in inner cities. Some was the result of emerging social consciousness. There was no shortage of good intentions, but good execution did not always follow. Limited public funding and the desire of many architects to work on other projects were ongoing problems.

About 500,000 federally supported public housing units were created in the United States during the early years of the 1960s; by the end of the decade, that total had almost doubled.[4] Units, of course, had their positive aspects: fireproof construction, good lighting, private bathrooms, equipped kitchens, and so forth. Yet a project like the Robert Taylor Homes in Chicago, by Shaw, Metz Associates (1962), with twenty-eight sixteen-story buildings, each identical, often proved dehumanizing, ultimately substituting one type of slum (better constructed, of course) for another.

Some serious efforts were made to be more sensitive to the psychological as well as physical needs of inhabitants. President Kennedy's commissioner of urban renewal, William Slayton, was directed to encourage better planning, and some progressive projects were constructed. They included The St. Francis Square, San Francisco, designed by Marquis and Stoller (1963); and Warren Gardens, Roxbury, Massachusetts, by Hugh Stubbins and Associates (1969). Both sought to escape the project look through such methods as variety in building materials and design, creative landscaping, and individual touches like front and back doors to each apartment and private yards. Major urban problems, though, did much to undermine these advances, including increased drug use, inadequate education and job training, and broken families.

As living situations changed in the 1960s, so did shopping behaviors. As Americans moved into the suburbs, urban businesses increasingly followed. Large department stores and other businesses found more money to be made by going where the people who had money lived. Inner cities, increasingly left to the poor, also became increasingly dangerous as drug use and crime spread. Improved highways facilitated the relocation of stores, as suburbanites preferred the comfort and flexibility of cars to public transportation. The exodus of businesses from downtown areas left citizens who lacked the money to move prey to fewer purchasing options and therefore higher prices.

These changes meant an enormous growth in suburban shopping centers. Realtors and builders worked closely together to construct shopping centers as they did with residential developments. Highways and cars made centers readily available even when at a distance from the consumer's home. As shopping centers proved profitable, architects were called on to create complexes that would provide pleasant shopping experiences.

One type of shopping center is the strip center, which was popular in the 1950s and 1960s, and returned to favor in the 1980s. A strip usually included a supermarket and a variety of other stores lined up with it. Many strips were built along highways, with the consumer able to survey the entire range of stores. Parking usually was available in front of the stores, sometimes also on the sides, with delivery trucks unloading at the rear.

A second type of shopping center was the campus center, designed as a freestanding complex, often out in the country, as shopping centers began to inch beyond residential and business areas. A true shopping center is not just a random collection of stores that gradually came together, but a group of stores designed and constructed together, often with shared management and marketing. It is one unit, much like a college campus, with green space and parking lots planned to add practical and aesthetic dimensions to the buildings themselves.

The campus shopping center created on a separate plot of ground permitted overall planning and invited greater participation from architectural firms. One of the finest examples from the 1960s is Century City, in Los Angeles, designed by Welton Becket Associates (1964). A shopping center has at least one anchor, a major store that draws large numbers of consumers, along with smaller stores to encourage impulse shopping. The anchor for the strip usually was a supermarket, sometimes with a department store as a second anchor; the campus anchor more typically was a department store. In the case of Century City, both anchors were department stores.

Shopping centers initially excluded stores that would undermine the family atmosphere, such as liquor and secondhand establishments. Nor were recreational buildings, including movie houses, and restaurants part of the complex. Before long, however, restaurants were added, with the pizza place particularly popular.

The primary problem with the campus center was that customers were subject to inclement weather as they moved from store to store. It therefore was inevitable that all of the stores within a shopping center would be enclosed. Thus was born the mall.

The first enclosed shopping mall was Southdale Regional Shopping Center, in Edina, outside Minneapolis, which opened in 1956. During the 1960s, the shopping mall began to assume its place as not only a shopping center but also a recreational center for the community, as well as a hangout for teens. An early, and simple, mall plan was the dumbbell design, with two large anchor stores at each end and an aisle between them. Smaller stores lined the aisle so shoppers could be enticed from both sides while making their way from one end to the other. The aisle had to be narrow enough for consumers to see window displays on both sides yet wide enough not to create a sense of overcrowding.

Malls quickly grew, with additional anchors, more complex designs to accommodate increased numbers of stores, two or more levels of shops, courtyards with plants and even trees, skylights, and escalators. Restaurants were added to encourage more hours at the mall, and therefore more purchases. The Paramus Park Shopping Center in Paramus, New Jersey (1962), added a food court, now a staple of shopping malls, which featured large shared seating for an array of fast-food franchises. Theaters helped the mall to become a day and night encounter, and the larger and more imaginative planners included other recreational opportunities, such as skating rinks.

The guru of shopping-center design was Victor Gruen, who designed Southdale. His *Shopping Towns U.S.A.: The Planning of Shopping Centers* (1960) became the bible of shopping-center planning and was followed in 1973 by Gruen's *Centers for the Urban Environment: Survival of the Cities*.

By the publication of Gruen's second book, city planners were trying to renew inner cities devastated by the exodus of businesses. Shopping centers had become primarily a suburban phenomenon, but they started to appear occasionally in city centers. San Francisco helped lead the way in restoring old buildings and transforming them into shopping centers, especially offering upscale shops selling fashions, crafts, and gourmet food. Ghirardelli Square, a block of industrial buildings along the north end waterfront in San Francisco, was redesigned by Wurster, Bernardi and Emmons (1964) into an inviting complex of shops and restaurants. At the end of the decade, the nearby Cannery project, by Esherick, Homsey Dodge and Davis, added similar opportunities.

Many Americans left the cities to live and shop elsewhere, but continued to work in them. In fact, the need for office space grew dramatically during the 1960s, a need in part filled by looking upward. Skyscrapers had long served as an important symbol of American ambition, profit, and prestige; so while many new offices opened in suburban office parks, others appeared in new buildings downtown.

Technological advances, including new building materials and computer designing, permitted great variation and innovation in skyscraper design. Mies van der Rohe, the master of the glass curtain wall (which seemed to drop from the top rather than bear structural weight) and champion of a minimalist approach (with relatively simple design), continued to create such skyscrapers as the One Charles Center in Baltimore (1963) and Chicago's

Federal Center (1964). With improvements in concrete, the curtain could convey a greater sense of solidity and make use of contrasts between light and shadow, as in New York City's Pan Am Building (later renamed MetLife), designed by Walter Gropius, Pietro Belluschi, and their respective associates (1963).

Other architects chose to highlight the skeleton rather than skin, bringing forward the steel structure in buildings like the John Hancock Center in Chicago, designed by Fazlur Khan of the highly respected SOM team (Skidmore, Owings, Merrill), constructed during the late 1960s and completed in 1970. A system of diagonal braces creates a kind of exoskeleton that helps to reduce effect of the wind. At its completion, the ninety-seven-story Hancock Center was second in height only to the Empire State Building; "Big John," as it is often called, remains the tallest mixed-use building in the world (including a hotel, offices, shops, and a swimming pool).

The concept of a tube within a tube became popular in tall buildings that went up in the late 1960s, some of them not completed until the next decade, including the John Hancock Center. A variety of refinements were employed, such as use of a central tube enclosing elevator and utilities, and an exterior tube composed of the outer walls, including tightly spaced columns, to distribute the structural load of the building (Brunswick Building, Chicago, SOM, 1965); bundling tubes together to gain support from common walls (Sears Tower, Chicago, SOM, 1974); and enclosing the surrounding sheer walls (the inner tube) with an outer tube of concrete columns and beams (One Shell Plaza, Houston, SOM, 1971).

PUBLIC BUILDINGS

The 1960s proved receptive to new public buildings, including government buildings, museums, and schools. The decade opened with a new sense of optimism concerning public service in response to the election of the first U.S. president born in the twentieth century. There was a widespread feeling that the country was moving forward, and President Kennedy's summons to explore a new frontier set the tone. Both the president and First Lady were keenly interested in the arts and encouraged creative exploration in how to bring architecture, painting, sculpture, music, and other arts before the public. The National Endowment for the Arts was born in 1965, and the Arts in Public Places program followed two years later.

Growth of suburbs necessitated new schools, especially at the elementary and secondary levels. Educational opportunities increased from preschool through adulthood, stimulated by such factors as the space race, integration of schools, and growing awareness of those who needed job training, remedial instruction, or help to overcome disabilities.

No one style dominated any of these public buildings, but for government buildings architects tended toward either a sort of modernist classic or abstract approach. Classic details often included use of the colonnade and/or elevated podium to create a quasi-temple look. The plaza also was popular. For example, the City Hall in Eugene, Oregon, designed by Stafford and Morrin, and James Longwood (1964), offers a formal approach to visitors who climb steps and pass through an encircling colonnade to enter the building, itself a circular construction surrounded by a square plaza. The Lincoln Center for the Performing Arts in New York, its buildings designed by Max Abramovitz, Wallace Harrison, and Philip Johnson (1962–66), offers colonnades, arches, and a geometrically designed plaza among other architectural details.

More abstract designs yielded other buildings of great beauty and usefulness, among them Boston City Hall, by McKinnell and Knowles (1969), with its sense of power through almost pop art configurations of vertical and horizontal concrete trusses, preceded by rectangular and diagonal walls; and the two joined Ys of the U.S. Department of Housing and Urban Development, by Marcel Breuer Associates (1968), in Washington, D.C.

Rising interest in art in the 1960s rendered many art museums too small and called for additions as well as new buildings. As Carole Rifkind has pointed out in her *Field Guide to Contemporary American Architecture*, art museums usually were constructed according to one of three general designs: the loft, the path, or the palace.[5] The loft construction offers open spaces that can be reconfigured with temporary dividers and that emphasize primacy of the artifacts themselves. Other museums lead visitors along a defined path, making the architecture part of the artistic experience. Still other museums invite visitors to wander among an array of rooms and corridors, similar to passing through a palace. Some museums, of course, employ a combination of these models.

The Whitney Museum of American Art in New York City, designed by Marcel Breuer and Hamilton Smith (1966), is an important example of the loft structure. With its exterior combination of overhanging sections and largely plain walls, and an interior utilizing an open grid ceiling, the museum gives the appearance of being an unusually aesthetic warehouse, which is what a loft-designed art museum really is.

Frank Lloyd Wright's Solomon R. Guggenheim Museum in New York City (1959) offers a spiraling exterior that parallels the spiraling interior ramp that viewers follow from level to level. Wright influenced many other museums, including I.M. Pei's Everson Museum at Syracuse University (1968), a geometrically complex structure with the spiraling concept leading into four large rectangular gallery spaces.

The palace museum included Philip Johnson's Amon Carter Museum in Fort Worth, Texas (1961), and Sheldon Memorial Art Gallery, Lincoln, Nebraska (1963). The nation's most complete examples of this type of museum, though, fall prior to and after the 1960s—for example, the truly palatial National Gallery of Art in Washington, D.C. (John Russell Pope, 1941); and the

J. Paul Getty Museum in Malibu, California (Langdon and Wilson, 1974), constructed along the lines of a magnificent classic villa.

Elementary and secondary schools quickly joined residents and shopping centers outside the city, with school boards favoring modern designs rather than the traditional two-story brick and stone structures that for previous generations symbolized a solid, uniform, no-nonsense education. Federal financial support made architectural experimentation easier, and some communities tried new approaches like open spaces rather than closed-in classrooms and windowless buildings to discourage distractions. Such innovations usually proved short-lived, but more permanent changes produced buildings that were lower, often one-story high (with the exception of the gymnasium), and spread out over a much larger expanse of ground. With the United States attempting to catch up to Russia in the space race and realize President Kennedy's goal of putting a man on the moon before the end of the decade, schools increased their emphasis on science and mathematics. New schools, with spacious and well-furnished science labs, reflected this national goal. In a more international world, schools also had to accommodate a boom in studying foreign languages, hence the language lab. And there was a lot more grass surrounding the building, artistically landscaped, while parking lots accommodated the large number of drivers, both staff and students.

The campus concept had been part of American universities and colleges since their inception, and that same approach increasingly was being taken toward shopping centers and suburban schools. The campus ideal, however, includes uniform planning, and in that area the university sometimes came up short. Most institutions of higher learning continued to grow, requiring new buildings, yet these additions in many cases reflected the individual genius of the architect more than the stylistic pattern of already existing buildings. That could create considerable controversy, as, for example, with Paul Rudolph's School of Art and Architecture at Yale (1964). Influenced by Walter Gropius, his Harvard mentor, Rudolph created a rugged surface by hammering raised ridges of concrete. The building has been called more of a sculpture than building, and its enormous variety in ceiling height and an interior that proved confusing to find one's way around in led to quite a bit of controversy, all the more so when heating and ventilating problems developed.

The main library at the University of Notre Dame, though radically distinct from other campus buildings, proved that contrast could be quite appealing. Opened in 1963 and designed by the Ellerbe Company, the Theodore M. Hesburgh Library (originally named the Memorial Library) rises over the Notre Dame campus, its two large main floors topped by a thirteen-floor tower. Open stacks, considerable open space for flexibility in use, and limited windows (especially in the tower) to reduce glare mark the interior. The exterior is highlighted by a huge Word of Life mural on

The Theodore M. Hesburgh Library at the University of Notre Dame features "Touchdown Jesus," made from eighty-one types of stones.

the south side often referred to as "Touchdown Jesus" because the image of Christ, arms raised not unlike the referee's touchdown gesture, is visible from the football stadium. The mural is based on a commissioned painting by Millard Sheets depicting teachers and scholars (with Christ presented as the ultimate teacher), the painting applied to the wall by the Cold Spring Granite Company as a mosaic consisting of eighty-one different types of stones from sixteen countries.[6] The stones could almost be seen as symbolic of the variety in architecture during the 1960s.

VATICAN II AND CHURCH ARCHITECTURE

The Roman Catholic Church was not alone among religions that found their members worshipping in new and innovatively designed houses of worship in the 1960s. In fact, churches and synagogues accounted for a significant percentage (the exact figure impossible to calculate) of creatively designed buildings in the decades following World War II. Some of this growth resulted from the need for new places to worship in the growing suburbs, with an often unhappy consequence being the abandonment of inner-city places of worship dear to the hearts of millions of American families.

A few of the new and aesthetically appealing houses of worship built in the 1960s are the Central United Protestant Church, Richland, Washington, designed by the Durham Anderson Freed firm (1965), with steeply pitched roof, angled ceiling, and nave and sanctuary joined as one space; the John Knox Presbyterian Church, Marietta, Georgia, by Amisano and Wells (1966), constructed simply with local materials and featuring a square skylight over the sanctuary area with rows of bench seats crowding closely on three sides; the First Unitarian Church and School, Rochester, New York, by Louis Kahn (1963), utilizing open space, individual chair seats, and light filtering in from the corners; B'Nai Jehudah Synagogue, Kansas City, Missouri, by Kivett and Myers (1967), its conical ceiling about eight stories high with strategically placed lighting to suggest the surrounding universe and the aspiring, eternal nature of humanity's search for God; and the Trinity Episcopal Church, Concord, Massachusetts, by Pietro Belluschi, a prolific builder of churches (1963), wedding old and new in its expression of Gothic characteristics in wood, such as arches and ribbed vaulting, while focusing worshippers' attention on the triangular stained glass window above and behind the altar.

The Catholic Church, however, was unique in the 1960s in that a watershed event precipitated enormous changes in the life of the church, including its liturgy, leading to major alterations in how Catholic churches were designed. This event was the Second Vatican Council, and its very existence, much less its impact, would have been almost impossible to predict at the beginning of the 1960s.

Pope Pius XII died in 1958 and was succeeded by John XXIII (Angelo Giuseppe Roncalli). John XXIII quickly endeared himself to Catholics and non-Catholics alike with his preference for the human touch and a lot less pomp than was customary with pontiffs. He was not, however, different only in style; he soon became one of the most reform-minded popes in history. John XXIII announced the Second Vatican Council in January 1959 and formally opened the proceedings on October 11, 1962. Although he lived for only the first of four sessions, the council continued until 1965 under Pope Paul VI. Vatican II was the twenty-first ecumenical (that is, worldwide) council, the second to be designated a Vatican Council (the first occurring in 1870). It included more delegates than any previous ecumenical council (about 2,600 bishops in attendance), was most representative (earlier councils having been European dominated), included the most non-Catholic and lay observers, and differed in its mission (to promote peace and unity rather than defend dogma or attack enemies of the church).

Vatican II produced sixteen documents, varying, of course, in significance. These documents redefined the Catholic Church as a community of the whole people of God rather than primarily as a hierarchical organization, expanded roles for lay members, and asserted that the church functions within rather than outside the world. One document produced during the first session of Vatican II is immediately relevant to church architecture—*The Constitution on the Sacred Liturgy.*

This document emphasizes the importance of liturgy in the life of Catholics as the "outstanding means by which the faithful can express in their lives, and manifest to others, the mystery of Christ"; and requires "that all the faithful be led to that full, conscious, and active participation in liturgical celebrations which is demanded by the very nature of the liturgy." *The Constitution* then discusses types of liturgy, beginning with the Eucharist, which is celebrated during the Mass, and which Catholics believe contains the real essence of Christ. Catholics should, the document continues, "participate knowingly, devoutly, and actively" in this "mystery of faith."[7] Clearly, changes were required to achieve these goals.

These changes included permission to use the vernacular language during Mass. Although continued use of Latin was permitted, it was not long before the vernacular replaced most of the Latin, enabling the congregation better to understand the Mass and participate in communal responses, prayers, and hymns.

With these new directives for the Eucharist, along with new emphasis on the collective "people of God," physical changes in Catholic churches were necessary. Priest and congregation must be closer together to jointly participate in the liturgy. In pre-Vatican II churches, the altar was against the front wall, and the priest "said" Mass with his back to the people, except for certain portions of the Mass, such as distribution of communion and preaching the epistle and gospel. In addition, an altar railing essentially fenced off the congregation from the altar.

Now the altar was turned around and simplified, with the priest facing the congregation, speaking across a low altar to worshippers able to see all of the priest's actions. In old churches, the previous altar might remain, but a new one was constructed for daily use. The altar railing disappeared, eliminating a symbol of separation. This sanctuary area is where much of the most essential change in architecture occurred within Catholic churches.

There were other areas of change as well. Older churches usually contained a wide array of statues, not just of Jesus, but also of Mary and other saints. Statues were still permitted, but *The Constitution on the Sacred Liturgy* urged limiting their number and moderating their impact. This call to greater simplicity encouraged more modern styles in the statuary, Stations of the Cross, and other artwork.

Furthermore, the document called for revision of the canons and statutes governing all of the material objects associated with liturgy—in essence, an invitation to greater creativity in the exteriors and interiors of churches, including construction of altars, tabernacles, and baptisteries. Also mandated were changes in the sacrament of penance to better express the nature of the sacrament.

Although it would take ten years before the new *Rite of Penance* would be promulgated (December 2, 1973), the revised liturgy for penance, now usually called the Rite of Reconciliation, would mean changes in the physical structure of the church. The old confessional typically was a small room with a central section for the priest and a section on each side for penitents separated from the priest by a wall with a window that could be opened by sliding a panel across to permit communication. The penitent confessed in anonymity, a process that did not encourage extensive dialogue. After Vatican II, especially from the 1970s on, new churches featured a reconciliation room where the parishioner and priest could speak face-to-face in more of a counseling format. In old churches, many confessionals were remodeled into reconciliation rooms.

The new vision of the role of lay Catholics and the nature of liturgical rites bore quick fruit in church architecture. Sacristy and nave came closer together, often almost merging when seats surrounded the altar on three sides, a common approach to bringing worshippers closer to the altar. Altars devoid of their previous ornate decorations moved down close to the congregation, with no altar railings intervening. Tabernacles, usually in the center of old altars, now moved off the altar, often to the side. Simplicity, light, and closeness dominated, while modern, often abstract images replaced the old brightly colored larger-than-life statues of saints. The choir, rather than being located in a high loft at the back of the church, was more likely somewhere in front, and the accompaniment was often a small organ or guitars rather than the grand pipe organs of the past. Triumphalism, the use of architecture and other arts to symbolize the power and grandeur of the Catholic Church, faded into history.

Post-Vatican II churches mushroomed during the 1960s, especially in suburbs. Some of the new buildings achieved considerable architectural renown, among them the Church of St. Jude in San Francisco, by Patrick Quinn and Dennis Shanagher (1969), with its almost square nave virtually merging with the sanctuary area, and with seating surrounding the forward altar on three sides; St. Patrick's, in Oklahoma City, from the firm of Murray Jones Murray (1962), its glass walls and open space uniting congregation and celebrant; St. Mary's Cathedral, San Francisco, by Pietro Belluschi (under construction from 1963 and completed in 1970), one of the first Catholic churches planned from inception according to Vatican Council directives, and despite its size maintaining a sense of closeness with no columns impeding the vision of the altar from the seating in front and along the sides; and St. Francis de Sales, Muskegon, Michigan, by Marcel Breuer, another prominent designer of churches (1967), combining soaring height with natural light from cut-in skylights, the height by contrast with the length of the nave making priest and worshippers feel closer together than they actually are. Vast numbers of existing churches, including cathedrals in Chicago and Indianapolis, were remodeled to facilitate new requirements of the liturgy and the vision of a community rather than hierarchy of participants.

PRESERVING HISTORY

The decade of the 1960s in many ways was a time of revolution, but regarding architecture there also was a strong desire to retain some of the great buildings of the past. The groundwork for addressing this problem had been laid in earlier decades with establishment of the Historical American Buildings Survey (HABS) under the Park Service to document the history of American buildings, and the congressionally chartered National Trust for Historic Preservation to preserve relevant information and coordinate preservation efforts. Nonetheless, destruction of historically important buildings continued to occur.

This decade was also a turning point in the struggle to retain buildings that were important within American history and culture. By the early 1960s, about 25% of buildings listed on the HABS had disappeared.[8] Consciousness, however, had been raised by Jane Jacobs, who in her book *The Death and Life of Great American Cities* (1961) argued for, as she entitled one of her chapters, "The Need for Aged Buildings." To Jacobs, buildings are important not just for their individual historical or aesthetic significance but also because they reflect a diverse way of life. A strong contingent of representative buildings must be preserved, she argued, not for their own sakes but for the different types of people who lived, worked, and played

Grand Central Station was a battleground for preservation efforts during the 1960s. Source: Corbis Corporation.

in them—buildings she described as "not museum-piece old buildings, not old buildings in an excellent and expensive state of rehabilitation—although these make fine ingredients—but also a good lot of plain, ordinary, low-value old buildings, including some rundown old buildings."[9]

One of these old buildings that stirred up considerable passion in the decade was New York's Pennsylvania Station, modeled somewhat on an ancient Roman bath complex. Utilitarianism won out, with the Pennsylvania Railroad demolishing the station in 1963. However, its loss helped lead to the New York City Landmarks Preservation Commission in 1965, charged with reviewing all buildings that had been standing for at least thirty years and designating those it deemed appropriate to be official landmarks. Owners who violated the commission's judgments were subject to penalties, including fines.

Other cities followed New York's lead by establishing similar commissions, among them St. Louis, Denver, and San Francisco. The U.S. Congress approved a National Historic Preservation Act to require preservation of historic architectural works. Financial incentives, including tax credits, supported preservation efforts, and financial assistance was made available to private groups through the National Trust for Historic Preservation.

One of the preservation battlegrounds was the Grand Central Terminal in New York City, a 1913 Beaux-Arts train station. The Landmarks Preservation Commission named Grand Central an official landmark in 1967. The owner, Penn Central Transportation Company, challenged the decision, arguing economic hardship for the corporation, and later, as it carried its battle to the nation's Supreme Court, that the original decision was unconstitutional. The battle continued until June 1978, when the Supreme Court upheld the landmarks law. A very public train ride featuring prominent architects and Mrs. Jacqueline Kennedy Onassis, the former First Lady, had helped to mobilize popular opinion behind the preservation effort. Where architecture was concerned, the 1960s had found common ground for both respecting the old and creating the new.

5

Fashion

If clothes make the man (or woman), then during the 1960s the United States was populated with a vast kaleidoscope of beings. The 1950s, a decade commonly associated with conformity, yielded to a decade rich in variety, including variety in clothing styles. The old order was breaking down, and as men, women, and the "young" started to think in patterns that diverged sharply from the past, they also started to dress differently. In an era reacting against the establishment, fashion both followed and precipitated political action. The fashion cart was both before and after the horse of social change.

In the old days, before the multifaceted revolution of the 1960s, fashion was set by an establishment ultimately housed in Paris, trickling down in diluted amounts to consumers across borders and oceans. The United States, however, had always to some extent gone its own way, having thrown off the shackles of European direction in the eighteenth century and reluctant to don them again through clothing dictates. Americans tended toward the practical and casual in clothing, though no less conformist for that tendency. The Sears mail-order catalog was more influential than Parisian haute couture, even if Sears and its competitors were not entirely free from foreign influence.

The mail-order business brought American fashion onto the farms and towns of the countryside, and only those who could not afford to buy what they saw remained outside the prevailing fashions. Changes, however, were occurring that would prepare Americans for radical alterations in clothing. World War II lured women out of their homes and into the workplace, many even dressing like men in blue jeans as they labored in defense plants to provide the means whereby the United States would rescue Europe from Hitler. After the war, many women were not prepared merely to resume their place in an Ozzie and Harriet world in which they stayed at home cooking and cleaning.

Also characterizing the years between that world triumph and the failure in Vietnam was a steady migration of farmers off the land and into towns and cities. Within cities, there was a parallel movement into the suburbs. At the same time, the U.S. population was both increasing and growing younger. From 1945 to 1960, the farm population declined from twenty-four million to fifteen million, dropping another five million by the end of the 1960s. By 1965, about one-half of the U.S. population was younger than twenty-five; and for the first time in the nation's history there were more students attending college than farmers working the land.[1] The country was younger, more urban (increasingly suburban), with a population of women ready to assert their individuality. The rules transmitted from the previous generations—in politics, religion, sexuality, the roles of the sexes, use of drugs, and in countless other areas—were growing more fragile by the day. Before the decade of the 1960s had reached its halfway point, for many Americans the only rule that remained was that there were none. Fashion was an important part of these changes.

THE INFLUENCE OF FRENCH HAUTE COUTURE

The arbiters of fashion in Paris, though less influential on American fashion than on European dress throughout the century, nonetheless were important as the 1960s began and continued to be part of the U.S. fashion world throughout the decade, although in an increasingly reduced role. The most important conduit for French style was the First Lady, Jacqueline Kennedy, who was the single greatest influence on the way American women dressed during the decade, especially in the early 1960s.

When the Kennedys visited Paris in 1961, the president, with only some exaggeration, introduced himself as the man who had accompanied Jackie. The Paris newspapers described Mrs. Kennedy, who had studied at the Sorbonne and spoke French fluently, as *charmante*, meaning charming. Glamorous and cultured, she exhibited impeccable taste in fashion as she did in the arts. American designer Oleg Cassini described her taste in fashion quite simply as the best.

That best in evening wear might be a Cassini gown, black on top with a gold skirt and large gold bow at the waist. The high-bodice, floor-length empire style was especially favored by the First Lady, leading her sister citizens, who could order their own empire evening gown through Sears for $25, to imitate her on their evening excursions.[2]

Then there was Jackie in a Chanel suit, with bouffant hairstyle and pillbox hat. A pillbox-hat craze swept over the United States, and again inexpensive versions were available for women of modest means. Sears featured

First Lady Jacqueline Kennedy set fashion standards for women throughout the country. Source: Photofest, Inc.

a variety of them in its catalogs at $3–$5, the higher price for a pillbox blooming in artificial roses.

Much photographed also in casual moments, Jackie could be seen sporting a riding suit complete with trousers or wearing wraparound sunglasses. The latter precipitated another fashion craze, with Purdy Opticians in Manhattan attempting to capitalize by claiming to have provided Jackie with her glasses. The White House forced Purdy to desist, but sunglasses were here to stay. The influence of Mrs. Kennedy on fashion began to decline after the assassination of President Kennedy left Americans with other, sadder images of the First Lady.

As the Johnsons replaced the Kennedys in the White House, the influence of haute couture on American fashion declined sharply, especially as much of the country turned increasingly antiestablishment. French designers, though, continued to have their moments, some of them through a wedding of fashion with painting. Yves St. Laurent borrowed Piet Mondrian's rectangular shapes for a 1965 line of straight jersey dresses. The Florentine Emilio Pucci and other designers borrowed from Op Art painters like Bridget Riley the black and white lines that created optical illusions of constant movement either on canvas or on a body. Pop Art, with its bright colors and bold but simple designs, also influenced fashion designers, such as the British popularizer of the miniskirt, Mary Quant.

Other innovations from time to time came forth from the world of haute couture. Paco Rabanne used aluminum, plastic, scrap metal, and even paper for his clothes. With the latter, he designed a disposable paper dress in 1967. Scott Paper Company had come up with the idea for a paper dress even earlier, an item of clothing labeled "the wastebasket dress" by *Life* magazine in 1966.

Two jackets for men, the Nehru and the Mao, had their time in the sun— or under the lights of night clubs and television studios. Pierre Cardin saw Sammy Davis, Jr., in a lapel-free jacket with a turtleneck shirt, and got the idea for a modification of the jacket (no lapel and a small stiff collar) worn by Indian Prime Minister Jawaharlal Nehru, who had died in 1964. The jacket had a serious vogue in 1967 and 1968, worn by celebrities such as talk-show host Johnny Carson, football star Joe Namath, and baseball pitcher Denny McLain. Sears included in their children's Winnie-the-Pooh collection a perma-press Nehru, even featuring it on the cover of their 1969 summer catalog. The Mao jacket, named after Chinese communist leader Mao Zedong (also spelled Mao Tse-tung) was similar to the Nehru but came farther down the legs. A Testa-Taroni creation, it fit a growing anti-American attitude that coincided with declining support for the Vietnam War.

At the beginning of the 1960s, the well-dressed serious man still favored a dark two-piece suit with white shirt. The more adventurous sported the three-piece Italian look. The major changes wrought in fashionable men's suits involved synthetic fibers and lighter weight. Short hair was the norm, although mothers might have their sons get a Prince Charles cut, named after the teen heir to the British throne. The style featured hair several inches long on top with a touch of a ducktail at back and hair falling forward and down about halfway on the forehead. In reality, the cut was only a modified version of the 1950s look associated with the actor Edd "Kookie" Byrnes. An even earlier antecedent had been called the French Cut some thirty years before.

Emanuel Ungaro, born in Aix-en-Provence to an Italian tailor, opened his own design house in the mid-1960s. The house of Ungaro was the last of the old-time haute couture enterprises. From then on, the self-contained world of high fashion could no longer dictate international fashion, and labels could not guarantee acceptance. Designers looked outward for inspiration, taking direction from what real people were wearing. Product followed demand; the market determined taste. The number of fashion houses enrolled with the prestigious Chambre Syndicale des Couturiers Parisiens dropped from thirty to seventeen,[3] and haute couture came increasingly to be viewed as old-fashioned.

AMERICAN INFORMALITY

The United States on the whole was not much given to formality. Its democratic spirit perceived all men (if not women) as created equal; a theoretically classless society might dress just about alike, and its members would not want to put on airs. Mail-order catalogs tended to homogenize fashion while making purchases easier and sometimes cheaper.

As much of the country benefited from increased postwar prosperity, the migration from farm to city to suburb picked up pace. Life in the suburb tended also to be somewhat uniform, and the backyard and patio encouraged easy informality among neighbors. Informal clothes fit the new lifestyle.

Sports also played an important role in American fashion. The outdoors had always been an important part of American life, although greater numbers of Americans by the 1960s were going outside to play rather than work. The spectator sports such as baseball and football were joined by a wide range of other athletic endeavors, among them skiing, hiking, boating, golf, and tennis. Sports such as golf and tennis became activities for more than just the wealthy. Participation in these sports called for clothing that was functional and comfortable. Before long, stretch pants and parkas had moved from ski slopes to everyday life—along with closets of clothes from other outdoor activities.

As Jackie Kennedy gave a kind of last-gasp rejuvenation to haute couture, the young, handsome president exuded informality, especially after his grandfatherly predecessor, Dwight Eisenhower. The American public was fed a steady diet of photographs of John Kennedy sailing or playing with his children, and of the Kennedy clan exercising their passion for touch football. Minus a tie, with an open-collar shirt and hatless, President Kennedy in these photographs helped to set a youthful, active, informal standard. Hat sales plummeted for men, and as the 1960s moved forward young women also eschewed head coverings, in their case less owing to a Kennedy than to changing hairstyles.

Haute couture had offered full ensembles, but the sportswear industry appealed to individual taste by serving up separates that consumers could mix and match as they wished. Sport coats began to replace traditional suits and did so in a variety of colors and designs, including prints, plaids, stripes, and checks. Men took to wearing them not only with dress slacks but with casual slacks and even jeans. The very nature of the suit began to change with the introduction of the oxymoronically named leisure suit, and the seersucker became a popular and light alternative for the man who chose to retain some degree of formality. Sears in the early 1960s offered matching his and hers seersuckers (for the woman, though, a skirt rather than slacks, and a double-breasted jacket with large buttons). A juvenile version was available for the boy in the family.

Much of the growing comfort in casual and semiformal wear resulted from the development of synthetic fibers. Lighter clothes that could be washed and worn without ironing or dry cleaning extended into all-day wear the desire for comfort and functionality previously found in clothes designed for recreational sports. Suits, sport coats, and slacks offered the ease of polyester, while the yielding polyester double-knit appealed to both men and women, especially those who were perhaps a bit overweight. Double-knit slacks and pant suits became enormously popular with women of all ages as the decade advanced.

Spandex clothes originally produced for sports, such as in stretch ski slacks, quickly migrated into everyday wear, even affecting undergarments. Lycra (a spandex trademark) yielded the Little Godiva step-in girdle, manufactured by the Warner Lingerie Company in 1960. By the end of the decade, though, the girdle would virtually disappear from the wardrobe of the young and would-be-young.

Growing passion for surfing induced many young women to trade in the bikini for the two-piece bathing suit, although the bikini, much to the delight of males, otherwise remained in place. Other popular casual items included culottes (women's trousers or long shorts cut to look like skirts), especially among coeds, and the simple "little nothing" black dress popularized by actress Audrey Hepburn in the film *Breakfast at Tiffany's* (1961) for an evening on the town.

The turtleneck became ubiquitous among men, worn for all occasions and with slacks, jeans, and sport coats. As the turtleneck rose in popularity, the tie declined. Even in the most formal of settings (except for an occasional restaurant that maintained traditional dress codes), the turtleneck minus tie with sport coat became the American look. Actors Paul Newman and Steve McQueen sported turtlenecks, and millions of other men could don the same apparel and imagine themselves just as handsome, sophisticated, and irresistible.

THE BRITISH ARE COMING, THE BRITISH ARE COMING

Just as Americans seemingly threw off the last vestiges of French haute couture, they succumbed (although only partly) to the British. Much of the credit (or blame) rested with four singers and musicians named George Harrison, John Lennon, Paul McCartney, and Ringo Starr, better known collectively as the Beatles. The Beatles came together in the early 1960s in Liverpool, England, recording their first single, "Love Me Do," in 1962. They arrived in the United States in 1964 and reached a national audience through an appearance on *The Ed Sullivan Show*, perhaps the most influential television program of its time. It is hard today to understand adults' opposition to a group singing "I Want to Hold Your Hand," but if adults were not sure about these visitors, teens took to them passionately. A new term was coined to describe the frenzy of the Beatles' fans—"Beatlemania."

The Beatles are discussed in more detail elsewhere in this book, but their relevance to fashion lay primarily in their hair. Because of the country's love affair with the Beatles, boys and young men in droves let their hair grow long enough to get a Beatles haircut. The mop-top look ushered in a decade of changing hairstyles for men and women, long for men, either super short or long and straight for women (although the Afro also became popular). Hair was no longer merely a matter of taste but a political statement. The 1960s was not the first time in American history when hair symbolized rejection of the older generation's social, political, and sexual attitudes (witness women's bobbed hair during the Jazz Age), but it was the period when hair reached its highest symbolic level, before antiestablishment trends in hair were adopted by the masses and became totally respectable.

The most popular British contribution to women's clothing styles (at least with men) was the miniskirt. The British designer Mary Quant deserves primary but not exclusive credit for the new style. Her innovation lay as much in process as product. Rather than look toward the traditional haute couture houses, she turned her attention to what young girls on British streets seemed to be wearing. Alert to market demand, she emphasized the short skirt worn anywhere from two to nine inches above the knee, at the same time giving the miniskirt a more legitimate place within fashion. André Courrèges did for France what Quant accomplished for England, but it was Quant who had the greater impact on American women. Many mothers and grandmothers, of course, along with a smattering of men, were scandalized by the revealing attire.

The London look created by Quant included miniskirt, patterned stockings, a short, tight ribbed sweater, and high boots. When *Seventeen* magazine featured Quant's clothes in the 1961 spring issue, and J. C. Penney followed the next year by marketing her designs, Quant's influence on American fashion was assured. A few years later, Quant helped to popularize the woman's pantsuit.

What really set off the miniskirt was a pair of go-go boots. Go-go bars and discotheques spread rapidly in the early 1960s from Paris to U.S. cities, usually featuring young women in very short dresses and very tall boots, dancing in a location readily visible, sometimes in a hanging cage. A U.S. singer brought the go-go boots out of bars and into countless closets—Nancy Sinatra, daughter of Frank. The song was "These Boots are Made for Walkin'," from 1966. Nancy often appeared in white miniskirt and white go-go boots as her song climbed to Number One on the charts.

In the same year that Nancy Sinatra was publicizing her boots, a waiflike teen named Leslie Hornby was refining the British mod look (bobbed hair, miniskirt, long eyelashes, bright colors, and a very slim, boyish figure). Twiggy, as she was known, came from a working-class London neighborhood and quit school to be guided by her boyfriend–manager, Justin de Villeneuve. She modeled for *Woman's Mirror*, was labeled the "face of 1966" by the *Daily Express*, and traveled to the United States in 1967. Americans were enchanted with Twiggy, and *Newsweek* called her hairstyle "the most

Designer Mary Quant wears one of her own miniskirts to a luncheon in 1966 to launch her book *Quant by Quant*. Source: Photofest, Inc.

radiant and evocative new image" of the year.[4] Her hair had been cut and styled by the famous hair stylist Leonard, but perhaps more influential overall as a hair stylist was Vidal Sassoon. Sassoon developed his boyish cut—short, sculpted, nape of the neck exposed, sideburns sometimes asymmetrical—for Mary Quant's mannequins.

Sears by 1967 was advertising its London look designs for women, including hip-hugging checked pants, a "Dapper Dot" shirt with wide pointed collars and wide dotted tie, and a visor cap to match or contrast. Men shared in this "peacock revolution," with bright colors and extravagant patterns. Textured vests and paisley shirts were in, and ties worked only if they were wide (3½–5 inches) and similarly colorful—the idea discarded that a man should wear a striped tie against a single-color, preferably white, shirt. Big was the order of the day—big collars, big lapels: big—like the influence of Britain on U.S. fashion.

THE YOUTHFUL LOOK

The designers, makers, and sellers of fashion were looking ever more closely at what young people wanted. The young were much of the fashion market, along with not-so-young individuals who turned to clothes and hairstyles to retrieve a bit of their youth. Developments like the short skirt previously worn by very young girls, the Twiggy look, and the slim ideal (such styles as hip-hugger slacks could be worn attractively only by the slim) taught the world that young was both beautiful and sexy. In many ways, the 1960s was a young decade—a youthful president, new frontiers in space, the Job Corps summoning men and women (primarily young) to help create a better world, the declining average age of U.S. citizens, even young lifestyles rooted in suburbia and the automobile.

At the beginning of the 1960s, there still remained the traditional view that the young were defined primarily within the context of their families. Sears proudly championed its "look-alike" fashions, identical dresses for all the women and girls in the family, above the knees, of course, only for the children. The assumption was that not much would please a child more than to dress like her parent. In its 1962 catalogs, Sears exhibited mothers and daughters barely able to contain their joy in identical dresses made of alternating squares of white and blue check gingham and beige saque cloth—the "patchwork pals." For play, there were matching sportswear sets of white poplin jackets and tapered slacks for mother, teen, and little girl. Boys were not left out; there was the Sears seersucker suit referred to earlier.

It was not long before the look-alike approach shifted to look-different, especially for teens. Sears continued its practice of reflecting changes in fashion, but as always eschewed extremes. Hippies, for example, would not make their way into Sears catalogs. However, the "urchin look" did, though true street urchins probably never looked so clean, healthy, happy, and moderate as those who graced a Sears page. By 1966, Sears urchins sported a scooped-neck dress with ribbed bodice and argylelike skirt just above the knee; or a turtleneck double-knit dress, ribbing to the hips, and again slightly above the knee. Sears urchins remained unfailingly modest.

Not so the young vulgarians, as they were called. These vulgarians were usually (in reality or through affectation) street-smart kids. They were most readily found in northern urban centers, fashion descendants of the James Dean-era rebellious youth of the 1950s. The 1960s youth, though, usually saw themselves as rebels with a cause, sometimes with many.

The female vulgarians took over the fashionable bouffant hairstyle of the late 1950s and early 1960, opting for its high beehive version, constructed laboriously with setting gel, big plastic rollers, hair dryer, rat-tail comb, and heavy-duty spraying with Aqua Net, to cite just a few of the requirements for creating the big-hair beehive. Heavy eyeliner complemented the hair nicely, along with white lipstick, a tight black miniskirt, padded bra, and a large mohair cardigan or high school letter jacket.

Male counterparts spent almost as much time getting their hair right, and tended to have almost as much hair, usually crisscrossed on the back in overlapping sections from nape to top, and a large wave curling far over the forehead. This style required a heavy application of hair grease such as Brylcreem (a "little dab" seldom sufficing). They favored tight sharkskin suits and leather raincoats while also proving fond of the wraparound sunglasses that Jackie Kennedy had made famous.

Both male and female vulgarians exhibited their hairstyles and dancing techniques on Dick Clark's *American Bandstand*, dancing to the songs of their favorites—Bobby Darin, Frankie Avalon, Bobby Rydell. Vulgarians also gave high marks to songs by a number of girls' groups: The Crystals' "Then He Kissed Me" (1963), The Shangri-Las' "Leader of the Pack" (1964) and "I Can Never Go Home Anymore" (1965), and The Shirelles' "Will You Love Me Tomorrow?" (1960) and "Soldier Boy" (1962).

The young vulgarian look faded by mid-decade, but the youthful ideal did not. Puritan, a New York manufacturer that had marketed a Gloria Swanson line, shifted at least two generations to introduce its "Youthquake" division. Paraphernalia opened for business on Madison Avenue in 1965, becoming a major player in youthful fashions for the 1960s. Throughout the decade, the youthful look continued to exercise its appeal in various manifestations.

THE ANTIESTABLISHMENT EARTHQUAKE

Reactions against the establishment took many forms in the 1960s, including sexual, racial, and political. The drug culture interacted with some or all of these factors to create the hippies. Then there was the growing antiwar movement that especially picked up steam after the Tet Offensive of 1968. All of these areas of reaction carried with them statements through clothing and hair fashions. To a great extent, how one looked reflected how one thought.

The "free love" movement emphasizing physical pleasure without traditional restrictions, aided by introduction of the birth control pill, is discussed in greater detail elsewhere in this book. It had, of course, its fashion dimensions. See-through blouses, the ubiquitous miniskirt, and even pierced earrings (considered symbolically more erotic than clip-on or screw-type earrings) reflected a greater openness about sexuality. Undergarments also changed, especially with young women, with bikini panties, panty hose, and tights in, girdles out.

Perhaps the most famous example of sexually liberated clothing, although in reality worn by few, was the topless swimsuit, officially called a monokini. Rudi Gernreich introduced it in 1964 as both a stylistic and ideological statement. Gernreich, who had fled Austria with his family while a teen to escape Hitler, was a strong supporter of nudism. He had viewed Hitler's ban against public nudity as a rejection of liberty and a reflection of fascism. For Gernreich, the topless swimsuit was both commercial and idealistic, a challenge to the idea that the body is essentially shameful.

Widely denounced and even outlawed, the monokini never caught on with the masses, although the *San Francisco Chronicle* printed a frontal photograph of a woman in monokini on its front page. When *Sports Illustrated* brought out its first swimsuit issue in 1964, the topless swimsuit was not included. The topless evening dress followed Gernreich's creation but proved even less popular. However, Gernreich's swimsuit did lead to a more lasting effect—the topless dancer. David Rosenberg came up with the idea of go-go dancers wearing the topless swimsuit, the owner of the Condor Club in San Francisco bought the idea, and the topless bar was born, never to die out completely. Such bars, of course, lacked any of Gernreich's ideological motivation, settling quite happily for mere commercialism.

Another fashion that followed liberalized sexual mores was the playboy bunny outfit. Hugh Hefner had started *Playboy* magazine in the 1950s, but as the next decade dawned decided to expand into playboy clubs. Hefner opened the first of his clubs in Chicago on February 29, 1960, with bunnies serving drinks in their tightly corseted swimsuitlike costumes with white collars, black bow ties, fishnet stockings, rabbit ears, and the most distinctive detail—a white bunny tail gracing each bunny's derrière.

Bunny costumes left nothing to the imagination regarding the gender of the wearer, but long hair on males, short hair on females, and high-heeled boots, hip-huggers, and ruffled shirts on either sex sometimes made it difficult to tell male from female. The question of gender might be leveled directly at the person under examination in order to express disapproval or merely to clear up confusion. Prominent among the clothing similarities between the sexes was a shared obsession with blue jeans, often worn skin-tight.

Motivation was seldom simple in the 1960s, with choice of a particular fashion usually impossible to reduce to just one factor. For example, one important reason for the mushrooming popularity of blue jeans during the decade was rejection of middle-class, materialistic norms. Jeans were initially working-class wear for farmers, miners, and others engaged in manual labor, although the name of the fabric used to manufacture them ironically derived from France. After Levi Strauss arrived in San Francisco in 1850, he went into business selling canvas for tents and wagon covers but quickly switched to pants. When he ran out of canvas, he turned to a tough twilled cotton fabric originally made in Nimes, France, hence from Nimes, or de Nimes, finally denim.

Quickly, however, jeans became associated with sexiness and turned fashionable. They came in a wide variety of styles during the decade, including hip-huggers, flared legs, bell bottoms, cuffed, patched, or cut off to make shorts. Because the tattered look was especially desirable, manufacturers began producing jeans that looked already seriously worn. New jeans also came with bright patches over imaginary holes. Quickly mainstream America took up the fashion, and men began wearing jeans with their sport coats and turtlenecks.

Also popular, although never to the extent of jeans, were bib overalls previously worn by farmers and train engineers. The same rejection of the middle class applied to overalls, but they lent themselves less readily to improvisational alterations, and even in an age when almost anything was acceptable, they never fit quite right with sport coats.

During the 1960s, African Americans started to switch from imitating white society to expressing their uniqueness. As they adopted the concept of "black is beautiful," they applied it in many ways, including hairstyles. Instead of bleaching and straightening their hair, many African Americans started wearing the Afro, viewed as a natural style with unstraightened curls cut in a somewhat rounded shape. The Afro, however, had little to do with Africa. Tanzania even banned the Afro as an example of Western colonialism. Nonetheless, the style became quite popular, worn by James Brown, Jessie Jackson, and Angela Davis, among countless others. Those who, like Diana Ross, preferred to keep their options open relied on an Afro wig.

The cornrow hairdo, with hair divided into sections and braided close to the scalp, conveyed the same pride in one's African American heritage. So did the dashiki (a loose, brightly colored African garment resembling a tunic) and caftan (similar to the dashiki but full-length). Some Americans, including whites, adopted these styles without much attention to the heritage, giving birth to a new radical chic. White designers started employing black models for other than African American markets. Paco Rabanne, noted earlier for his unusual fabrics, introduced black women into haute couture modeling in 1966. For that he was almost expelled from the Chambre Syndicale de la Couture Parisienne.

Members of the drug culture especially liked bright colors and patterns that visually paralleled their hallucinogenic experiences with LSD. Psychedelic shirts and ties (when they were worn) were popular, along with almost anything else psychedelic, such as posters. Day-Glo colors that glowed in daylight appeared in clothing as well as on posters, guitars, and vans. Then there was the tie-dyeing craze.

Tie-dyeing could be done with any clothes, but T-shirts were the most common. They were cheap enough to warrant experimentation, could be worn almost anytime, and were readily visible in order to convey a political or social statement. Tie-dyeing is an ancient process, practiced by Chinese and Nigerians many centuries ago. It involves knotting the fabric and dipping the cloth into dyes to create clothing with splotches of color. Repeated dippings yield ever more hallucinogenic effects. The tie-dyed T-shirt scored high on several counts with hippies and others rebelling against traditional values: it was cheap, homemade (in the dyeing), was something anyone could do, ended up individually unique with no two quite identical, yet united wearers in a sort of community.

As with anything popular, commercialism reared its head and nonhippies adopted the trend. Best Foods, maker of Rit dye, sent out half a million booklets showing how to tie-dye clothes and saw its dye sales jump sharply. Department stores threw tie-dye parties. Burlington Industries started manufacturing clothes already tie-dyed, and customers could wander among aisles of tie-dyed items at Macy's.

The hippie culture—consisting of students, artists, and others who dropped out of mainstream society, and who also were known as flower children—was in full swing by 1967, when a June 16–18 concert in Monterey, California, inaugurated the Summer of Love. Hippies had been birthed two years earlier in the Haight-Ashbury section of San Francisco. Seeking a nonmaterialistic, peace-loving society in which they could be their natural and individual selves, they adopted certain fashions in clothing as well as in lifestyle. An easy openness toward sex, rejection of nine-to-five jobs, and adoption of communal living by some were a few of the behavioral characteristics of hippies.

Long, straight hair dominated among female hippies, fashioned after the folk singers Joan Baez and Mary Travers; and many males also wore their hair long, often adding beards and mustaches. Granny dresses and granny glasses were popular, the latter with both sexes. Apparently it was only the previous generation that was especially distasteful, as young women hopped over that one to choose dresses they imagined their ancestors might have worn. They usually either purchased the dresses in thrift shops or made them, but in either case the dresses were long and full—the antithesis of the miniskirt and mod look. Granny glasses, also known as Ben Franklin spectacles, received a huge impetus from Roger McGuinn of the Byrds, who wore them to protect his sensitive eyes from stage lights. The glasses usually were small, sometimes square, with partial wire rims.

When granny dresses were not the fashion of choice, blue jeans usually were—often hip-hugging and very tight with bell bottoms. Bright colors on shirts and blouses, working-class and ethnic clothes such as bandannas and Native-American style jackets and vests, love beads, peace jewelry, and flowers in one's hair—sung about by Scott McKenzie in his 1967 hit song

The popular and controversial Broadway musical *Hair* flaunted new elements of youth counterculture fashion. Source: Photofest, Inc.

"San Francisco (Wear Some Flowers in Your Hair)"—all helped to identify the hippie. Many members of the older generations, and, in fact, many of their own generation, were repelled by the drop-out mentality of hippies and even by how they looked. Future president Ronald Reagan, then governor of California, the state with the largest population of hippies, offered his definition of a hippie as a person "who looked like Tarzan, walked like Jane, and smelled like Cheetah."[5]

Vietnam War activists may often have looked like hippies, and many once were, but they tended in some ways to be the opposite of the flower children. Rather than drop out, they became actively involved in opposing the Vietnam War through demonstrations, sit-ins, teach-ins, flag burnings, and other activities designed to raise America's consciousness against the war. These efforts increased after the Tet Offensive of 1968, which, although a major defeat for the communists, was perceived in the United States as proof that no place in Vietnam was secure from enemy attack and that the United States was no closer to winning the war than it had been years before.

There was little to distinguish Vietnam War protesters from hippies in appearance except for the overt symbols of their protest: military jackets adorned with flags and antiwar statements, antiwar buttons, the omnipresent antiwar symbol of the upside down bomber within a circle, the V for peace sign made with fingers, and perhaps an armful of posters or pamphlets. If the antiwar movement added little to the world of fashion, it added much to the nation by helping to bring about the end of the Vietnam War. When the war finally ended for the United States in the following decade, Americans lived in a world radically different from the United States of the 1950s. Some of those changes were very visible because they were worn at home, in the office, and at play every day.

The future would continue to reflect the decade's changes, fashion and otherwise. Perhaps the most universal change in fashion, though, has not yet been mentioned, its impact greater than that of the miniskirt or blue jeans, and more gender neutral than any unisex product—the disposable diaper.

Men and women who reared children in the 1960s or even 1970s remember well the cloth diapers, cost effective to be sure because they could be used almost forever, and able to serve a variety of other purposes long after babies had grown into teenhood. Yet rinsing and washing dirty diapers was pleasing to no parent. So life became much simpler with diapers that could be used and discarded. With the spread of family automobile trips in the 1960s, the throwaway diaper was especially practical, and many parents who continued to use cloth diapers at least made use of the disposable variety on family outings.

Procter and Gamble was first into the disposable business in 1961 with its Pampers, which proved so popular that when other companies introduced their own versions, many consumers went right on calling all of them "pampers." Before long, diaper services, which supplied families with clean cloth diapers, seemed headed along with barbers into oblivion. Ultimately, both would survive, but with reduced roles; parents concerned with protecting the environment opted for reusable diapers, and many barbers transformed themselves into hairstylists. By the end of the twentieth century, almost every parent, however, made some use of disposable diapers, and most used nothing else. Even those who find almost nothing good to say about fashions of the 1960s owe a debt of gratitude to the creative spirit of the times that saved them from rinsing out dirty diapers.

6

Food

Food, as a basic requirement for life, cuts across all social and economic classes. At the same time, what, how much, and how often people eat divide classes. That was true in the 1960s, as it always has been. For those with sufficient money, the decade was a time of new favorites when eating out or dining in. International influences became important, especially French, and increasing numbers of relatively affluent Americans, including new suburbanites, turned to cookbooks and television programs to learn how to make their dinner tables *au courant* (up-do-date).

Changes in how Americans ate reflected other changes in American society. With increasing numbers of men, women, and children on the move—commuting between home and work, driving to school (or being driven there), shopping at suburban shopping centers (including the new indoor malls with their food courts), going on long vacations in new automobiles—eating habits also became more mobile. The 1960s witnessed a tremendous growth in fast-food restaurants that did not seriously slow down customers from their other pursuits.

Many other food-related developments came along in the 1960s. Farming continued its slide from small family farms to large agribusinesses, along with the overall demographic shift of Americans from rural to urban (or suburban). An unceasing stream of purchases and mergers occurred among food-related businesses. Technology affected the farm, food processing, marketing, cooking, and consumption.

At the same time, the United States was a place of considerable poverty and malnutrition, even if few Americans were actually starving to death. That fate, however, befell great numbers of people in other lands. Much to the credit of Americans, a growing social consciousness, aided by print and television exposés, led to serious attempts at home and abroad to address the terrible problem of hunger.

DINING IN STYLE

Everybody her (or his) own chef was a common attitude in the 1960s. Being a good cook was not enough; that was for one's mother and grandmother, for cherry pies, chocolate cake, mashed potatoes and gravy. Home-style cooking, unless ethnic, was out, and nouveau cuisine (sort of) was in. The influences were many, including French cuisine, instant foods, the microwave and freezer, the Kennedy administration, and Julia Child.

Americans were busy and mobile in the 1960s. They spent a lot of time on the road living their new suburban lifestyle, and while they aspired to elegant dining, time was often an enemy. So it was important to prepare fine meals and party foods without devoting the whole day to the enterprise. Instant foods and increasingly popular kitchen appliances such as the freezer and microwave helped. Freezers had been around for years, and a new compact microwave from Amana went into widespread distribution in 1967.

On the shelves of the pantry and the freezer were the makings of dinners homemakers could serve with pride. Cans of condensed soup made many things possible, and so did a variety of other cans and boxes. Boxes of dried soup mixes were almost as helpful as their canned cousins. With a freezer at hand, there was no need to rush off to the supermarket to buy a nice cut of meat. Suburban chefs in doubt about how to proceed needed look no farther than the helpful 1960s cookbook, *Cooking from the Pantry Shelf*. The title of another useful guide, *Easy Gourmet Cooking*, struck cooking purists as an oxymoron, but summed up the direction that multitudes of new kitchen artists happily took. *Mary Meade's Magic Recipes for the Electric Blender* and Marian Tracy's *Parties from the Freezer* made no bones about using the latest technological shortcuts.

So what fashionable delicacies might a family have served in the 1960s? This question is answered with special indebtedness to Sylvia Lovegren's enormously informative *Fashionable Food: Seven Decades of Food Fads*, whose recipes resurrect many a mouthwatering memory.[1]

The more dramatic the main course, the simpler the salad might be—quite possibly iceberg lettuce with an occasional slice of tomato and cucumber. Roquefort dressing was popular, but so were Thousand Island and French, the final choice, given its name, always a safe bet. The cold, simple flavors of such a salad cleansed the palate after the inevitable preliminaries of cheese, crackers, dip, and chips, consumed with some pleasant pre-meal conversation. Cheese balls were popular, as was Edam cheese in its red wax shell. Lipton's dried onion soup mix was on virtually everyone's shelf, ready, combined with sour cream, to make the ubiquitous California dip. Ridged potato chips, the most famous being Ruffles, proved much sturdier than traditional chips for dipping the dip.

A with-it alternative to traditional soup was gazpacho, a Spanish dish. A cold blend of vegetables (with a dominant tomato taste) and such readily accessible items as red wine vinegar, olive oil, and Italian or French bread crumbs, this was an easy creation. The blender did all of the hard work, and after sitting in the refrigerator for a few hours gazpacho was almost always a hit.

Of all vegetable dishes served with home-prepared meals, none equaled green beans amandine for ease, popularity (those two qualities, of course, having something to do with each other), and an inoffensive taste. Almonds were everywhere in the 1960s and made this dish more than just green beans. Melt a little butter, toss in the almonds, heat for a while, add beans, and the dish was ready to serve. If potatoes were part of the meal, they usually were baked, especially with steaks as the entree. A dab of sour cream completed another easy portion of the meal, requiring nothing more complicated than turning on an oven and making sure to slit the potato a time or two to avoid potato explosions.

The main course, however, might take more effort. Two favorites of the Kennedys were beef stroganoff and beef Wellington. The former, given the availability of canned gravy, canned mushrooms, canned minced onions, even canned roast beef, could be prepared with limited difficulty. The latter, though, was hard to do well. That difficulty did not deter Americans, with whom the dish enjoyed great popularity. With a background in France and the British isles, beef Wellington had an international cachet about it. For busy gourmets, frozen beef tenderloin and frozen puff pastry could be thawed. Most instant chefs found a great challenge in getting the pastry flaky and, at the same time, the beef done as they wished it, preferably rare. The Kennedys' White House chef, René Vergon, undoubtedly fared better, but presumably not with frozen ingredients.

Campbell's mushroom soups were much used in the 1960s, even more so after the company released its Golden Mushroom version. If beef dishes were not the order of the day, the suburban chef might turn to chicken, adding Golden Mushroom Campbell's to make skillet-cooked chicken that both looked and tasted good. If green beans amandine became tiresome, Campbell's Golden Mushroom could come to the rescue. A string bean casserole graced many a dinner table in the 1960s, requiring only some of the most common 1960s ingredients in addition to string beans: mushroom soup, sherry, instant minced onions, and slivered almonds. Canned French-fried onions sprinkled on top perfected the dish.

Wine, of course, accompanied the meal. It was probably from France, but those in the know might serve a special California vintage.

Then came dessert. Grandmother's pies and cakes were decidedly too old-fashioned. The 1960s featured cheesecakes topped by fruit pie fillings, fruit cocktail cakes, and grasshopper pies, among other super sweet concoctions with or without various alcoholic additives.

Of course, there were many other options. Fire was big in the 1960s. Flambéing, dousing food with liquor and then setting it afire, could be a bit dangerous, but it made quite an impression, whether the food was a steak, cherries jubilee, crêpes suzette, or anything else combustible.

Fire, at a low, steady pace, helped to provide one of the most popular party dishes—fondue. A community-building approach to eating, fondue seemed French (the name deriving from the French verb *fondre*, to melt), but actually originated in Switzerland as a means of salvaging hard cheese and stale bread. The point was to melt cheese (with some other ingredients) and dip French bread into it. People would sit around the fondue dish and take turns dipping. Variants of this approach included dipping chunks of meat into boiling oil or pieces of cake or fruit into hot chocolate.

The credit (or blame) for much of this nouveau cuisine lay with the association of culture, including stylish food, with the French—and the popularity of a pioneering teacher of fine cooking made easy, Julia Child. Along with co-authors Simone Beck and Louisette Bertholle, Child published *Mastering the Art of French Cooking* in 1961. The following year, she began her televised show, *The French Chef*, on a Massachusetts public broadcasting station. Before long, channels throughout the country were carrying her.

Like good teachers everywhere, she made the difficult seem easy—or at least understandable. She relied on ingredients that normal people would reasonably have in their kitchens or at least be able to find in their local grocery stores, and she led her viewers through the cooking process in a clear and methodical way. Countless households began to enjoy their own creations of bœuf bourguignon and chocolate mousse, and along the way they learned the importance of fresh ingredients rather than items pulled from the freezer.

The interest in international cuisine also led to a quality series of international cookbooks from Time-Life Books. Using series editors and one principal editor per volume, Time-Life in 1968 alone produced M.F.K. Fisher's *The Cooking of Provincial France*, Waverley Root's *The Cooking of Italy*, Emily Hahn's *The Cooking of China*, Jonathan Norton Leonard's *Latin American Cooking*, and Dale Brown's *American Cooking*.

As the decade progressed, increasing interest developed in ethnic and health foods. Soul food became popular with large numbers of white Americans who sympathized with civil rights movements or who merely wanted to appear hip. Ham hocks, collard greens, corn bread, chitterlings (a pig's small intestines), black-eyed peas, and sweet potato pie were a few of the choice items. This interest gave rise to soul-food restaurants such as the famous Sylvia's in Harlem, which quickly became so popular that proprietors Sylvia and Herbert Wood had to move to a larger building and add on a new dining room.

Julia Child wields her knife while teaching television watchers how to prepare mouthwatering meals. Source: Photofest, Inc.

Japanese food also grew in popularity; the number of Japanese restaurants in New York increased from seven in 1959 to thirty-six in 1969.[2] At Japanese steakhouses, Americans could combine their love for steak and the exotic while watching the chef prepare and cook the food before their eyes. Performed at a spacious table around which diners sat, with a large grill on the chef's portion of the table, the preparation and cooking offered an exciting and dramatic experience for the audience. Sushi bars began to appear in certain areas of the country, especially on the West Coast. By offering raw fish on small cakes of cooked cold rice, sushi bars at first enticed generally only the most daring of American diners.

Other ethnic groups also contributed their foods to American tables, both at home and in restaurants. Dishes from India not only proved exotically romantic but presented new tastes for palates unaccustomed to Eastern spices that could bring tears to diners' eyes. In some restaurants, diners would sit on cushions on the floor, soaking up the environment and imagining themselves far away from their daily problems. Southeast Asian restaurants, featuring Vietnamese, Cambodian, or Thai foods, started appearing in the 1960s, but their numbers increased dramatically in the following decade as refugees fleeing communist Indochina in the postwar years found in the restaurant business a way to make a decent living in their new country.

Health food had a long history by the 1960s, but in that decade it became especially associated with countercultural types. Many ingredients popular (or at least accepted, often without scrutiny) in previous eras—such as white sugar, monosodium glutamate, bleached white flour, processed cheese, canned vegetables and fruits—were rejected with the older generation's political and religious values. Organic food was good, eschewing chemicals applied to soil or added to the food. Brown rice, yogurt, whole wheat flour, sunflower seeds, and similar natural delicacies were championed. Many Americans became vegetarians, for political as much as health issues, seeing in the nation's devouring of red meat another manifestation of the lust for violence and slaughter that produced the Vietnam War.

The most famous restaurant for antiestablishment figures may have been one that existed for less than a year in the middle 1960s but inspired one of the era's most popular resistance songs. Alice Brock started (and closed) her restaurant, The Back Room, in Stockbridge, Massachusetts, in 1965. It was a simple luncheonette where Brock baked her own bread and served health food. Arlo Guthrie, son of folk singer Woody Guthrie, encountered the restaurant and created out of that experience a song called "Alice's Restaurant," which he sang at the 1969 Woodstock festival. The restaurant came to stand for a world of peace, hope, harmony, and rejection of establishment values. A movie was based on the song in 1969, and Alice Brock wrote *Alice's Restaurant Cookbook* (1969) and returned to the restaurant business, serving, of course, healthy, antiestablishment food.

During the 1960s, health-food advocates were not alone in being concerned about health issues relating to food. Other aspects of that concern are discussed in a later section of this chapter.

FAST-FOOD RESTAURANTS AND OTHER DEVELOPMENTS

As Americans looked toward the seemingly incongruous mixture of instant food and French cuisine, they also frequented fast-food restaurants to such an extent that these establishments mushroomed, especially along highways and in shopping malls. Hamburgers, chicken, tacos, pizza, and a variety of other goodies, accompanied by French fries and soft drinks (or pop or sodas, depending where one lived) were among the favorites.

McDonald's, born during 1940 in a California drive-in owned by Richard and Maurice MacDonald, enjoyed tremendous growth after Ray Kroc bought out the brothers in 1961. Kroc had been operating MacDonald's franchises since 1955, had about 230 when he purchased exclusive rights to the name, and would have 700 by 1965, along the way dropping the initial "a" from "MacDonald's." McDonald's introduced its Big Mac sandwich in 1967; also during the decade it began to export its golden arch throughout the world, cementing its position as number one among hamburger chains.[3]

Burger King also enjoyed considerable growth during the 1960s but remained behind McDonald's. Having begun in 1954 in Miami, Florida, with its Whopper introduced three years later, Burger King operated 274 restaurants by 1967 and would grow to about two thousand franchises by the middle of the 1970s. Hardee's joined the hamburger competition in 1961 in North Carolina, using a then-rare charcoal broiler, and had two hundred outlets by the end of the decade. Wendy's came along in 1969 in Ohio, begun by David R. Thomas, who had been successful running Kentucky Fried Chicken franchises and who named the new chain after his daughter.

Harland "Colonel" Sanders had started establishing his Colonel Sanders' Kentucky Fried Chicken restaurants in 1955, selling "finger lickin' good" chicken made with his "secret blend of herbs and spices." In 1964, with over six hundred franchises, Sanders sold the business but continued with Kentucky Fried Chicken as a good-will ambassador.

Varying the fast-food menu, Arby's specialized in roast beef, opening its first restaurant in Ohio in 1964, and adding its first franchise the following year. Taco Bell, named after its creator, Glenn Bell, began in California in 1962 and quickly spread eastward. Busy travelers could dine on seafood at Long John Silver's Fish 'n Chips starting in 1969 in Lexington, Kentucky. Thomas Monaghan, a former seminarian and Marine, opened his first Domino's Pizza restaurant with brother Jim in 1960. Originating in Detroit, Domino's specialized in delivering phone orders within thirty minutes, making pizza definitely fast food. By the end of the century, enormously wealthy and having recently sold his pizza business, Monaghan turned his attention to bankrolling a new law school in Ann Arbor, Michigan.

Another new chain in the 1960s, although not quite as fast as those just mentioned, was Red Lobster, which began in Florida in 1968—the creation of William Darden, who had begun his career as manager of The Green Frog in Georgia about thirty-five years earlier. Red Lobster was especially popular as a family type of restaurant. Howard Johnson's restaurants had been around since the mid-1930s and by the early 1960s numbered over six hundred, many located near highways and exit ramps.

All of this eating and driving was bound to result in weight gains, so it was inevitable that a chain like Weight Watchers would arise. Jean Nidetch, a Queens, New York, housewife who had shed seventy pounds, began helping other people to lose weight through group therapy and careful dieting. The idea was to take the weight off and keep it off. In 1966, Nidetch published her *Weight Watchers Cookbook*.

Diners needed something quick to drink with their fast food, and a number of new soft drinks entered the market in the 1960s. Coca-Cola introduced Sprite in 1967 to do battle with the old favorite 7-Up. Royal Crown's Diet-Rite became the first sugar-free soft drink distributed nationwide in 1962, appealing to the growing numbers of people concerned with dieting. Coke countered with Tab in 1963 to contest the cyclamate-sweetened market, and two years later PepsiCo introduced Diet Pepsi.

Other drinks also were new to the scene for the modern-minded. Consumers who needed to move fast in the morning could drink their breakfast, courtesy of Carnation Company's Carnation Instant Breakfast (introduced in 1964); people aspiring to great heights could emulate the astronauts in drinking orange-flavored Tang (marketed nationwide in 1965), hoisting a glass to toast the 1969 moon landing, which Neil Armstrong and crew could reciprocate, having Tang along in their galley; and athletes and would-be athletes started turning to Gatorade in 1965 to replace fluids lost during physical exercise. Gatorade was named for the University of Florida Gators because a university kidney specialist, Robert Cade, developed it after testing fluid loss through perspiration by the university's football players.

Coffee also was a growth industry in the 1960s. General Foods started marketing Maxim, a freeze-dried instant coffee, in 1964. Taster's Choice freeze-dried instant, from Nestlé, arrived in 1966 and quickly became Number One among instants. Instant coffees had been around since the early 1940s, but the new freeze-dried process became more popular with coffee drinkers, who found freeze-dried more like the real thing. There also were developments in what to put in the coffee. Coffee Rich nondairy creamer (named after its developer, Robert Edward Rich) gave coffee drinkers in 1960 a milk or cream substitute that would not quickly spoil. All good things give rise to competitors, and the following year Coffee-Mate from Carnation entered the market.

Among the multitude of other new food products in the 1960s were Pop-Tarts (1964), Lucky Charms cereal (1964), the horn-shaped snack Bugles (1964), Shake 'n Bake to coat chicken and fish (1965), Cool Whip to replace whipped cream with fewer calories and a product that would last longer (1965), and Pringles (1969).

Margarine gradually supplanted butter as the bread covering of choice in the 1960s despite the best efforts of dairy farmers. Wisconsin, the dairy capital of the world, finally permitted yellow margarine to be sold within its borders in 1967.

Changes in containers also occurred in the 1960s. Consumers by then were buying most of their milk in stores rather than receiving home delivery, and that milk increasingly was in waxed paperboard cartons rather than glass bottles. Aluminum cans meanwhile were becoming popular for beer and soft drinks. First used in 1960, their popularity was greatly enhanced by development of steadily improved self-opening tabs on the cans.

The growing business of food production was also visible in the steady stream of business transactions involving companies. Just a few of the purchases in the 1960s: Coca-Cola bought Minute Maid, Campbell Soup bought Pepperidge Farms, Proctor and Gamble bought J.A. Folger, H.J. Heinz bought Starkist (and created Charlie the Tuna to sell its product), Pepsi-Cola bought Mountain Dew, Borden bought Cracker Jack (of baseball fame). H.W. Lay and Frito merged to become Frito-Lay, and then Frito-Lay and Pepsi-Cola merged to become PepsiCo Incorporated.

Government and religion also were involved in what people ate. Concerned about truth and safety in relation to food, the U.S. government passed the Fair Packaging and Labeling Act in 1966 to require accurate and clear labeling of food weights, and the U.S. Federal Meat Inspection Act in 1967 to improve the safety of meat products reaching America's tables. The fish industry worried in 1966 when the Roman Catholic Church dropped its ban on eating meat on Fridays (one of many changes in church practice growing out of Vatican II), but there was no clear damage done. In fact, many restaurants would continue for decades to offer Friday fish specials.

AGRICULTURE AND DEMOGRAPHICS

Turning to the production of food, one sees that effectiveness can be a two-edged sword. That surely has been the case with farming, where increasing efficiency and productivity have wiped out jobs in a manner parallel to increased technology in urban industry. Although the population of the United States continued to increase during the 1960s, and the amount of land devoted to agriculture remained fairly constant, fewer farmers were necessary to meet the food needs of the country. The needs of the world, however, were another matter.

Farmers improved their productivity not solely because of hard work but also due to increased use of technology in the form of more advanced farm implements and greater use of fertilizers, pesticides, and herbicides to increase crop yield and reduce loss to insect and weed infestation. By 1963, the average farmworker was producing enough food for thirty-one people, twice the number an individual farmer supported in 1950, and the U.S. corn crop exceeded five billion bushels, two billion more than at the beginning of the century. The corn crop leaped to nine billion bushels by 1965. Toward the end of the decade, farmers, who had been able to grow only twenty-five bushels of corn per acre at the time of World War I, were routinely getting one hundred, often far more. By 1969, a Wisconsin cow was producing ten quarts of milk per day rather than the six her ancestor yielded in 1940; overall, the average farmworker was now able to provide enough food for forty-seven people.[4]

As the decade wound its way toward a conclusion, the farm population dropped from over 15.5 million to under 10 million. The number of farms decreased from almost four million to under three million, while the average size of farms increased from about 300 acres to over 370 acres.[5] Increasingly, large agribusinesses were squeezing out the family farm, a process that would accelerate in future decades. Adding to the farmer's plight was his income; by the end of the 1960s the farm family's median income was approximately $3,700 beneath the median income of nonfarm families.[6] The changes were not confined to the nation's heartland, for major transformations were also occurring in the South with consolidation of farmland and increased industry. The drop in farm population also involved African Americans who chose to move northward or were pushed off farms by the new economic realities of the South. Many were tenant farmers or sharecroppers no longer needed with the widespread use of mechanical cotton pickers.

Farmers' own productivity worked against them by yielding large surpluses, which depressed prices. Two partial answers to their financial problems were exports and subsidies. During the 1960s, half or more of America's wheat, rice, and soybeans traveled abroad, along with at least one-fourth of cotton and tobacco. Serious famines struck, especially in Asia, and the United States responded with large shipments of grain, with one-third of U.S. grain exports in the mid-1960s going to India. President Kennedy in 1963 approved the sale of two million tons of grain to the Soviet Union and, despite Republican opposition, President Johnson delivered on his predecessor's promise.[7] Opposition to communism, though, reduced the country's willingness to trade extensively with communist nations. President Eisenhower effectively ended trade with Castro's Cuba in 1960, and in 1965 American longshoremen resisted loading grain for shipment to Russia.

Farm subsidies had existed in various forms since the Agricultural Adjustment Act of 1933 during the Great Depression. President Franklin Roosevelt's New Deal approach to helping farmers combined subsidy payments with removal of land from production to avoid large surpluses. Roosevelt followed in 1941 with a plan whereby prices would be maintained at a certain percentage of parity (prices shortly before World War I). The support program tied to parity was ended by President Eisenhower amid considerable controversy in 1954.

During the 1960s, federal agricultural policy included a combination of guaranteed price, soil conservation, land set-asides, and use of food surpluses in food-stamp and school-lunch programs. The Food and Agriculture Act of 1962 created price support payments to farmers making up the difference between former and current world price levels for their product. Cash payments to remove cropland from production continued throughout the decade. Farmers benefited from these programs, receiving an average of one thousand dollars, thousands of farmers much more, yet in the middle of the decade, Americans were spending just 18.5% of their income on food, compared to 24.4% ten years earlier. No people in the world were paying out less of their income for food.[8]

Despite the assistance given to America's farmers by the government, large numbers of agricultural workers received no help beyond what their own hands provided. Migrant workers, many of them Mexican American, were worst off, working excruciatingly long and hard hours picking vegetables and fruit for whatever owners wanted to pay them, their poverty giving them little choice. That began to change in the early 1960s as the CBS documentary *Harvest of Shame* (1960) publicized the plight of migrant workers, and César Chávez founded the National Farm Workers Association (1962). By 1968, Chávez and the union were receiving strong public support for both their strike and their proposed boycott of table grapes. His fasts both dramatized the boycott and brought a moral power to the effort, encouraging prominent political leaders such as Robert Kennedy, Eugene McCarthy, and Hubert Humphrey to add their support. In 1970, the boycott ended, with most table grape owners having agreed to recognize and negotiate with the union, now known as the United Farm Workers (UFW) after NFWA's merger with the Agricultural Workers Organizing Committee. Migrant workers, however, were not alone among America's rural in suffering poverty amid plenty.

POVERTY AND POLLUTION

Michael Harrington's *The Other America: Poverty in the United States* (1962) was one of the most important books published in the 1960s. Writing of "a culture of poverty" within the affluent United States, Harrington brought to public consciousness the existence of a nation within a nation, one easy to overlook because few Americans were actually dying of starvation, and because poverty and hunger tended to be camouflaged by urban development and the green fields of rural America.

Subsequent books, government studies, broadcast documentaries, and demonstrations brought hunger and poverty more clearly into the light of day for middle-class and wealthy Americans. William and Paul Paddock sounded an alarm concerning future international famines in *Famine— 1975!* (1967). President Johnson's Science Advisory Committee released in the same year a massive study entitled *The World Food Problem*, examining the effects of growing populations and demands by the wealthy on food supplies. The 1968 CBS documentary *Hunger in America* explored hunger in the prosperous United States, especially focusing on malnutrition among infants, including Native Americans. In that same year, after the assassination of its original organizer, Dr. Martin Luther King, Jr., the Poor People's March on Washington protested hunger in this rich land and inadequate efforts to solve the problem. Further evidence of the continuing crisis came in the same year when the Citizens Board of Inquiry into Hunger and

Malnutrition in the United States reported that only 18% of the country's poor were being helped by federal food programs.

Arnold E. Schaefer, a nutrition expert, asserted in 1968 that malnutrition was as serious in parts of the United States as in India, and that vitamin deficiencies put large numbers of American children at risk of blindness. Unfortunately, much of Schaefer's data was effectively buried by being transferred to computers at the Centers for Disease Control that were not compatible with the Washington computers initially storing the information. Jean Mayer, founder of the National Council on Hunger and Malnutrition, chaired a White House Conference on Food, Nutrition and Health in 1969, testifying before a Senate Select Committee chaired by Senator George McGovern, who would be the Democratic Party's nominee for president three years later.

The evidence of widespread hunger in the United States generated enough compassion and outrage to bring about changes that helped large numbers of Americans but, of course, did not completely eradicate the problem. Shortly after publication of Harrington's book, President Kennedy signed into law the Public Welfare Amendments to the 1935 Social Security Act. These amendments fixed federal support to states at 75% of the expenses for counseling, job training, and placement for individuals on public assistance.

Food-distribution programs had been in place since 1949, but their primary objective was to reduce farm surpluses rather than eliminate hunger. The food stamp program, established in 1964 with the Food Stamp Act, worked better by getting needed and varied food into the hands of families. The Agriculture Department administered the program, and people applied as households rather than as individuals for food stamps. Through eligibility criteria, officials attempted to ensure that those who needed the stamps would receive them. By the end of 1967, 2.7 million Americans were benefiting from food stamps, and food stamp funding continued to rise.[9]

Meanwhile, the National School Lunch Program, inaugurated in 1946 to meet one-third the Recommended Daily Allowance (RDA) of calories, minerals, and vitamins, was helping 21 million U.S. children by the end of the 1960s. Almost 4 million children received lunch either free or at a much reduced price, with the number continuing to rise.

Hunger and malnutrition were not the only food-related crises in the United States during the 1960s. Increasingly, developments in manufacturing, technology, and use of chemicals in farming were impacting the safety of food and the welfare of the environment. Rachel Carson's *Silent Spring* (1962) did for the environment what Michael Harrington's *The Other America* accomplished regarding poverty. A book whose influence continued throughout the century, *Silent Spring* warned that pesticides such as DDT (dichloro-diphenyl-trichloroethane) were causing great damage to wildlife and, by extension, to humans. Likening the effect of heavy use of pesticides to nuclear fallout, she cautioned against a silent world in which the birds have been poisoned along with the poisoned insects they ate. Concealing her own breast cancer for fear that knowledge of her illness might undermine her effectiveness, Carson bravely carried forward the torch of a responsible approach to the environment. She died two years after the publication of her book; five years later, in 1969, Congress passed the National Environmental Policy Act mandating that federal agencies provide environmental impact reports. By that time, her warnings about DDT had been widely accepted. Studies subsequent to publication of *Silent Spring* demonstrated that DDT accumulated in fatty tissues, increasing in concentration up the food chain, and caused cancer in test animals. Coho salmon in Michigan lakes were found to have concentrations of twenty parts per million of DDT in 1969; indeed, 90% of fish sold in the United States were discovered to be contaminated with the pesticide. Perhaps even more troubling for consumers, milk also began to test positive for DDT, the result of cows eating grain sprayed with it. By the end of the decade, DDT was outlawed by several states and was being phased out by the federal government. With few exceptions, it was not available for use in the United States after 1972.

DDT, however, was not the only contaminant endangering America's food. Cesium-137 from nuclear fallout was found in 1960 to have migrated from lichens to caribou to the Alaskan Eskimos who ate the caribou. Eating pork from pigs that had ingested mercury fungicide from contaminated millet seed caused some of the children in the Ernest Lee Huckleby family to suffer blindness and brain damage in 1969. Monosodium glutamate (MSG), a flavor enhancer, was added to baby foods until 1969, when several manufacturers of baby food, following tests showing that baby mice suffered brain damage from MSG, discontinued its use.

Manufacturers of diet soft drinks used cyclamates as a sugar-substitute sweetener. In fact, by the end of the decade Americans were consuming 20 million pounds of cyclamates per year when it was learned that tests showed large quantities of the sweetener to cause bladder cancer in rats. The Food and Drug Administration then banned their use.

Another food additive eventually found to pose a substantial health hazard was Red No. 2 food dye. First approved by the Food and Drug Administration in 1960, the dye contained amaranth sodium salt (composed of sulfur and naphtha), which studies indicated caused cancer in animals. Despite growing scientific awareness of the danger, Red No. 2 dye was not banned until 1976.

Food is a basic good, necessary for sustaining life. It also offers considerable enjoyment. During the 1960s, though, Americans increasingly came to understand that it was not a universal good, for millions of people within the most affluent nation on earth lacked sufficient nutritious food to sustain health. In addition, Americans were putting into the environment and directly into the food substances that posed enormous health risks. There clearly were more problems surrounding food than simply the concern of many dieters—that one can get too much of a good thing.

THE 1960S

7

Leisure Activities

The decade of the 1960s was a period of war abroad and social upheaval at home, but there remained time for play. From the most popular of professional sports to children's toys, and through a variety of fads and hobbies that also exhibited America's spirit of play, the nation found itself at least at times able to turn away from its concern with political and social divisions to revel in pastimes long associated with a lighter aspect of human nature. Yet so strong were the social dynamics of the decade that even play could gravitate toward the ideological, sometimes mirroring conflicts and preoccupations that were threatening to unravel the social fabric of the country.

The lines of demarcation among fads, games, toys, hobbies, and sports are often difficult to draw. A particular game or toy that proves briefly popular may be considered a fad; one person's hobby is another individual's serious, even professional sport; and a game that draws neighbors or friends together to play on a Saturday night may be a productive career for others. Thus, something of an exclusionary criterion has been employed in categorizing the practices discussed in the following sections. If the type of behavior was popular but relatively short-lived in its popularity, and if it seemed not to fit the other categories, it was deemed a fad. In addition, fads that relate directly to topics considered in other chapters, such as music or clothing fashions, are discussed there.

FADS

A fad, or craze, is any custom or activity that enjoys great, but temporary popularity. The 1960s included a great many fads, perhaps more than in many other decades because of the nation's general prosperity during the decade. More disposable money meant that less thought needed to be given to the long-term value of a purchase. Inclinations could be satisfied, and often were.

Most homes, for example, did not want for light, but individuals seeking maximum pleasure and profit from their moments of relaxation and meditation increasingly added a Lava Lite. Originally known as an Astrolight in Germany, where it was invented, the Lava Lite was cylindrical and contained a yellow wax heated by a coil. The Lava Lite was not bright enough to be a reading light; its purpose, instead, was to set a mood, regardless of what mood was desired. In living rooms and college rooms, the light provided visual delight as the wax took on varying forms and hues. Many people found it also a mood-setting accompaniment to whatever drugs they were taking.

The Lava Lite was not the only item that could set a mood. The water bed, invented by Charles Hall to provide something more comfortable than the then popular beanbag furniture, became instead a major sex symbol of the late 1960s. It appealed to the counterculture and to the very rich. Hugh Hefner established a king-sized model in his Chicago mansion. Water beds, however, had an unfortunate tendency in their early days to collapse floors and spring leaks that proved dangerous to the electrical heaters that kept the water warm. One story circulated about a couple making love in their water bed on their balcony, only to have the balcony collapse under the weight of the water (and perhaps their strenuous activity), crushing the lovers to death.

Individuals tripping on LSD were fond of "black lights," which could be purchased in "headshops" along with fluorescent paints and dyes. Fluorescent clothes or posters in the presence of black light bulbs created a visual counterpart to the effect of LSD. Restaurants and nightclubs installed black lights to appeal to those seeking drug (or druglike) effects. Day-Glo dyes and paints were attractive to the same individuals who favored black lights. Incandescent pigments of orange, red, and yellow would glow brightly in normal daylight, giving the visual effect the name of "Day-Glo." Posters, sides of vans, guitars, and countless other types of objects were painted in Day-Glo. Since the 1960s, Day-Glo colors have moved from the level of fad to standard issue in such everyday items as swimsuits and highlighting markers used in huge numbers by students. Colors also made their way to people's bodies during the 1960s, as body painting achieved short-lived but well-publicized exposure.

Buttons proclaiming slogans or favorite political candidates have been worn for a long time, but they achieved a level of popularity in the 1960s never enjoyed before or since. At the same time, bumper stickers became a staple of the automobile. The more serious messages on these buttons usually were antiwar or in some other way reflective of social attitudes. "Make love, not war"; "Tune in, turn on, drop out"; "Kill a Commie for Christ"; and countless other statements were intended at least to express one's opinion if not convert others. Many buttons addressed the increasingly liberal attitudes toward sex, such as "Cure virginity." Sometimes the button might address both the political and sexual: "Lay, don't slay." The most popular message on buttons was the antiwar symbol, expanded from its antinuclear origins—a somewhat abstract bomber pointed straight up. Many buttons, of course, were strictly frivolous: "Mary Poppins is a junkie."

Bumper stickers were more evenly divided between the established culture and the counterculture. Individuals, often older, expressed their opposition to the new culture while affirming traditional values: "God bless America"; or "Support your local police." As buttons have declined in popularity over the subsequent decades, bumper stickers have spread ever more widely. Following a car on a city street today, drivers can learn far more than they care to know about the lead driver's past destinations, political preferences, and attitudes toward other drivers, as well as the academic accomplishments of the driver's children. Bumper stickers may prove to be a fad, but, if so, at the beginning of the twenty-first century, they have become a long-lived one.

GAMES AND TOYS

The spirit of play in the United States continued unabated even as the political climate of the nation changed dramatically in the second half of the 1960s. So popular and varied were games and toys that only a sampling can be given here.

Many of the older games, such as cards and checkers, continued to be played by young and old. Poker and euchre were common across the age spectrum, with bridge usually associated with an older and more upscale crowd. College students enjoyed cribbage, and increasing numbers of students and young adults turned to chess. Considered by some to be a sport, and so categorized in the *Sports Illustrated 2000 Sports Almanac*, chess received a great boost from Bobby Fischer, the first chess player to become widely recognized in the United States. Robert James Fischer taught himself chess at the age of six and won the U.S. Junior Championship and the U.S. Championship by fifteen. He was U.S. champion every year from 1958 to 1967 with the exception of 1962. His most defining moment, though, came in the following decade, in 1972, when he defeated Russian Boris Spassky for the World Championship.

By the middle of the decade, Tarot cards, representing virtues and vices and used in fortune-telling, had become popular, in part responding to growing interest in alternative forms of spirituality. Similar impulses toward antiestablishment norms helped to popularize the Ouija board, which includes a planchette that, when touched, allegedly moves to spell out spiritualistic messages by pointing at letters on the board.

Adult board games introduced during the 1960s tended to mirror real-life situations and/or appeal to the supposed intelligence of adults. Acquire and High Bid were stock market games. Jeopardy posed answers and required players to supply the questions. Diplomacy, invented by an MIT professor, included a board with seven European countries on it. The seven players attempted to take each other's countries with their armies and navies, or by forming alliances with other players. Bar-Spreezy included the bonus (or penalty) of having to sip a drink for each point won, although drawing "Intoxicards" permitted the player to skip a sip. A tamer but more intellectual game was Scrabble, which included small squares with letters on them and demanded creation of words; the person with the best vocabulary was most likely to prove victorious. Acting out words was the point of charades, a popular party game that called for a bit of acting ability and willingness to make a fool of oneself in public. Many hosts found it an effective ice-breaker.

A game for children of all ages, and much more than just a toy, was the slot car. Over three million Americans were playing with slot cars by mid-decade, including Robert Kennedy and CBS anchor Walter Cronkite.[1] Universities, including several Ivy League schools, were home to slot-car teams. The small (usually two-inch) plastic car derived its name from a slot in the track on which the cars were raced. A projection under the car fit into the slot, and electricity powered the vehicles. When Ford brought out its Mustang in 1964, Aurora Plastics introduced a slot-car version. By 1967, however, the slot-car craze was heading downhill.

Games and toys are hard to separate, for children have always played games with toys. One of the most popular toys of the 1960s was the super ball. The super ball was a small, dense ball with the capacity to rebound almost the same distance as that from which it was dropped and continue bouncing much longer than other balls, about sixty seconds. Wham-O sold the ball for less than a dollar, and adults as well as children bought it in such numbers that Wham-O was producing 170,000 balls per day at the height of the craze.[2] McGeorge Bundy, National Security Advisor to President Lyndon Johnson, purchased super balls for sixty members of his staff, apparently as much to help them reduce stress as for entertainment. Skateboarders liked to bounce a super ball while they skated down the street, and children used it while playing jacks. Wham-O also created such other classics as the Frisbee and the Hula-Hoop, both of which, introduced in the late 1950s, remained popular through the next decade. Early in the 1960s, children and adults alike found themselves caught up in another game involving some physical exertion, if only by the hand and wrist—the yo-yo craze.

An all-1960s grouping of toys would be heavy on dolls, with two very opposite dolls heading the list: Barbie and G.I. Joe. Mattel produced its first Barbie in 1958. Within five years, there were nine million Barbies residing in little girls' rooms and anywhere else girls happened to be.[3] The doll received five hundred letters per week, although no record exists regarding how many she successfully answered. Barbie had expensive tastes, with

Barbie's outfits even included a workout suit so that she could stay thin and beautiful. Source: Photofest, Inc.

her clothes multiplying in numbers and styles. Some of her clothing items in the 1960s, such as a red velvet coat, cost more than the doll did (about three dollars). Keeping the doll inexpensive was a brilliant marketing strategy to hook youngsters and then induce continuing expenditures to keep Barbie in style.

So that Barbie would not feel alone, Mattel came up with pals for Barbie, the male Ken and the female Midge. Both of them also wore clothes, lots of them. Critics saw in the Barbie phenomenon a symbol of much that was wrong with the United States, including its commercialism and gender stereotyping. Many a parent, though, saw her or his objections crumble before a child's ardent longing for her own Barbie.

G.I. Joe was another popular and controversial doll, created in 1963 but seemingly out of sync with the growing antiwar sentiment of the second half of the 1960s. By 1966, G.I. Joe was in ten million homes. Sales of the doll did slide toward the end of the decade, with Dr. Benjamin Spock condemning it in his *Baby and Child Care*, and the doll's role was transformed into more of an explorer and adventurer, later resuming its overt combat persona. Hassenfeld Brothers put considerable thought into creation of their doll, creating Joe's face from a composite of twenty actual Congressional

Medal of Honor winners. Like Mattel with Barbie, the manufacturer kept the price of the doll low (about four dollars), while the full range of clothes, equipment, and weapons ran to about two hundred dollars.

A popular theory behind Stanley Weston's development of G.I. Joe is that the purpose was to detach boys, enamored with Barbie's curvaceous characteristics, from their secret playing with her. Better guns than breasts, violence rather than sex, hence G.I. Joe, an American hero.

Other dolls did not approach Barbie and G.I. Joe in sustained popularity but had their moments. The Troll Doll, also known as the Dammit Doll after its inventor, Thomas Dam, became a favorite of college women in the 1960s. By the end of the decade, only Barbie was outselling the Troll Doll, two dolls that could not have been less alike.[4] Unlike the sexy Barbie, the Troll was an ugly gnome with big ears and a wide nose, so ugly as to be cute. Not only college students favored the doll, which was supposed to bring good luck. Pilot Betty Miller had a Troll Doll co-pilot on her duplication of Amelia Earhart's 1935 flight, and Lady Bird Johnson shared the White House with her husband and one of the gnomes.

As pressure to achieve equal rights regardless of race picked up steam in the later 1960s, so did the movement make its way into the world of toys. Baby Nancy, from Shindana, appeared in time for Christmas 1968. Nancy was clearly African American in features, color, and hair, and sold for five to six dollars. The Black Doll Toy Company produced "Soul Babies" and black equivalents to previously white dolls, such as astronauts. Barbie and G.I. Joe appeared as Afro-Americans, while Remco put on the market such supposedly realistic black dolls as Baby-Grow-a-Tooth and Li'l Winking Winny, the latter with an Afro hairstyle.

Other popular toys during the decade included James Bond dolls and cars. During the early 1960s, JFK coloring books helped millions of young children learn more about the young president and his family. A child's version of disposable pop art was available with the Etch-A-Sketch, which permitted drawing on a screen by turning two knobs; shaking the screen removed the picture in preparation for the next creation. "Mr. Machine" was a robot that children could take apart and, at least in theory, reassemble without tools. The toys, of course, went on and on, in an unlimited stream.

HOBBIES

A variety of noteworthy hobbies in the 1960s, some of them closely allied to sports and games, occupied large numbers of Americans. The most physical of these pastimes included bowling, sailing, surfing, skateboarding, and touch football. If tennis at the beginning of the decade was a country-club sport, bowling, in the minds of many, was strictly a lowbrow and low-income pastime. In reality, large numbers of people who deviated from one or both of those categories enjoyed bowling. Its popularity was sufficient to induce ABC to begin televising tournaments in the early 1960s. Don Carter, Billy Hardwick, and Dick Weber were the most prominent male bowlers in the 1960s, with Carter twice named Male Bowler of the Year during the decade, and Hardwick and Weber winning or sharing that distinction three times each. Among women, Shirley Garms was Bowler of the Year in 1961 and 1962, with Dotty Fothergill achieving that distinction in the final two years of the decade. Less accomplished but no less enthusiastic were the many men and women who bowled, informally with friends or relatives, or in leagues, at a local bowling alley. Teams often were sponsored by a business, which received advertising on the backs of the team members' shirts.

Americans who favored outdoor hobbies could take their lead from the Kennedy administration, which increased the popularity of both sailing and touch football during the early 1960s. It was not unusual to see photographs of President Kennedy skippering his family sloop off Hyannis Port, family members aboard, with daughter Caroline sometimes sitting in his lap helping to keep the boat on course. The coastlines, rivers, and lakes of the United States meanwhile offered relaxation and adventure to millions of less famous boaters. Touch football was another Kennedy pastime, with Attorney General and later Senator Robert Kennedy often in the middle of the game. Hardly a sport for sissies, touch football, Kennedy style, was a rugged and highly competitive endeavor shared by enthusiasts on college campuses and residential lawns.

Few outdoors activities are more associated with the 1960s than surfing. An ancient sport that almost died out in the nineteenth century, surfing was reborn in Hawaii early in the twentieth century and became popular in California during the middle of the century. Surfers were an important division of the counterculture of the 1960s, adopting a distinctive attire (typically striped shirts, white jeans, and sunglasses for the males), a peculiar jargon (phrases like "daddy-o" and "kook"), and a fanatical core of true believers in sufficient numbers to warrant their own magazines (e.g., *Surfer*, started in 1960 and still in existence at the beginning of the new century). So popular was surfing, even among millions of people, not all of them young, who never came within yelling distance of a wave, that it inspired a new genre of surfing movies and gave rise to a unique kind of music (called "surf music") transported around the world by the Beach Boys and other groups. Among the songs glorifying surfing were the Beach Boys' "Surfin' USA" and Jan and Dean's "Surf City."

Skateboards evolved from roller skates but actually have more to do with surfing than roller-skating. In the early 1960s, surfers devised an earthbound version of the surfboard to keep in practice when they were away from the waves. By 1963, skateboards had caught on and have stayed around ever since. The original mass-marketed skateboards were made of

Collecting baseball cards was a popular hobby during the Sixties, practiced more for love than money.

wood or plastic with wheels underneath; the board is controlled by knees and shifts in body weight to simulate the act of surfing.

Still other outdoor activities were much practiced in the 1960s. A 1966 poll showed approximately fifty-nine million bikers, forty million volleyball players (many of whom played indoors in gyms), and thirty-six million fishers and campers in the United States.[5] Many people also took up jogging, an activity not often seen prior to the 1960s. More than a few of the participants were encouraged in these activities by the call of young President John F. Kennedy in 1961 for Americans to exercise more and become more physically fit.

Americans who preferred their hobbies indoors had many options, one of which was collecting baseball cards, which remained popular with young baseball fans. Buying packages of cards with pink gum continued in the 1960s, as youngsters looked for their heroes: Willie Mays, Hank Aaron, Mickey Mantle, Sandy Koufax, Bob Gibson, Tom Seaver, Frank

Robinson, and many others. Although collecting baseball cards remained primarily a love-of-the-game hobby throughout the decade, the commercialization of card collecting had already started. The pivotal moment in this transformation was the publication of Jefferson Burdick's *The American Card Catalog* in 1967. From then on, card condition, price, and value began to shove aside the old traditions of collecting, trading, and playing imaginative games with the cards. Even young fans started to look at baseball cards as financial investments.

Building model planes and ships remained popular hobbies, primarily with boys, but also with some adults. With the space race blossoming in the 1960s, space vehicles joined lower-flying aircraft on tabletops with diagrams and bottles of glue. Scientifically inclined youngsters also enjoyed science kits, which were especially popular as Christmas presents from parents anxious to encourage their children's academic pursuits.

Photography received a boost as a hobby from development by Kodak of its Instamatic camera in 1963, which used a cartridge and required no real expertise. The musically inclined increasingly turned toward the guitar, mirroring the resurgence of folk music among professionals.

Some of the hobbies already mentioned were at least borderline sports. Watching professional, college, and Olympic sports was a hobby shared by many millions in person or through the media of radio and television. The sports themselves are discussed in the following section.

SPORTS

Professional Football

Perhaps the two most dominant figures in American sports during the 1960s were two individuals who at first glance could hardly have seemed more opposed: Vince Lombardi, the coach of the Green Bay Packers in the National Football League, and Muhammad Ali (formerly Cassius Clay), the heavyweight boxing champion.

"Winning isn't everything, it's the only thing," Vince Lombardi is credited with saying. That remains his signature quotation, although others made the statement before him.

In an increasingly urban America, Lombardi, a New Yorker, settled in a relatively small town in the football hinterlands, Green Bay, Wisconsin. There he built a dynasty starting in 1960. During the next seven years, Lombardi's Packers won five NFL championships and the first two Super Bowls, which were played in January 1967 and 1968.

Lombardi, with his insistence on hard work and discipline, and his unswerving commitment to winning, seems an anomaly in the turbulent decade of the 1960s, a throwback to an earlier era even as he brought innovation to professional football. Yet, as his biographer David Maraniss

In Super Bowl III, the AFL's New York Jets scored an historic upset win over the NFL's Baltimore Colts. Clockwise from top left: Jim Turner kicks a field goal; Kyle Rote interviews Joe Namath; Namath prepares to take a snap from center; announcer Curt Gowdy covers the game. Source: Photofest, Inc.

points out, he was progressive in his attitudes toward race relations and homosexuality. He insisted that African American players on his team be treated the same as white players, refusing, for example, to house his team at hotels that would not accept African Americans and insisting on employing Native American caddies at a Green Bay golf course year-round when it was customary to lay them off in the summer in favor of white youngsters. While coaching the Washington Redskins later in the decade, he threatened to fire anyone who belittled a gay Redskins player because of his sexual orientation.

One might say, regarding professional football in the 1960s, paraphrasing the famous Lombardi quote, that the Green Bay Packers were not everything; they were the only thing. However, it only seemed that way. The two greatest players of the decade were not Packers, but quarterback Johnny Unitas of the Baltimore Colts and fullback Jimmy Brown of the Cleveland Browns. The most exciting player probably was halfback Gayle Sayers of the Chicago Bears, who scored twenty-two touchdowns in 1965, six of them in one game. The expansion Dallas Cowboys began their rise from mediocrity to become "America's Team." The American Football League was born in 1960, competing and finally merging with the older National Football League by 1970. The Super Bowl, conceived in the competition and then cooperation between the two leagues, began its ascendancy toward its eventual status as America's most spectacular sports event. The contest that set it on that track, though, was neither of Green Bay's triumphs, but Super Bowl III, when quarterback Joe Namath of the upstart New York Jets of the AFL predicted a victory over the NFL Colts and then made good on his promise.

The National Football League, winner of the first two Super Bowl games by decisive margins, was the prohibitive favorite to extend its winning streak in the third meeting between the league champions. Joe Namath, known as "Broadway Joe" for his flamboyant lifestyle, was the quarterback of the American Football League champion New York Jets. Namath, showing little respect for the older league and unfazed that his own Jets were seventeen-point underdogs, guaranteed victory. On January 12, 1969, Namath delivered on that guarantee, showing that the new league was the NFL's equal and setting himself on a path that would lead to the Pro Football Hall of Fame.

Boxing

Sharing top billing with Vince Lombardi among 1960s sports figures is Muhammad Ali. The young Cassius Clay, light-heavyweight gold medalist at the 1960 Olympics and heavyweight champion of the world at twenty-two, was an "in-your-face" person, predicting the round in which he would win and celebrating his greatness with whimsical verse of his own creating (such as his self-description: "float like a butterfly, sting like a bee"). Yet beneath the surface of that apparent arrogance, Muhammad Ali proved greater than even he recognized.

Clay met Sonny Liston, a huge bear of a man and a heavy favorite, in a 1964 fight for the heavyweight championship of the world. Liston had won the title with a first-round knockout of then-champion Floyd Patterson in

Cassius Clay (later Muhammad Ali) won the heavyweight boxing championship from Sonny Liston in 1964. Source: Photofest, Inc.

1962 and retained his title with another one-round demolishing of Patterson the following year. Faced with Clay's speed and taunting, though, the older fighter could not connect, and when the seventh round began, the champion remained seated in his corner. The stunning upset was followed by an even more bewildering rematch in 1965, with Liston going down for the count in the first round, victim of a "phantom" punch that no one saw land. Rumors circulated that Liston had thrown the fight.

By the second fight with Liston, Clay had converted to the Nation of Islam and changed his name to Muhammad Ali. The Nation of Islam advocated black separatism and encouraged its adherents to reject their old names, often given to ancestors by their slave masters. As Ali spoke out against racism, the media began to turn against him, even as he continued his mastery of the boxing world.

By 1967, Ali had established himself as one of the greatest heavyweight boxers ever, if not the best. He also had become increasingly outspoken against the Vietnam War, which he saw as a racist war against another colored race. Ali was drafted into military service and sought unsuccessfully to receive a conscientious objector classification. Denied that status, he refused induction. The penalties were heavy. At the very peak of his career, Ali was stripped of his heavyweight title. He was brought to trial for refusing induction, convicted, and sentenced to five years in prison. Ali appealed the conviction, but in the meantime was deprived of his career. He traveled widely throughout the country, much in demand as a public speaker, especially on college campuses. As the decade approached its conclusion, increasing numbers of African Americans shared Ali's view, asking why they should fight in Vietnam for a government that back home refused them the rights for which they supposedly were fighting and dying to provide for the Vietnamese. As opposition to racism and the war merged in the minds of large numbers of African Americans, Muhammad Ali steadily grew in stature, an inspiring force within the Black Power movement.

Ali in the next decade would see the Supreme Court overturn his conviction and return to boxing, twice more becoming world champion. As the years passed, Ali continued to rise in popularity, assuming by the end of the twentieth century an almost mythic stature. He became one of the most loved figures in America, invited to light the torch at the opening ceremonies for the Atlanta Olympics in 1996.

Another prize fighter who earned headlines as an exemplar of the 1960s was Rubin "Hurricane" Carter. A top middleweight challenger, Carter was arrested with another man, John Artis, for the shooting murder of two men and a woman at the Lafayette Bar and Grill in Paterson, New Jersey. The shootings occurred on June 17, 1966, and the arrests came several months later as the result of testimony by a local criminal. The arrests occurred despite Carter's having passed a lie detector test, neither man being identified by the surviving victims or meeting the physical descriptions given of the assailants, and both having alibis and earlier being exonerated by a grand jury.

An all-white jury convicted both Carter and Artis on May 27, 1967. Later reports claimed that witnesses were frightened by police into not testifying or testifying incompletely. The two men received three life terms, and during imprisonment Carter lost sight in his right eye because of inadequate medical attention. Carter's book, *The Sixteenth Round*, published in 1974, elicited interest in his case (Bob Dylan, for instance, composed a song, "Hurricane," about him), and two men who claimed to have seen Carter at the murder scene recanted, claiming that police pressure and financial payoffs had induced their false testimony. After the convictions were overturned by the New Jersey Supreme Court in 1976, another trial found them guilty again as the prosecution was permitted to introduce a new line of argument, that the murders had been racially motivated. Although Artis was paroled in 1981, not until November 1985 was Carter released from prison when Judge Lee Sarokin of the U.S. District Court in Newark ruled that the second trial had convicted Carter and Artis on "racism rather than reason, and concealment rather than disclosure."[7] Carter's conviction was representative of the view that most blacks and many whites had of American justice at the time—that justice was far from color-blind.

Baseball

Professional baseball looked about the same as ever in the 1960s except for the growing number of teams, but those appearances were deceiving. The winds of change were also buffeting baseball, although not until the next decade would the public clearly see what those winds had been blowing up.

The decade opened with Bill Mazeroski, the great defensive second baseman of the Pittsburgh Pirates, hitting a ninth-inning home run in game seven of the 1960 World Series to give his Pirates the championship and put a dent in the New York Yankee dynasty. The Yankees continued, though, to be the Yankees of old through 1964, when another Series loss, this one to the St. Louis Cardinals, temporarily ended the long run of Yankee successes.

The most important on-field baseball happening of the 1960s featured Roger Maris, the Yankees' right fielder, at a time when the greatest active Yankee hero was still Mickey Mantle. Maris did the unthinkable, breaking the beloved Babe Ruth's home-run mark, which had stood at sixty since 1927. Maris did not wear his heroic role comfortably, suffering badly under the stress of media attention and considerable fan unhappiness that the great Bambino's record was falling. For most fans, if the record had to fall, it should have been broken by Mantle. The commissioner of baseball, Ford Frick, a former newspaperman and ghostwriter for Babe Ruth, did his best to retain Ruth's status by adding the most famous asterisk in history to Maris's record, indicating that he had played a 162-game schedule, eight more games than in Ruth's time.

Not only the single-season home-run record fell in the 1960s. A year after Maris clubbed his sixty-one, Maury Wills, shortstop for the Los Angeles Dodgers, took on another legendary star, Ty Cobb, outrunning Cobb's single-season stolen base record 104 to 96. The year 1962 also was remarkable for other events. A young fireballing lefthander, Sandy Koufax, struck out eighteen batters in a game for the Dodgers, tying the all-time single-game record. Casey Stengel, let go after the 1960 season by the Yankees, resurfaced to manage the expansion New York Mets, and lost 120 games.

For fifty years, from 1903 until 1953, the same sixteen teams in the same sixteen cities had constituted the major leagues. That changed in the mid-1950s as several teams changed residences, including the flight of the Dodgers and Giants from Brooklyn and New York to Los Angeles and San Francisco. Yet the number of teams remained fixed at sixteen until the 1960s. In 1961, the Los Angeles Angels (who moved to Anaheim in 1966) and the second version of the Washington Senators were added to the American League. The following year came the Houston Colt .45's (later Astros) and New York Mets to the National League. Four additional teams joined the majors for the 1969 season, the Kansas City Royals and Seattle Pilots (later the Milwaukee Brewers) in the American League, and the San

Roger Maris broke Babe Ruth's record by hitting 61 home runs in 1961.
Source: Photofest, Inc.

Diego Padres and Montreal Expos in the National League (the latter marking the first inclusion of a major league team from another country). Also in 1962, Jackie Robinson, the first African American player in the modern major leagues, was inducted into the Baseball Hall of Fame at Cooperstown, New York. The enshrinement of Robinson was especially significant in the decade that witnessed so much striving after racial justice.

No major league team would completely replace the Yankees in the 1960s, but many would try, with the Los Angeles Dodgers coming closest. The Dodgers won the National League pennant in 1963, 1965, and 1966, and captured the World Series after the first two of those pennants. The Dodgers were led by the best pitcher of his time, and one of the greatest ever, Sandy Koufax, who won twenty-five to twenty-seven games three times in four years, struck out a then-record 382 batters in 1965, threw four no-hitters, including a perfect game, captured three Cy Young and one Most Valuable Player Awards, and retired at his prime with an arthritic elbow after the 1966 season.

Warren Spahn, who spent most of his career with the Boston and Milwaukee Braves, winning twenty or more games thirteen times, completed his career in 1965 with 363 wins, the most ever by a left-hander. Two players won Triple Crowns in the 1960s, leading their league in home runs, runs batted in, and batting—Frank Robinson of the Baltimore Orioles in 1966 and Carl Yastrzemski of the Boston Red Sox in 1967.

The 1968 campaign was the year of the pitcher. Denny McLain won thirty-one games for the World Series champion Detroit Tigers, the first pitcher to reach thirty since Dizzy Dean of the Cardinals in 1934. Don Drysdale of the Dodgers set a record by pitching $58\frac{2}{3}$ consecutive innings without allowing a run. Bob Gibson of the Cardinals compiled a phenomenal earned run average of 1.12. Don Wilson of Houston recorded eighteen strikeouts in a nine-inning game, and Luis Tiant of the Cleveland Indians fanned nineteen in ten innings.

The remarkable decade ended with one of the most improbable stories in baseball history. The previously hapless Mets, by now one of twenty-four teams and playing in a divisional structure that introduced a preliminary playoff prior to the World Series, went the distance behind their great young pitcher Tom Seaver to capture the World Series.

Perhaps the most significant development in baseball during the 1960s occurred off the field, while not many fans noticed. The Major League Baseball Players Association in 1966 hired Marvin Miller as executive director. Within a decade, Miller would transform a fraternal organization into one of the most powerful unions in the world. Before the 1960s were over, Miller had negotiated a collective bargaining agreement with major league baseball. The following decade would see the end of free agency, with the resulting player mobility producing vast leaps in player salaries. Four player strikes followed over the final three decades of the century; umpires, who organized in 1968, became embroiled in major labor-management conflicts; the cost of attending a game skyrocketed; and money became as much a defining character of major league baseball as the home run or the strikeout. All of this can be traced back to the 1960s.

Basketball

Basketball took its place next to baseball and football as the third most popular sport during the 1960s. Professional basketball was a dynastic sport during the decade, dominated by the Boston Celtics and two players huge in physical stature as well as talent. The Celtics were National Basketball Association champions every year during the decade except 1967. That year marked the first season for Bill Russell, the Celtics' center, as player-coach, succeeding the legendary Red Auerbach, who left coaching to enter Boston's front office. Russell brought his team back to the top in 1968 and 1969 before retiring. A master rebounder and defensive player, Russell brought defense into the forefront of basketball, changing the game forever. Along the way, he won five Most Valuable Player Awards and became the first African American head coach in any major professional sport in the United States.

The one blemish on the Celtics' record in the 1960s was caused by the Philadelphia 76ers, led by Wilt "The Stilt" Chamberlain, the most prodigious scorer in basketball history. In Chamberlain's first season (1959–60), he set a new scoring record with 37.6 points per game. He won seven consecutive scoring titles, averaging an astronomical 50.4 points per game in 1961–62. In one game that season, he scored one hundred points against the New York Knicks. Also a great rebounder and playmaker, Chamberlain won the Most Valuable Player Award four times in his career and led his team twice to the NBA championship, in that 1967 season and with the Los Angeles Lakers in 1972. Throughout the 1960s, the greatest matchup in the NBA was between Russell and Chamberlain, two powerful and proud individuals. Although Russell's team usually prevailed, which player was greater continues to be debated.

College Football

At the college level, football remained popular, while basketball joined it in the public consciousness. A small number of college powerhouses, but no one team, ruled the gridiron. The University of Alabama won two national championships and shared a third during the 1960s, while the University of Texas finished atop the polls twice. The University of Southern California won two national titles and featured two Heisman winners, more notably O.J. Simpson, who would go on to a record-setting career in the National Football League and in the 1990s become part of one of the most sensational murder trials in history. The University of Notre Dame, under coach Ara Parseghian, returned to prominence, with the Fighting Irish capturing a national title in 1966 while playing one of the most famous games ever, a 10–10 tie with Michigan State—also one of the most controversial games, as Notre Dame, its starting quarterback and halfback out with injuries, elected to run out the clock. In the 1960s, service academies still produced top-flight teams. Navy was edged by Missouri in the 1960 Orange Bowl, 21–14, but featured the Heisman Trophy winner, Joe Bellino. Three years later, Navy had another Heisman winner, quarterback Roger Staubach.

College Basketball

Triumphs were spread around the world of college football, but much less so in basketball. As with professional basketball, the college sport featured a dynasty in the 1960s, the University of California at Los Angeles (UCLA). The National Collegiate Athletic Association (NCAA) championship belonged to Ohio State University, the University of Cincinnati, and

Loyola of Chicago during the first four years of the 1960s. In 1964, UCLA took over, ruling as NCAA champions for the rest of the decade (except 1966) under John Wooden, possibly the greatest college basketball coach of all time with ten national titles in twelve years during the 1960s and 1970s. After Texas Western interrupted UCLA's reign in 1966, the California university returned to the top with a new superstar, center Lew Alcindor, college player of the year in each of his three varsity seasons (1967–69). A player for the ages, Alcindor also became a man for the times in 1968, assuming the role of activist for racial justice. He became a Muslim and, as Cassius Clay had done earlier, chose a new name—Kareem Abdul-Jabbar. As the decade closed, Abdul-Jabbar, now with the professional Milwaukee Bucks, was winning the Rookie of the Year Award for 1969–70 and starting on a career that would last until 1989 and include six Most Valuable Player Awards, six NBA championships (one with Milwaukee and five with the Los Angeles Lakers), and the all-time career scoring record.

Hockey

Hockey was growing in popularity during the 1960s, although in most of the United States it remained behind baseball, football, and basketball. A sign of the sport's growth was the expansion of National Hockey League clubs from six to twelve for the 1967–68 season. The new teams were all American: Los Angeles, Minnesota, Oakland, Philadelphia, Pittsburgh, and St. Louis. Except for the two ends of the decade, though, Canadian teams dominated, with the Toronto Maple Leafs and Montreal Canadiens capturing the Stanley Cup. The Chicago Blackhawks won the championship in the 1960–61 season, and the Boston Bruins in 1969–70. The great players on U.S. teams during the 1960s included Bobby Hull and Stan Mikita of the Blackhawks, Gordie Howe of the Detroit Red Wings, and, by the end of the decade, Bobby Orr of the Bruins.

Golf

Two sports largely associated with America's country clubs took on more of a popular, if not populist, tone during the 1960s. They were golf and tennis. At the beginning of the decade, golf, despite such famous stars as Slammin' Sammy Snead and Ben Hogan, was perceived as pure country club. That image faded at the skilled hands of Arnold Palmer and Jack Nicklaus. Palmer, son of a greenskeeper, set the golfing world on its head with his talent and charisma. Winning six major professional tournaments between 1960 and 1964, Palmer excited large numbers of fans, "Arnie's Army," who exulted in his patented late drives for victory, the so-called "Palmer's Charge." Although past his prime by the decade's midpoint, he continued to play good golf throughout the rest of the decade, never losing the public's goodwill.

Following Palmer into the golfing limelight was Jack Nicklaus, whose blond hair and sturdy physique earned him the nickname "the Golden Bear." In his early twenties, he won the U.S. Amateur and U.S. Open tournaments. Between 1959 and 1967, he brought home nine major titles. Like Palmer, he continued to compete throughout the century while maintaining the respect and admiration of his fellow golfers and the public.

Palmer and Nicklaus were the best of the 1960s, but they were not alone. A long list of fine golfers, among them Julius Boros, Billy Casper, Ken Venturi, and Lee Trevino, helped golf come of age. As the decade progressed, television viewers could sit at home and watch matches on the weekend, while *The Wonderful World of Golf* offered golf tournaments especially created for television. Not until the next decade, however, did women's golf, featuring the incomparable Nancy Lopez, attain a level of popularity in any way approaching that of men's golf.

Tennis

Tennis traveled a similar path. At the beginning of the 1960s, tennis was as locked in tradition and conservatism as any sport could be, with most of the major tournaments still played on grass, players compelled to wear all white (the participants themselves just as white), and for most of the decade major tournaments limited to amateurs in an attempt to maintain the purity of the sport. Yet, as with golf and so many other areas of American life, the winds of change were blowing through tennis.

In the latter part of the 1960s, tournaments began to admit professionals in order to offer the best talent available. Metal racquets became popular with many of the top players. Meanwhile, two figures brought vitality and diversity to the sport: Billie Jean King and Arthur Ashe.

Billie Jean King helped popularize women's tennis and bring the sport closer to parity with men's tennis in media attention and financial rewards. Playing an aggressive game that was copied by most top women players, King compiled a remarkable string of tournament victories, including twenty Wimbledon titles by the end of the 1970s. She won her first Wimbledon doubles title in 1961, when she was just seventeen, and added additional doubles titles at Wimbledon in 1962, 1965, 1967, and 1968, plus the Wimbledon mixed doubles title in 1967 and the singles from 1966 to 1968. Among her many other victories were the U.S. Open singles, doubles, and mixed doubles in 1967. That same year she was named Associated Press Female Athlete of the Year. In 1973, she struck another blow for women by defeating Bobby Riggs in a tennis match labeled the "battle of the sexes."

Although Arthur Ashe did not dominate men's tennis the way Billie Jean King did the women's game, his achievement may have been even more important. Ashe, an African American, came early to tennis, then an almost totally white game. As the son of a parks supervisor in Richmond, Virginia, he had access to parks and became an outstanding tennis player while still a child. By the age of ten, he was touring under the sponsorship of the American Tennis Association. A tennis scholarship took Ashe to UCLA, where he became the national collegiate singles and doubles champion.

Arthur Ashe's fame was secured with his 1968 triumphs in the U.S. Open and as a member of the U.S. Davis Cup team. In a society and sport still imbued with considerable racism, Ashe became the first African American to be recognized as a top tennis player. A turning point for Ashe came in 1969 when he was denied a visa to travel to South Africa to play in a tournament. After that rejection, he became more involved in political action, increasing the public's awareness of the evils of apartheid.

Ashe's later years were filled with work on behalf of human rights and educational efforts, including a three-volume book entitled *A Hard Road to Glory: A History of the African-American Athlete* (1988). After contracting AIDS through a blood transfusion while undergoing heart surgery, Ashe worked diligently to raise public awareness of the disease and of its impact on those infected and their families. Arthur Ashe was a man of great courage and dignity, and his impact on tennis, while great, was transcended by his contributions to the larger society.

The 1960s Olympics

Some of the most exciting sports events occurred in the three Olympics of the 1960s, and a considerable portion of that excitement was driven as much by political issues of the time as by popular interest in the sports themselves. The 1960 Olympics came during the height of the Cold War, and in the middle of an international incident seriously affecting United States–Soviet Union relations. Between the winter and summer Olympics, the Russians shot down an American U-2 spy plane flown by Gary Powers. Even more than usual, competition between the U.S. and Soviet teams came to be viewed as a contest for national pride and ideological supremacy.

For Americans, the highlight of the winter games was the gold medal won by the U.S. hockey team in a stunning upset of the Soviet Union and Czechoslovakia, all the sweeter for being held within the United States, in Squaw Valley, California. The U.S. basketball team, paced by future basketball immortals Jerry Lucas, Oscar Robertson, and Jerry West, took home a gold medal in the summer games in Rome. Cassius Clay (the future Muhammad Ali) won the gold as a light heavyweight boxer. Rafer Johnson finished first in the decathlon, and Wilma Rudolph captured three gold medals, in the 100-meter and 200-meter races, and as the anchor of the 400-meter relay event.

Wilma Rudolph had contracted polio as a child and, unable to walk, was forced to wear a brace. Gradually, she recovered, became an outstanding high school athlete, won a bronze medal at the 1956 Olympics, and made history in Rome. She was the first African American woman to capture three gold medals in track and field, along the way setting a new record in the 100 meters. In 1962, she received the Zaharias Award, given to the individual considered the best athlete in the world.

The Olympic summer games were held in Tokyo in 1964 amid the continuing Cold War. Americans did especially well in track and field, with Henry Carr, Mike Larrabee, and the future pro football star Bob Hayes winning two gold medals each. Don Schollander won gold medals in the 100-meter and 400-meter freestyle events and two golds in relays as the U.S. team took thirty-seven medals in swimming and diving. Joe Frazier won the gold in heavyweight boxing.

The best remembered of the three 1960s Olympics is the 1968 one. The games that year came as antiwar sentiment was increasing in the United States and much of the country was aflame, metaphorically and literally, over racial injustice. African American athletes threatened to boycott the Olympics if South Africa were permitted to participate, and eventually the Olympic Committed decided to ban South Africa from the games. The winter games in Grenoble, France, were reasonably nonconfrontational, with U.S. figure skater Peggy Fleming and French skier Jean-Claude Killy among the best known victors. The win was bittersweet for Fleming, after the death of her coach and the U.S. skating team in an airplane crash seven years before.

By the summer Olympics, held in Mexico in October, both Martin Luther King, Jr., and Robert F. Kennedy had been assassinated. After Dr. King's death, riots erupted in many U.S. cities. The Tet Offensive early in the year had made it clear that victory in the Vietnam War was far away, if it were ever to come. African Americans increasingly came to the realization, as Muhammad Ali and Dr. King had done, that the Vietnam War should be seen within the context of racism.

With South Africa and its system of apartheid excluded from the games, African American athletes competed, but many still looked for a way to make a political statement. Two, Tommie Smith and John Carlos, did so very publicly. After winning the gold and bronze medals respectively in the 200-meter race, they mounted the victory stand shoeless but wearing black socks, and each with a black glove on one hand, representing black poverty in the United States and black power. They raised their black-gloved hands and bowed their heads, gestures that led to their expulsion from the rest of the Olympics.

Reactions to Smith and Carlos's demonstration varied widely. The U.S. Olympic Committee promised severe penalties for any athletes who engaged in political demonstrations during the Olympics. Many sports enthusiasts and others argued that the Olympics should be nonpolitical, although many who felt that way were happy to see their country capture more gold medals and more total medals than the Soviet Union in the games that year. Others saw the demonstration by Smith and Carlos as both brave and appropriate, given the continuing failures at home to establish racial equality.

There were other, less controversial medals for American athletes. For the fourth straight Olympics, Al Oerter won the gold in the discus throw. George Foreman, like Ali and Frazier a future world heavyweight champion, finished first among heavyweight boxers. Dick Fosbury won the gold medal in the high jump with a new backward, head-first technique. Bob Beamon took the broad jump. Debby Meyer captured the gold in three swimming events, while Mark Spitz won four medals, two of them gold, as a prelude to his seven gold medals in the next Olympics. A U.S. athlete who did not gain the gold was perhaps the most important male runner of the decade. In 1964, Jim Ryun had become the first high school runner to break the four-minute mile. Although defeated in the Tokyo Olympics, he smashed the world record for the mile in 1967, running it in 3:51.1, a record that would endure for eight years. The high altitude of Mexico City hurt him in 1968, and he finished second. He would try again in 1972, but fail to win a medal. Nonetheless, Ryun achieved widespread fame in the United States during the decade and inspired countless individuals to take up running. He later was elected to the U.S. House of Representatives from his native Kansas.

Horse Racing

The "Sport of Kings" featured an impressive stable of fine horses in the 1960s but perhaps no legends. Kelso may have been the most noteworthy, named Horse of the Year five years running (1960–64). There were no Triple Crown Winners in the decade, but several came close. Five horses won both the Kentucky Derby and the Preakness: Carry Back (1961), Northern Dancer (1964), Kauai King (1966), Forward Pass (1968), and Majestic Prince (1969). Chateaugay won the Belmont and Kentucky Derby in 1963, and Damascus captured the Belmont and Preakness in 1967. Jockey immortals Bill Shoemaker and Bill Hartack continued to accumulate victories, with Shoemaker the top money-winner among jockeys every year from 1958 through 1964.

Throughout the various major sports of the 1960s, memorable individuals, teams, and contests attracted large numbers of followers. At the same time, sports continued to evolve into big business. Participants may have been playing games, but those games in both talent level and financial ramifications were far from child's play.

THE 1960S

8
Literature

This chapter discusses fiction, creative nonfiction, poetry, and magazine and newspaper publications of the 1960s. Drama, although universally recognized as literature, is also a performing art and is examined in the chapter on performing arts.

The world of fiction saw many of its giants pass from the scene during the 1960s, leaving the arena to newer voices. Ernest Hemingway, who revolutionized fiction in the 1920s in both style and subject, succumbed to depression in 1961, committing suicide at his home in Ketchum, Idaho. He would permanently be known for his commitment to short, powerful declarative sentences, for making famous the Lost Generation of American expatriates living in Paris during the 1920s, and for his depictions of bullfighting in Spain and fishing in Michigan. William Faulkner, the chronicler of post–Civil War southern society, including a series of novels about the Snopes family of Yoknapatawpha County, Mississippi, died in 1962. John Steinbeck, the third of this great triumvirate, all of whom won a Nobel Prize for Literature in their careers, passed away in 1968. Steinbeck, who set many of his novels in his native California during the Great Depression, and remains best known for *The Grapes of Wrath* (1939) about Oklahoma sharecroppers driven from their land by 1937 Dust Bowl storms, earned his Nobel in 1962. He was the only U.S. author to receive a Nobel Prize for Literature during the 1960s, an award usually given more for lifetime accomplishments than a single work. Although the decade was rich in American fiction, as in poetry, most of the best-known younger writers had not yet secured the long list of writing successes required for a Nobel Prize.

As in fiction, there was a changing of the guard in American poetry during the 1960s, a process demonstrated no more definitively than by the number of giants of American poetry who died during the decade. They included H.D. (Hilda Doolittle), who died in 1961, e.e. cummings (1962), Robinson Jeffers (1962), Robert Frost (1963), William Carlos Williams (1963), Theodore Roethke (1963), T.S. Eliot (1965), and Carl Sandburg (1967). Charles Olson just survived the decade, dying in 1970. Some poets achieved fame during the 1960s only to die in the same decade. Sylvia Plath, just into her thirties, committed suicide in 1963, and Frank O'Hara, a few days after his fortieth birthday, was struck and killed by a beach-buggy on Fire Island, New York, in 1966.

Creative nonfiction joined fiction and poetry as an important literary genre during the 1960s. Creative nonfiction, by now a common term in literature, refers to nonfiction prose that aspires to literature. It uses language not merely to inform clearly or to persuade but with the nuances, connotations, and complexities with which language serves fiction and poetry. Creative nonfiction usually includes a specific voice at its creative core, as do fiction and poetry.

The most important types of creative nonfiction during the 1960s were New Journalism (also called the nonfiction novel) and the personal essay. New Journalism replaced the ideal of objective reporting and a distancing of writer from subject with the subjective involvement of the author and a clear authorial voice. It also included conventions traditionally associated with fiction, but not with journalism, including character development, plot, narrative techniques such as the flashback, and use of dialogue to explore emotions as well as actions and to draw suppositions in addition to clarifying facts. Essayists tended to use many of the same approaches but with the more limited focus demanded by the shorter form. A subject that came into its own in American writing during the decade was nature, so the final section of this chapter examines, in a shift from form to subject, nature writing by several important U.S. writers of nonfiction.

The 1960s witnessed as well great interest in magazines and newspapers. Some of the old standards, like *Time* and *Life*, remained popular, while being joined by magazines that appealed to special segments of society—*Ebony* and *Jet*, for example, directed toward the African American community, and *Ramparts* for a generally antiestablishment reading audience. The decade was a time of great activity in newspaper journalism, with so-called underground newspapers sprouting throughout the country. Generally staffed and read by a young audience, underground newspapers usually adopted strong political positions on such vital issues of the day as the Civil Rights Movement and the Vietnam War while also offering news on music, drugs, and fashions for their youthful readers.

FICTION

With the passing of such novelists as Hemingway, Faulkner, and Steinbeck, new voices arose, often challenging traditional political, social, and literary norms. Many looked toward new lifestyles for their subjects, explored different ways of constructing narratives, and reexamined the very nature of what it means to write a novel. The Beats, African American and Native American authors, and proponents of what came to be known as metafiction contributed engaging and often highly successful novels. A number of Jewish authors brought to public consciousness the Jewish-American experience. On college campuses throughout the country, certain books from a broad range of perspectives, in some cases written prior to the 1960s, achieved widespread popularity.

The Beats came to prominence during the 1950s, but continued to wield great influence on the literary scene in the following decade. Jack Kerouac achieved fame and something of cult status with his *On the Road* (1957), which captured the wandering, nonconformist mood of large numbers of his generation. The heavily autobiographical book (the main characters Sal Paradise and Dean Moriarty were based on Kerouac and a friend, Neal Cassady) has been likened to Hemingway's *The Sun Also Rises* (1926) for effectively depicting a generation's rejection of traditional mores. Throughout the 1960s, *On the Road* remained popular, its treatment of drug and sexual experiences appealing to a new generation of young men and women. Although Kerouac published several more books during the 1960s, none achieved *On the Road*'s influence. Before the end of the decade, both Kerouac (1969) and Cassady (1968) were dead, the former of alcoholism, the latter of exposure after a drug overdose.

William S. Burroughs, who established friendships at Columbia University in New York City with fellow Columbia students Allen Ginsberg and Jack Kerouac, and Ken Kesey were also important novelists of the Beat generation. Burroughs's *The Naked Lunch*, first published in Paris in 1959, appeared in the United States in 1962. The heavily scatological content and explicit treatment of drug use stirred the fires of censorship and led to a four-year legal battle in Massachusetts that ultimately failed to suppress the book. Using hallucinatory effects in his narratives and looking inward at the writer's own identity as well as outward at society, Burroughs followed *Naked Lunch* with *The Soft Machine* (1961), *The Ticket that Exploded* (1962), and *Nova Express* (1964).

Kesey used his experiences working in a psychiatric ward and volunteering in a government experiment with LSD and other drugs in writing *One Flew Over the Cuckoo's Nest* (1962). The novel focuses on Chief Bromden, a Native American mental patient forced to undergo multiple shock treatments; a rigidly authoritarian Nurse Ratched; and the hero of the story, Randle Patrick McMurphy, whose nonconformist but humane attitude induces the patients to gain some joy from each other. Chief Bromden finally escapes from the "cuckoo's nest" while McMurphy is subjected to shock treatments and a lobotomy. The novel questions who the insane ones really are and attacks the conformist powers of institutional society. The story became a successful film in the 1970s starring Jack Nicholson as McMurphy.

With Richard Wright, author of *Native Son* (1940), dying in 1960; and Ralph Ellison, creator of *Invisible Man* (1952), undergoing a fictional hiatus during the 1960s, the strongest black voice in American fiction during the decade was James Baldwin. Baldwin secured an important position in fiction and social protest with his novel *Go Tell It on the Mountain* in 1953. The novel was widely read during the 1960s and was followed by *Giovanni's Room* in 1955 and *Another Country* in 1962. Baldwin's fiction explores the difficulties of being a member of two minorities: African American and homosexual. Baldwin spent much of his time in France, but despite his rightful anger over racial injustice, continued to believe in the possibilities of American society. His essays, gathered in such collections as *Notes of a Native Son* (1955), *Nobody Knows My Name* (1961), and *The Fire Next Time* (1963), are viewed by many critics as better than his fiction. They certainly had an important effect on readers, gaining support for enforcing civil rights on behalf of black Americans. Baldwin's rejection of racial separatism and plea for love over hatred elicited both praise and condemnation, depending on readers' political points of view.

As Baldwin was a powerful advocate for understanding the plight of African Americans, N. Scott Momaday sought to bring both himself and modern society to a greater understanding of Native American history and culture. Momaday, son of a Kiowa father and Cherokee mother, both of whom were artists and teachers, learned firsthand of life on reservations and was educated in the ways of both his native people and the broader American society. His novel *House Made of Dawn* (1968) won a Pulitzer Prize (the first novel by a Native American to be so honored) and helped to introduce what has been called the Native American Renaissance, a rich harvest of outstanding fiction, poetry, and nonfiction by Native American writers that continues to this day. The protagonist of *House Made of Dawn* is Abel, a returning veteran of World War II whose life reflects the alienation, alcoholism, and difficulty finding a good job that afflict many Native Americans whose culture has been systematically destroyed by white Americans bent on conquest. Finally, Abel overcomes, reuniting with his grandfather as the old man dies, and going out for a run across the countryside, singing as the dawn rises. The title of the book is from a poem that is part of a Navajo religious ceremony.

The nonfiction *The Way to Rainy Mountain* (1969), like the privately printed *Journey to Tai-me* (1967), gains its inspiration from the death of Momaday's grandmother, who had been present at the last Kiowa Sun Dance, in 1887. *The Way to Rainy Mountain* is an attempt, using a variety of genres (myth, folk tales, family stories, history, poetry, songs, and drawings by his father), to discover the history of the Kiowa people and, therefore, Momaday's own heritage.

The Jewish American experience also yielded an impressive body of fiction, by such writers as Bernard Malamud, Saul Bellow, and Philip Roth.

Malamud's 1950s novels, *The Natural* and *The Assistant*, established his popularity, and *The Fixer*, published in 1966, secured his lasting reputation as both an outstanding chronicler of Jewish life in the United States and one of the country's foremost novelists. *The Fixer*, about a seemingly ordinary man accused of the ritual murder of a Christian child, won both a Pulitzer Prize for fiction and a National Book Award.

Saul Bellow, who later was awarded the Nobel Prize for Literature (1976), excelled in, as the Nobel citation stated, "human understanding and subtle analysis of contemporary culture." He grew up in Quebec, but set most of his fiction in Chicago and New York City. His highly successful novel of the 1960s, *Herzog* (1964), narrates the story of Moses Herzog, a sort of everyman who complains, charms, is deceived, but survives his personal crises.

Philip Roth has proved more controversial than Bellow. His *Portnoy's Complaint* (1969) features Alexander Portnoy's memories, especially of childhood, with a heavy emphasis on sex. Many readers were put off by the descriptions of young Portnoy's skills at masturbation and criticized Roth for moving away from middle-class Jewish subjects to depict Jewish characters as bizarre, even grotesque.

Kurt Vonnegut achieved great success in the 1960s, especially on college campuses, not for reflecting a particular ethnic background, but for combining social criticism with highly innovative approaches to storytelling that pulled apart the traditional concept of narrative as a coherent, cause-to-effect, beginning-middle-end plot. Vonnegut broke through the curtain of popular acceptance with his novel *Cat's Cradle* in 1963, a strong indictment of contemporary science, religion, and politics. Vonnegut's structural experimenting reached its apex, though, with the later *Slaughterhouse-Five or The Children's Crusade: A Duty-Dance with Death* (1969). In it, the main character, Billy Pilgrim, comes unstuck in time, moving among three worlds: his past as a prisoner of war in Dresden during the World War II firebombing of the city, his present as a husband and father, and a fantasy realm on the planet Tralfamadore (where he is mated with another earthling, porn star Montana Wildhack). At one point, Billy Pilgrim (his name representing his time travels), watches a war movie backward, which makes everything turn out better as the flyers return safely to their bases. Billy imagines the film continuing, with the soldiers turning in their uniforms and becoming happy high school students again; even Hitler is transformed into an innocent baby. The novel is both an antiwar book and an assault on contemporary society's dehumanizing impact, summed up in the phrase of acceptance repeatedly appearing in the story: "So it goes."

Other novelists also looked closely at not only the story as artifact or product, but as a process intimately related to its author. Such writers as John Barth, Thomas Pynchon, Robert Coover, and Richard Brautigan thus gave rise to what critics have labeled metafiction, an approach to fiction that parallels the rejection of traditional values and expectations found

Kurt Vonnegut attracted readers with his comic and satiric novels, including *Cat's Cradle* and *Slaughterhouse-Five*. Source: Photofest, Inc.

throughout American society during the 1960s. The relevant meaning of "meta" in this context is going beyond or transcending. Metafiction goes beyond traditional views of fiction by being self-reflective, by looking closely at the act of writing and the writer. Metafiction usually is highly personal, grounded in the belief that the most important reality is personal reality. Metafiction thus transcends tradition by looking inward at the author and exhibiting the mind of the writer and the writer's personal sensory experiences. Style often becomes more important than plot and characterization. Heroes tend to become antiheroes—that is, nontraditional types of protagonists often far removed from what readers are accustomed to viewing as heroic. It is often said, borrowing a verse from Ecclesiastes, that there is nothing new under the sun. That is true with metafiction as well, which owes much to eighteenth-century fiction such as Laurence Sterne's self-reflective *The Life and Opinions of Tristram Shandy, Gentleman*, and the epistolary novels of Samuel Richardson.

The clearest connections to the antecedents of metafiction are found in John Barth's novels, such as *Giles Goat-Boy* (1966), with its comic scenes, self-conscious footnoting, parodies, deliberate confusion of art and life, transformation of academic life into an allegory of the world, and even its great length (eighteenth-century novels were often published in multiple volumes). Thomas Pynchon's *V* (1963) and *The Crying of Lot 49* (1966) overturned most fictional expectations, creating labyrinthine plots that tend toward the absurd, repeatedly running serious moments into comedy, and imitating other writers' styles with exuberant humor rather than satiric intent.

Robert Coover's *The Universal Baseball Association, Inc., J. Henry Waugh, Prop.* (1968) is a comic and allegorical novel featuring J. Henry Waugh, who devises a baseball game in which every move is determined by throwing dice. For Waugh, unfulfilled in his job as an accountant, the Universal Baseball Association becomes not only the perfect game with its exact balance of offense and defense, but one in which he increasingly invests his own imagination and psychic life until the game becomes his all-consuming reality.

Among the writers associated with metafiction, Richard Brautigan was perhaps the most popular during the 1960s, especially among college students and young people living in communes and otherwise withdrawing from mainstream society. His books included the volume of poetry *The Pill Versus the Springhill Mine Disaster* (1968) and the novels *A Confederate General from Big Sur* (1964), *Trout Fishing in America* (1967), and *In Watermelon Sugar* (1968). A reclusive writer seldom seen in public or photographed, Brautigan served as a role model for the 1960s dropout. His works of fiction consisted of loosely ordered prose pieces, not much of a plot, criticism of modern society's destruction of nature, and a consistently irreverent tone. *Trout Fishing in America*, for example, includes such elements as a "Kool-Aid wino," many references to the narrator and the book itself, personification of Trout Fishing in America as someone the narrator meets at the Big Wood River near Ketchum, Idaho, just after Hemingway's death (ironically linking the book with the great chronicler of fishing in America, Hemingway), a surrealistic satire on destroyers of the environment in which a trout stream is cut up and sold by the foot (waterfalls, birds, ferns, and trees sold separately), and a concluding chapter entitled "The Mayonnaise Chapter" because the narrator says that he "always wanted to write a book that ended with the word Mayonnaise."

Seldom does a title work its way into the popular lexicon. That, however, occurred with the title of Joseph Heller's World War II novel *Catch-22*

(1961), a novel that became something of a commentary on what many increasingly saw as an irrational political and military system in the United States during the 1960s, even though the novel is set in a previous war. Captain John Yossarian tries to escape certain death from following the insane orders of his squadron commanders by claiming insanity. His doctor, though, points out the Catch-22 principle, that a flyer must be insane to be excused from combat, but the fact that he wants to escape from the mission proves his sanity. Conversely, Doc Daneeka acknowledges that Yossarian's tentmate, Orr, is crazy but that Orr must request to be grounded, which he does not do precisely because he is crazy. Unable to function logically within a crazy system, namely the war-making apparatus, Yossarian deserts. Other characters take other approaches. Orr utilizes cunning while pretending to be merely a not very bright joker to thwart the efforts of Colonel Cathcart, the ultra-authoritarian villain of the novel. An important symbolic character is the nameless Soldier in White, bandaged mummylike over his whole body and kept alive while fluids enter his body at one end and are secreted at the other in a grotesque joke that stands for the impersonal manipulation of individuals by the institutions of modern society.

The novel is one of the most important and lasting antiwar writings of American literature, but it also transcends war to comment on the essential irrationality of the human condition. Countless readers and people who have never even heard of the novel continue to use the phrase "catch-22" to express irrational but irrefutable contradictions that put people in no-win situations.

Not all novelists during the 1960s wrote against the traditional grain. Two who followed mainstream paths but with the individual talents and vision that characterize every good artist were John Updike and William Styron. Updike published ten volumes of fiction (novels and collections of short stories) during the 1960s while also writing poetry and book reviews. *The Centaur* (1963) depicts a high school teacher during a three-day period within a narrative heavy in mythological allusions, starting with the mythical part-human, part-horse beast of the title. It brought Updike a National Book Award and considerable critical acclaim. *Rabbit Run* (1961), more rooted in social realism than *The Centaur*, introduced Harry "Rabbit" Angstrom, a former high school basketball star disenchanted with his present life and what he feels are a stultifying town, job, and family. Harry would appear in several more novels in the following decades. Updike's most controversial novel during the 1960s was *Couples* (1968), which chronicles suburban sexual relationships heavy on adultery.

Styron encountered controversy, not for experimentation with narrative form, but because of his depiction of Nat Turner in *The Confessions of Nat Turner* (1967). In real life, Turner led a slave rebellion in 1831 that resulted in the deaths of over fifty whites in Virginia. The novel opens with Turner in jail, where he reflects on his past life. His owner, Samuel Turner, supposedly had promised Nat his freedom, but went broke and sold Nat to a Reverend Mr. Eppes. Having promised to free Nat, Eppes reneged and sold him to slave traders. As the novel progresses, Nat becomes increasingly filled with hatred, has a homosexual affair that induces considerable guilt, and undergoes a religious conversion that propels him into a prophetic state in which he believes he is ordained to kill whites. *The Confessions of Nat Turner* won a Pulitzer Prize for fiction but engendered great opposition from many African American writers and critics who believed the novel inaccurate and racist. One reaction was a book entitled *William Styron's Nat Turner: Ten Black Writers Respond* (1968), edited by John Henrik Clarke, a prominent teacher of African American history.

Although men were in the majority among leading novelists during the decade, a number of women also left their lasting marks on the American reading public. They included Flannery O'Connor, Katherine Anne Porter, Harper Lee, and Joyce Carol Oates.

O'Connor brought her Roman Catholic background and Georgia heritage to her explorations of character. Her often rural figures rise above their commonplace situations as O'Connor lays bare their eternal yearnings. Her stories are rich in religious symbolism and revelations of the humanity within characters that some critics have labeled grotesques. O'Connor is considered one of America's finest short story writers as well as an effective novelist. She died in 1964 at the age of thirty-nine after a long struggle with disseminated lupus, a disease that also claimed her father. Her second and final novel, *The Violent Bear It Away*, appeared in 1960; a second collection of short stories, *Everything That Rises Must Converge*, was published the year after her death. Despite her early death, O'Connor's reputation continued to rise. *The Flannery O'Connor Bulletin*, dedicated to the study of her life and work, originated in the 1970s and was upgraded to *The Flannery O'Connor Review* in the year 2001.

Katherine Anne Porter achieved critical acclaim for her short stories in the 1920s. In the following decades, she produced additional short stories and an occasional novella while the literary world awaited her long-anticipated first novel. That first novel, which would also be her last, finally was published in 1962. *Ship of Fools* is set on a ship traveling across the Atlantic to Germany in 1931. The confined setting permits a close analysis of a wide range of characters and relationships. In structuring her novel, Porter worked within a long established tradition of confining characters within a situation that encouraged self-revelations (Chaucer's *Canterbury Tales* from the fourteenth century is just one of many earlier examples) and at the same time consciously viewed the ocean crossing, as she noted in a preface to the novel, as an allegory of the world's journey toward eternity. Porter's *Collected Stories* appeared in 1965, earning her several important awards, including a National Book Award and a Pulitzer Prize for fiction.

Porter lived to the age of ninety, dying in 1980, enjoying her fame, but completing no more novels.

Students throughout the 1960s and beyond were likely to encounter a novel by Harper Lee on a reading list for at least one English course. Published in 1960, *To Kill a Mockingbird* presents a story of racism and injustice set in 1930s Alabama. The narrator, Jean Louise "Scout" Finch, who ages from six to eight during the story, recounts the case of Tom Robinson, an African American on trial for allegedly raping a white woman. Convinced of his innocence, Jean's father, Atticus Finch, defends Robinson. Atticus demonstrates his defendant's innocence, but the white jury finds him guilty anyway. Robinson subsequently is killed trying to escape. Another important story line involves Boo Radley, who despite being treated as an outcast, even something of a monster, by his neighbors, rescues Scout and her brother Jem when the father of the woman Robinson was accused of raping tries to kill the children to exact revenge on Atticus. The novel's powerful questioning of racial and social justice, as well as institutional hypocrisy, earned Lee a Pulitzer Prize. The novel was made into a film (1962) starring Gregory Peck, who won the Academy Award for his performance as Atticus.

One of the new fictional voices in the 1960s was Joyce Carol Oates. Her first collection of short stories, *By the North Gate*, was published in 1963, and was followed by the novels *With Shuddering Fall* (1964), *Expensive People* (1968), and *them* (1969). Since *them*, which won a National Book Award, she has been one of the country's most famous and prolific writers. She is especially well known for writing about the physical and emotional violence with which seemingly ordinary people find themselves afflicted.

The 1960s, as this discussion shows, witnessed considerable variety in fiction. And there were still other works that caught the attention of large numbers of readers, including college students, who were at the heart of much that was happening in social, even revolutionary action during the 1960s.

J.D. Salinger remained popular on college campuses and in college English courses. His *Catcher in the Rye* had been published in 1951, but it retained its hold on youthful readers and writers. Sixteen-year-old Holden Caulfield justified alienation from family and adult society, and his creator expressed a similar disenchantment with contemporary life by withdrawing from the public eye during the 1960s, becoming one of America's most famous recluses. His collections of stories, *Franny and Zooey* (1961) and *Raise High the Roof Beam, Carpenters, and Seymour—An Introduction* (1963) were followed by a cessation of publishing that continued to fascinate Salinger fans as well as the media, critics, and general reading public into the twenty-first century.

Also present in large numbers on college campuses were copies of Robert Heinlein's science fiction novel *Strangers in a Strange Land* (1961), depicting the story of Michael Smith, a Martian-raised earthling who returns to his native land only to find himself an outcast in a totalitarian society. Smith, whose common name helps establish him as an everyman despite his powers of telekinesis and telepathy, establishes a new church. The principles of this new institution, mirroring youthful concerns of the 1960s, call for recognition of the self as divine, rejection of private property, and advocacy of sexual freedom and a spiritual union of people. Smith finally is martyred for his beliefs.

Hermann Hesse's *Steppenwolf* was published in 1927, but the German novel, which shares some of the concerns found in Heinlein's novel, made a strong comeback in the United States during the 1960s with college students. The protagonist, the middle-aged Harry Haller, is a steppenwolf—that is, a wolf of the steppes, or a wanderer seeking his true identity. Music, drugs, and sex are some of his avenues toward that understanding, as well as the dreams that he encounters in the "Magic Theater." Haller perseveres to discover youth, love, and freedom in a rejection of bourgeois materialism.

Also set in another land but with many lessons that youthful readers of the 1960s found relevant to their own searching was the fantasy fiction of British medievalist J.R.R. Tolkien. The works that stirred readers' imagination so strongly during the decade had appeared earlier: *The Hobbit* in 1937, and the three volumes that compose *The Lord of the Rings (The Fellowship of the Ring, The Two Towers, The Return of the King)* in the 1950s. As with *Steppenwolf*, a key to the popularity of these books was their issuance in inexpensive paperback editions during the 1960s. *The Hobbit* describes a place called Middle-earth, and the trilogy picks up the story about fifty years later in the same realm. Middle-earth is a simpler place than contemporary America with the struggle between good and evil rendered in concrete terms. Tolkien, drawing on his knowledge of linguistics and the Middle Ages, creates not only a new place but a language, mythology, and society to make it come alive. The major story line throughout the trilogy is the effort, finally successful, to destroy a ring containing such power that its possessor could control the world of Middle-earth.

During the late 1960s, Tolkien societies and discussion groups became common, while Tolkien's stories helped to legitimize fantasy as a mode of fiction to be taken seriously by readers and literary critics alike. In some respects, Tolkien's fiction sums up in very concrete terms much of what was happening in U.S. fiction throughout the 1960s: an attempt to engage readers in examining contemporary institutions and values while also establishing through the power of imagination a world at once entertaining and challenging.

Many of these novels occupied prominent places on the best-seller lists, if not always nationally, at least with certain segments of American society, such as college students. Best-seller lists, in fact, included an extraordinary range of novels. Early in the 1960s, readers were also devouring copies of the political novel *Advise and Consent* by Allen Drury; the long historical novel, *Hawaii*, by James Michener; Irving Stone's story of artist Michelangelo, *The Agony and the Ecstasy*; and lots of sex, from Henry Miller's *Tropic of Cancer* to Harold Robbins's *The Carpetbaggers*.

By 1962, in the year of the Cuban Missile Crisis, novels of nuclear confrontation and political intrigue at the highest levels excited the general public. Two of the leading sellers of the year were *Fail-Safe*, an account of a mistaken nuclear attack on the Soviet Union by the United States, by Eugene Burdick and Harvey Wheeler; and *Seven Days in May*, about an attempt to overthrow an American president viewed by military leaders as too soft on communism, by Fletcher Knebel and Charles W. Bailey II.

Morris L. West proved that a novel about a Catholic pope, *The Shoes of the Fisherman*, could make the best-seller lists in 1963, perhaps helped by public interest in the Second Vatican Council and the wide popularity enjoyed by Pope John XXIII. Spy novels such as John Le Carré's *The Spy Who Came in from the Cold* and *The Looking Glass War* and Ian Fleming's *You Only Live Twice* and *The Man with the Golden Gun* continued to be popular. Jacqueline Susann hit it big with *Valley of the Dolls*, a supposed exposé of Hollywood in the mid-1960s which appealed to readers who liked a vicarious mix of sex, drugs, and other sins; she followed with *The Love Machine* at the end of the decade, moving her focus from Hollywood to television.

Novels that broke through in the latter years of the decade included the supernatural spellbinder *Rosemary's Baby*, by Ira Levin; Arthur Hailey's *Airport*, about a plane in danger of being blown up by a mad bomber; Michael Crichton's story of the dangers of bacteriological warfare research, *The Andromeda Strain*; and Mario Puzo's account of the Mafia in *The Godfather*, which tended to portray murderers and similar types as almost sympathetic if not admirable, and was made into a series of three popular films.

CREATIVE NONFICTION

Truman Capote's *In Cold Blood* (1966) was one of the most influential and controversial examples of New Journalism, also known as the nonfiction novel. Originally published in four installments in *The New Yorker* in 1965, *In Cold Blood* recounts the 1959 murders of Kansas farmer Herbert Clutter, his wife, Bonnie, and their children, Nancy and Kenyon, by Dick Hickock and Perry Smith. What excited controversy was not so much the retelling of the murders but that Capote deepened his narrative into a sociological examination of the small-town milieu in which the Clutters lived, a psychological portrayal of the murderers, and an indirect indictment of capital punishment. Capote became close to the murderers during his research, which may have helped lead to the double reference of the title—to the slaying of the farm family and the governmental execution of the convicted killers.

Truman Capote arrives for a party in New York's Plaza Hotel with *Washington Post* publisher Katherine Graham in 1966. Capote's *In Cold Blood* blurred the distinctions between true-crime writing and serious literature. Source: Photofest, Inc.

Capote viewed his book as a nonfiction novel, an apparent oxymoron that led some critics to question how much of the account originated in the author's imagination. Capote uses clearly literary devices, such as beginning the account in the middle of the story, well after the murders, and presenting the crimes as a flashback after the capture of Hickock and Smith. He also included long passages of dialogue that he said he was able to recall from memory. *In Cold Blood* received the 1966 Mystery Writers of America's Edgar Allan Poe Award, usually given to a work of fiction. Despite the controversy, Capote's book stimulated other mixed-genre works that staked out a middle ground between journalism and fiction. It also helped, along with Capote's flamboyant lifestyle and personality, to make him a major celebrity in both the literary and social scenes.

No less flamboyant and controversial was Norman Mailer; nor was he less important as a practitioner of New Journalism. Mailer originally gained fame with his first novel, *The Naked and the Dead*, in 1948. By the 1960s, he had turned increasingly to politics and creative reportage. A run for mayor of New York City was thwarted when he stabbed his second wife at a party, fortunately not fatally. A major celebrity who appeared regularly on late-night television talk shows, Mailer published during the decade, among other works, *Armies of the Night* and *Miami and the Siege of Chicago*, both in 1968. The former grew out of Mailer's participation in an antiwar demonstration at the Pentagon in 1967; the latter was in response to the political conventions of 1968 that nominated Richard Nixon in a placid event in Miami and Hubert Humphrey amid a massive storm of antiwar demonstrations in Chicago. The books discarded the objective ideals of traditional reporting and featured the author as a major character within the narrative plots.

Another popular nonfiction novel was Tom Wolfe's *The Electric Kool-Aid Acid Test* (1968), about novelist Ken Kesey's travels, both physical and drug-induced. In 1964, Kesey set off in a 1939 Day-Glo-painted International Harvester bus with a group of friends known as the Merry Pranksters. The trip included lots of LSD and filming of their experiences. Kesey and company interacted with the Hell's Angels motorcycle group and staged acid tests, which were multimedia happenings that included LSD, dancing, strobe lights, and rock music. Wolfe's account of Kesey's experiences was a subjective treatment that used fiction techniques, including typographic oddities to convey inner reality and selective descriptive details combined with authorial conclusions (often guesses as to what observed characters are feeling and thinking). The effect is to convey not only the action but the spirit of the times.

Also important in the development of New Journalism was Hunter S. Thompson, a journalist during the first half of the decade for such prestigious publications as *Time*, the *New York Herald Tribune*, the *National Observer*, and the *Nation*. A turning point in his career and in the genre was an article that Thompson wrote for the *Nation* in 1964 on motorcycle gangs. Thompson disagreed with the common perception of Hell's Angels as a bunch of thugs and spent much time with the group in the mid-1960s. The result was a book about them called *Hell's Angels: A Strange and Terrible Saga* (1967). His approach helped to popularize participant-observer reporting, a departure

Norman Mailer published *Armies of the Night* and *The Siege of Chicago* in 1968. Source: Photofest, Inc.

from the objective reporting generally in vogue. Thompson as journalist became part of the story, blurring the line between source and reporter. His type of unorthodox treatment of subjects usually given little serious treatment in the press would come to be labeled "gonzo journalism."

Joan Didion and Susan Sontag were among the essayists who brought a new creativity to analyzing important events and movements of the 1960s. Didion, also a novelist, was one of the first journalists to look seriously at countercultural types, including the hippies of Haight-Ashbury in San Francisco. Effective description, a keen sense of dialogue, and the ability to convey the essence of her "characters" were on display in essays that she wrote for *The Saturday Evening Post* in the 1960s. Her collection of essays, *Slouching Towards Bethlehem* (1968), with its title borrowed from the Irish poet William Butler Yeats, conveys a sense of the apocalyptic regarding the direction of a modern society involved in a fighting war in Southeast Asia as well as in a myriad of social, racial, and class conflicts.

Susan Sontag came to public attention as a social critic in the middle of the decade with essays in such magazines as *Partisan Review, The Evergreen Review*, and *Commentary*. She followed with a book collection entitled *Against Interpretation and Other Essays* (1966). In her essays, she ranged over many subjects, including science-fiction films, pornography, and art criticism. Sontag traveled to North Vietnam during the war, itself a highly controversial act, and published an account of her experiences in *Trip to Hanoi* (1968). Another collection of essays, *Styles of Radical Will*, appeared in 1969. Sontag combined her reporting and analyses with a leftist political point of view that challenged many actions and pronouncements of the government and other American institutions.

The 1960s witnessed a growing interest in protecting and living in harmony with nature, an attitude increasingly evident in the creative nonfiction of the decade. Lorein Eiseley grew up in Nebraska early in the twentieth century and developed an abiding love for nature and nature writing. His professional training as an anthropologist at the universities of Nebraska and Pennsylvania, combined with a personal commitment to protecting nature, led to a number of books, beginning with *The Immense Journey* (1946). Eiseley produced several books during the 1960s—*The Firmament of Time* (1960), *The Mind of Nature* (1962), *The Unexpected Universe* (1969)—that revealed a deep human connection to the surrounding natural world. Eiseley wrote in a manner accessible to nonscientists in which his personal values came through clearly.

Other important nature writers during the 1960s included Edward Abbey, John McPhee, and Edward Hoagland, all of whom in their writings combined science with a strong sense of self and a commitment to appreciating the natural environment. Abbey committed himself to political activism on behalf of the environment. He argued for ecocentrism, the view that nature existed for itself rather than to serve humankind, and condoned ecodefense, including environmental terrorism, to protect the environment. The 1968 *Desert Solitaire*, which reflects Abbey's longtime residence and interest in the American Southwest, is usually considered one of his most important books. McPhee, much less political than Abbey, helped to sensitize readers to the small details of nature in such books as *Oranges* (1967) and *The Pine Barrens* (1968). Hoagland's focus was primarily on animals in novels such as *The Peacock's Tail* (1965) and in the nonfiction that he began to write late in the 1960s and that would produce many nonfiction books beginning with *The Courage of Turtles* (1971). That much of the best nature writing was antiestablishment, resisting political and economic pressures to use the land for profit, helped to secure its position in American culture during the 1960s.

POETRY

Robert Frost was the most famous and beloved poet in the United States at the beginning of the decade. His white hair blowing in the January 1961 wind, he read his poem "The Gift Outright," a celebration of westward expansion and the people's surrender to the land that he saw as defining the

Robert Frost presents Kennedy with a book of his poetry at a ceremony honoring the poet with a Congressional medal on
March 26, 1962. Source: Photofest, Inc.

new nation, at the inauguration of President John F. Kennedy. Very much
a traditionalist, Frost used formal conventions, but filled them with colloquial speech. A poet of nature and New England, he perpetuated the myth
that real America was rural New England while comparing outer nature
with the inner self.

Generations of schoolchildren had come of age, and were still coming of
age in the 1960s, reading, reciting, and even memorizing such Frost classics
as "The Road Not Taken," "Birches," "Mending Wall," "The Death of the
Hired Man," and "Stopping by Woods on a Snowy Evening." Readers pulled
great truths of life from the poet's references to something not loving a wall,
the divergent paths from which people must choose, and the promises to be
kept before the eternal sleep of death. Countless valedictorians quoted Frost
in their speeches. There was a Frost line somewhere for everyone.

The United States, however, had changed greatly during the almost nine
decades of Robert Frost's life. The country was increasingly urban, truths
seemed increasingly less absolute as well as harder to decipher, and the individual self stepped forward in a more materialistic world in place of the
collective we.

More reflective than Robert Frost of the changing times were the Beats,
who came to prominence during the 1950s and continued to wield great

influence in poetry, fiction, and society during the 1960s. The term "Beat" typically carried as many as three meanings. It connoted a visionary, even spiritual perspective, borrowed from the term "beatitude," referring to blessedness or happiness. (*Beatitude* was also the title of an early 1950s magazine put out by Lawrence Ferlinghetti.) The term also conveyed the sense of being beat, or fed up with, or having had it with contemporary society. Finally, there was an association with the beat of jazz, a relationship that would endure with Allen Ginsberg in his later years performing onstage with jazz musicians.

The Beats tended toward a bohemian lifestyle, rejected many of modern society's standards and values, and sought enlightenment and freedom through love (and sex), drugs, and Eastern religions, especially Zen Buddhism. When the Vietnam War heated up, they opposed it, while typically supporting progressive social movements, such as civil rights. The Beats congregated more or less in San Francisco, fusing the Beat movement with a San Francisco renaissance of the arts.

Allen Ginsberg may have been the most important of the Beat poets. He had considerable knowledge of earlier poetic traditions and retained respect for much of early poetry, even incorporating some aspects of it into his own new directions in writing. The long line is one major example. Ginsberg underwent a visionary experience in which he seemed to hear the eighteenth-century British poet William Blake, himself given to visions, and adopted an unusually long poetic line in imitation of Blake, Walt Whitman, Christopher Smart (another eighteenth-century British poet), and the Bible. He popularized the approach in his groundbreaking long poem, "Howl," published in 1956 in *Howl and Other Poems*.

After graduating from Columbia University in 1948, Ginsberg pled insanity and spent eight months in an institution to avoid being prosecuted as an accomplice to theft; a friend, Herbert Huncke, had used Ginsberg's apartment to store goods that he stole. By the 1960s, Ginsberg was widely known as a revolutionary poet, an antiwar activist, a student of Buddhism in India, and a popular reader of his poetry on college campuses throughout the United States. His important books of poetry in the decade included *Kaddish and Other Poems* (1961), with the title poem about his mother's suffering and death; *Reality Sandwiches* (1963); and *Planet News* (1968).

Other important Beat/San Francisco poets during the 1960s were Lawrence Ferlinghetti, Gregory Corso, and Gary Snyder. Ferlinghetti's *A Coney Island of the Mind* (1958) remained enormously popular throughout the decade, especially among college students. Ferlinghetti published additional books during the decade, such as *Starting from San Francisco* (1961), poems about the poet's travels to Cuba as well as to other spots in the United States and Latin America; and the heavily satirical *Tyrannus Nix?* (1969) attacking Richard Nixon. He included a record of himself reading his poetry with *Starting from San Francisco*, thus encouraging the idea that poetry should be heard and helping to popularize the growing phenomenon in the 1960s of poets giving public readings of their works. Much of his time, though, he devoted to publishing other poets. In the 1950s, Ferlinghetti was co-founder of City Lights in San Francisco, an all-paperback store; and publisher of City Light Books, the Pocket Poets Series, and the magazine *Beatitude*. The fourth book in the Pocket series was Ginsberg's *Howl and Other Poems*, and Ferlinghetti continued publishing other poets throughout the 1960s.

Corso had a difficult youth, spending most of it in foster homes, orphanages, or prison. In the 1950s, he was released from prison, having been incarcerated for theft, and met Allen Ginsberg, who befriended Corso and strongly encouraged him in the poetry that he had started writing in prison. Corso moved to San Francisco in the mid-1950s and began to establish himself as a poet, publishing several books over the next two decades, including *The Happy Birthday of Death* (1960), *Long Live Man* (1962), and *There Is Yet Time to Run Back Through Life and Expiate All That's Been Sadly Done* (1965). Despite his difficult life, Corso brought a sympathetic and comic touch to his poetry, as in one of his most famous poems, "Marriage," a meditation on whether marriage is in the cards for him. He imagines, for example, his wife's many relatives at the wedding, and his few friends "all scroungy and bearded." Or in "Dream of a Baseball Star," with the poet encountering Ted Williams weeping against the Eiffel Tower and assuring the slugger that he too is a kind of poet.

Snyder was part of the San Francisco scene but difficult to categorize. He studied Eastern religions and Native American cultures, learned Chinese, traveled to Japan, communed deeply with the natural world, and helped introduce Oriental poetic forms, including haiku, into English-language poetry. He published poetry—*Myths and Texts* (1960), *The Back Country* (1968), *The Blue Sky* (1969)—and essays in *Earth House Hold* (1969).

The Beats are often credited with helping to spawn the beatniks and hippies. The columnist Herb Caen used the term "beatnik," derived from "beat," in a *San Francisco Chronicle* column on April 2, 1958. The term caught on, usually in a derogatory, sometimes comic way. Images of the beatnik reached a wide audience through the character Maynard G. Krebs (played by Bob Denver) on the television series *The Many Loves of Dobie Gilis* (1959–63) and through *MAD* magazine, with its satiric mock magazine *Beatnik: The Magazine for Hipsters* (September 1960). The line of descent from Beats to hippies is traced through such common ground as support for peace, love, drugs, and sexual freedom, and opposition to conformity and received authority.

As the Vietnam War dragged on throughout the 1960s, the large majority of America's poets, not just the Beats, turned against it, with many engaging quite actively in antiwar efforts. Robert Lowell, who came from an old Boston patrician family and had been sentenced to a year in New York's

West Street jail for opposing America's war efforts during World War II, helped lead protestors against the Pentagon in 1967. He believed that a poet should also be a public person who takes seriously one's obligations to society. A tireless craftsman who revised almost endlessly, Lowell became, through collections like *For the Union Dead* (1964) and *Notebook 1967–1968* (1969; revised as *Notebook* in 1970), and for his social commitment, one of the most respected poets of his time.

Antiwar activism also drew British-born Denise Levertov, whose poetry through such books as *O Taste and See* (1964), *The Sorrow Dance* (1967), and *Relearning the Alphabet* (1970) became increasingly political. Adrienne Rich sought unification in her poetry of her various identities—woman, poet, political activist, mother, wife. Some of the titles of her books are indicative of personal issues important to her: *Snapshots of a Daughter-in-Law* (1963), *Necessities of Life* (1966). The collection *Leaflets* (1969) expresses Rich's growing involvement with politics. In the following decade, she would turn her attention even more emphatically to feminism.

Robert Bly believed that poetry should be simple in diction, concrete in image, and direct in expression in order to combine the external landscape (often his native Minnesota) with the mystical or imaginative landscape of the mind. That direction later would lead him to write prose poems (compositions that look like short prose pieces but utilize many of the rhetorical conventions of poetry). During the 1960s, living out his conviction that the poet should be society's conscience, Bly helped to create American Writers against the Vietnam War and organize the series "Poets Reading Against the Vietnam War." Important collections of his 1960s poems include *The Light Around the Body* (1967), *The Morning Glory* (1969), *The Teeth-Mother Naked at Last* (1970), and *The Shadow-Mothers* (1970).

Social activism in poetry also included a growing commitment to other major movements of the decade, such as black consciousness and the Civil Rights Movement. At the beginning of the 1960s, Langston Hughes was the best known and most respected voice among African American poets. Known as "the bard of Harlem" and acclaimed for his use of jazz and African American rhythms in his poetry, Hughes remained productive until his death in 1967. He edited anthologies of younger black writers in his last decade, *New Negro Poets* (1964) and *The Best Short Stories by Negro Writers* (1967); and served as lyricist on the musicals *Black Nativity* (1961), *Jericho-Jim Crow* (1964), and *The Prodigal Son* (1965), which brought gospel music to the stage. His final volume of poetry, *The Panther and the Lash: Poems of our Times* (1967), demonstrated his growing involvement in civil rights and the black power movement.

Hughes's successor as the most widely known black poet in America was Gwendolyn Brooks, the first African American writer to win a Pulitzer Prize, which she received in 1950 for her collection of poetry *Annie Allen* (1949). The late 1960s marked a major turning point for Brooks, who earlier in her career had written for a mainstream audience in traditional poetic forms such as the sonnet. In 1967, she attended the Black Writers' Conference at Fisk University, an experience that motivated her to focus more directly on a black audience and experiment more widely in her poetry both in form and language (emphasizing, for example, jazz rhythms, African chants, and a more consistently colloquial diction). She also began to publish with African American presses. Such volumes as *In the Mecca* (1968), consisting of poems about African Americans living in poverty in Chicago, and *Riot* (1969), written in response to the assassination of Martin Luther King, marked her growing political consciousness. In a dramatic sign of changing attitudes in American poetry, Brooks followed the venerable Carl Sandburg as poet laureate of Illinois in 1968.

Younger African American poets also came to the fore. Imamuu Amiri Baraka, formerly known as LeRoi Jones, achieved prominence in poetry and in drama. The volumes *Preface to a Twenty Volume Suicide Note* (1961) and *The Dead Lecturer* (1964), written before he changed his name, demonstrate preoccupations with death and suicide. The later *Black Magic* (1969) shows a decided turn from victim to proud revolutionary, as represented in the titles of the book's three sections: "Sabotage," "Target Study," and "Black Art." The volume includes Baraka's call for a "Black Poem" and a "Black World."

Nikki Giovanni, while a college student in the early 1960s, helped to revive the Student Nonviolent Coordinating Committee (SNCC) at Fisk University, where it had been banned. After graduating, she published *Black Feeling, Black Talk* (1968) and *Black Judgement* (1969), volumes that established her as one of the country's most notable young poets and a powerful voice of urban African Americans. Sonia Sanchez moved from Alabama to Harlem, New York, in 1943 to live with her musician father, Wilson L. Driver. There she met jazz luminaries like Billie Holiday and Count Basie; her subsequent poetry, as with many African American poets, borrowed from jazz rhythms. Ideologically, her great influence was Malcolm X. She published her first book of poetry, *Homecoming*, in 1969, using such devices as slashes and omitted letters to simulate African American spoken English, and worked with the Congress of Racial Equality (CORE) on a variety of civil rights issues. Deeply interested in education, she encouraged development of black studies programs in higher education.

As poetry moved more deeply into the great swirl of social action in the 1960s, the poet's public persona in the United Stages became more varied. James Dickey, for example, published successful volumes of poetry during the decade—*Drowning with Others* (1962), *Helmet* (1964), *Buckdancer's Choice* (1965)—and occupied the chair of poetry at the Library of Congress (1967–69). At the beginning of the next decade, he published a powerful novel, *Deliverance* (1970), later made into a popular film (1972), about businessmen on a weekend outing who must battle natural and human forces out to destroy them. Yet Dickey's lifestyle seemed at times even larger than his writings—heavy drinking, fast motorcycles, and a fondness for publicity fostering a Byronic persona of the poet as a larger-than-life risk-taker.

One of the most widely read poets of the 1960s was Rod McKuen, derided by critics for his sentimental poetry but a mass-marketed best-seller devoured by youthful readers who responded to his sensitive persona and love-filled lyrics. Also a songwriter and singer, McKuen often performed his own works. His 1960s collections of poems included *Stanyan Street and Other Sorrows* (1966), *Listen to the Warm* (1967), and *In Someone's Shadow* (1969).

The image of the sensitive, troubled poet too fragile to cope with the pressures of everyday life was both persona and self for Sylvia Plath. As a student at Smith College, Plath suffered a nervous breakdown and attempted suicide. Her autobiographical novel *The Bell Jar* spoke for young modern women resisting traditional self-defining roles of wife and mother. Originally published in England in 1963, the book was released in the United States in 1971 and became extremely popular with young American readers during the 1970s. During the 1960s, however, most American readers knew Plath as a poet, author of the collections *The Colossus and Other Poems* (1962) and *Ariel* (1966); as wife of the British poet Ted Hughes; and for her death by suicide in 1963. In London with her two young children, and her marriage having broken up in 1962, Plath composed the *Ariel* poems. Although some of the poems express a mother's love for her children, others convey their creator's anger against the major male figures in her life, her husband and father. In the poem "Daddy," almost heartbreaking in its angry intensity and daughterly longing, the poet writes, "Daddy, I have had to kill you./You died before I had time." Building from her father's German ancestry, she likens herself to a Jew transported to a concentration camp, her father to a Nazi. "I was ten when they buried you," she writes. "At twenty I tried to die/And get back, back, back to you." Having worked on the *Ariel* poems until February 1963, she tried again to die, this time successfully.

MAGAZINES AND NEWSPAPERS

Americans continued to read old standbys during the 1960s in both magazines and newspapers. *Time* and *Newsweek* brought readers national and international news as well as a wide range of departments on a variety of aspects of American culture, including music, books, films, business, medicine, and religion. These popular news magazines also kept Americans abreast of prominent Americans who had died recently and other topical events. One of the publishing highlights of the year was *Time*'s designation of its "Man of the Year." *U.S. News & World Report* differed from *Time* and *Newsweek* by focusing almost completely on hard news, with primary attention given to politics and the economy. An unusual dimension of *U.S.*

News & World Report was that from 1962 until well into the 1980s it was employee owned.

Life and *Look*, large-format weekly magazines (approximately $10\frac{1}{2}$ by 14 inches), specialized in large photo spreads with easy-to-read stories that more often than not dealt with celebrities. *The Saturday Evening Post* differed most noticeably in its long tradition of publishing fiction and featuring covers by American painter Norman Rockwell. In 1963, the magazine used the last of its Rockwell covers, its 317th, dropping cover paintings as part of an updating designed to boost readership. The effort did not succeed, and the magazine went out of business in 1971.

Ebony was a *Life* for the African American community, substituting black models in the ads and features on subjects of interest to a mainstream black readership. Johnson Publications, producer of *Ebony*, also brought out *Jet*, a news magazine that was more cutting-edge in its approach to social issues than *Ebony*; *Tan*, marketed to African American homemakers; and *Negro Digest*, somewhat in the mode of the more white-oriented *Reader's Digest*. Both digests featured a wide range of articles, fillers, fiction (sometimes condensed versions), and cartoons.

Women were the targets of many large circulation magazines. *Ladies' Home Journal, Better Homes and Gardens*, and *McCall's* were especially for the stay-at-home mom and wife to help her beautify the house, prepare tasty meals, and sew skillfully. If she wanted a little vicarious adventure, she could read *True Confessions* and other romance magazines. *TV Guide* offered her and the rest of the family a weekly guide to what was playing on television. The man of the house could enjoy his sports on the page as well as on television, thanks to *Sport, Baseball Digest*, the venerable sports paper *The Sporting News*, and a variety of other sports publications. *National Geographic*, the magazine that seemingly no one ever threw away, was available for traveling to exotic places without leaving the comfort of one's easy chair.

Changing times were reflected in many magazines, including *Playboy, Cosmopolitan*, and *Ramparts*. Hugh Hefner's *Playboy* proposed a sexually free lifestyle minus commitment, along with centerfolds of young women devoid of clothes. *Cosmopolitan*, edited by Helen Gurley Brown, attempted to justify a similar philosophy for women, defending sexual pleasure apart from marriage and motherhood for the career woman. As *Playboy* and *Cosmopolitan* both reflected and contributed to a rejection of traditional sexual attitudes, *Ramparts* broke ground politically. A radical magazine, *Ramparts* featured articles by such activists as Eldridge Cleaver; printed exposés, including a report that the Central Intelligence Agency had channeled funds to religious, educational, and other cultural institutions to counter left-wing political action; published the diaries of Argentinian revolutionary Che Guevara, who had helped Castro come to power in Cuba; and argued at length that the John Kennedy assassination was a conspiracy being covered up by the government.

Major newspapers, especially eastern papers, continued to exercise considerable sway over public opinion, among them *The New York Times*, *Washington Post*, and *Boston Globe*. In smaller cities and throughout the country, a typical family received the local daily, usually delivered by a neighborhood paperboy or papergirl. The average citizen also valued his or her hometown weekly for local news and neighborly gossip. During the 1960s, though, a new type of newspaper came to prominence, usually written, produced, and primarily read by young men and women, mostly leftwing in their political, social, and cultural attitudes.

The *Los Angeles Free Press* was one of the early underground papers, originating in 1964. Many others followed: the *Berkeley Barb*, the *San Francisco Oracle*, *The Great Speckled Bird* in Atlanta, and many more. According to Robert J. Glessing, there were over four hundred fifty by the end of the decade.[1] In addition, untold numbers of high school students operated underground papers or newsletters, most of them short-lived. University campuses, home to plenty of students with some writing ability, spawned a large number of the underground newspapers. The new, inexpensive offset printing made production relatively easy and affordable.

The underground papers varied enormously in quality and professionalism, yet common political and cultural positions bound them into a journalistic movement of significance. The papers reported news with a strong left-wing, often radical, point of view. The papers were almost unfailingly antiwar. They championed the rights of women and minorities. Sex was good and should be expressed freely, although at the same time editors and writers were faced with trying to balance concepts of free love with respect for women's rights and opposition to dehumanizing behaviors.

Many aspects of the popular arts found their way into underground papers, including poetry, film reviews, and articles on rock music. Respecting the natural environment was important, as the movement contributed to the growth of environmentalism in the country. Alternate lifestyles, such as communal living, were described in positive terms. Much information on drugs appeared as underground newspapers played an important role in the expanding drug culture. New approaches to spiritualism received considerable exposure as well.

Radical youth tended to consider commercialism bad, but the underground newspapers found it increasingly difficult to stay aloof from it. Producing issues cost money, and advertisers were ready to provide funds to help the paper continue. Head shops (selling drug equipment), bookstores, coffeehouses, and record companies were among the advertisers buying space in the papers. Most of the papers died out quickly, but the underground publications helped to form and express the voice of much of America's youth during the second half of the 1960s and beyond.

THE 1960S

9

Music

Three terms that especially apply to music in the 1960s are variety, innovation, and quality. The decade was a time of enormous change in music, with musical performers turning both to the past and to the new. A blending of tradition and revolution ushered in an exciting and rich range of music, although commentators in later decades tended to ignore the traditional dimensions of 1960s music in favor of the very real changes occurring in rock and jazz.

The 1960s witnessed a rebirth of interest in folk music, with folk singers making the guitar as commonplace in the 1960s, especially for the young, as the piano was for their parents and grandparents. Folk music traditionally had been antiestablishment, and its revival in the 1960s wedded folk to protest even more securely as folk singers joined the vanguard in protesting the Vietnam War and demanding equal rights for people of color.

Country music gained a greater degree of respectability in the decade as it spread from southern and rural regions into all parts of the country. New directions in musical instruments, new approaches to phrasing, and very talented performers made it all right to be country, even in the most urban of settings.

Classical music declined somewhat in popularity during the 1960s but was far from dead. It opened itself to African American artists and embraced popular culture. Leonard Bernstein pushed classical music for children and used Beatles songs to exemplify its characteristics. Jazz meanwhile became a medium for some of the most innovative trends in music during the decade while also entering the political world as a vehicle for black aspirations and a repository of black cultural traditions.

Soul music also came to the fore, expressing the black experience in often emotionally powerful songs. Before long, Motown Records was wedding soul to pop, making soul a musical movement that really sold, with white audiences as well as black.

Rock, though, was the most powerful force in music during the decade. Elvis Presley returned from the army, but his role as leader of the rock movement evaporated even as he retained the honorary title of the King of Rock and Roll. The new revolution in rock was triggered by a British group with the strange name of the Beatles. The Beatles ushered in a new love for most things British, including British clothing and hairstyles. "Love me do," the group sang in its first single back in 1962, and within two years the United States had done just that. Much else also happened in rock, from San Francisco to Woodstock, and everywhere in between.

In addition, there was always an opening for a musical phenomenon that fit no category. Tiny Tim, for example, tiptoed through the tulips and onto Johnny Carson's *The Tonight Show* in 1969 (where he very publicly married his "Miss Vicky," Victoria May Budinger), squeezing temporary fame from long, stringy hair, a small ukelele, a falsetto voice, and an old tune entitled "Tiptoe Through the Tulips." In the 1960s, almost anything was possible in music.

FOLK MUSIC

Folk music declined in popularity during the 1950s, in part because much of folk music since the Great Depression had been antiestablishment. Senator Joseph McCarthy, the House Un-American Activities Committee, and others were attempting to hunt down musicians and other artists who seemed sympathetic to communism. To criticize the United States struck such witch-hunters as playing into the hands of the red menace.

By the late 1950s, however, folk music, especially commercial folk music, was making a comeback. The Kingston Trio led the way with their 1958 hit rendition of a North Carolina murder ballad, "Tom Dooley," and continued with a string of successful songs, including Pete Seeger's "Where Have All the Flowers Gone?" The Kingston Trio formed in 1956 when Dave Guard, Bob Shane, and Nick Reynolds came together in California. Guard and Shane had been reared in Hawaii, where they became interested in native music; Reynolds had learned folk songs from his father, a navy captain. True folk music, of course, is part of the oral tradition, handed down by word of mouth from generation to generation. Yet even in earlier decades, commercial folk had emerged with folk-song giants like Woody Guthrie and Pete Seeger composing many new songs in the folk mode.

Pete Seeger reestablished his position as one of America's great folk-song artists in the 1960s, although not without difficulty. Seeger and the Weavers, a group he helped form, ran into trouble in the 1950s because of their left-wing politics. Seeger left the Weavers in 1958, and the group disbanded in 1963. Seeger himself was convicted of contempt for Congress in 1961 as a result of his refusal to answer questions before the House Un-American

Activities Committee in the mid-1950s. The conviction was overturned in 1962, but Seeger continued to be blacklisted from network television. His political difficulties, however, endeared him all the more to the folk music crowd, and he was vitally important in the folk music revival of the 1960s. Woody Guthrie, incapacitated by Huntington's chorea, was unable to perform during the 1960s and died in 1967. His songs, however, remained popular, with "This Land Is Your Land" becoming a rallying cry for those struggling for freedom and equality during the 1960s. Cisco Houston, a close friend of Guthrie's, continued to popularize his friend's songs and became something of a transitional figure between the previous generation of folk singers and those who came of age in the 1960s. Houston performed at the 1960 Newport Folk Festival but, already suffering from cancer, had to give up singing not long after and died in 1961. Other singers popular with folk music enthusiasts who favored a natural, close-to-the-people sound were Bill Monroe with his bluegrass music, and Dewey Balfa and his Cajun fiddling.

Woody Guthrie's son, Arlo, took his own place in folk music during the 1960s. His song, "Alice's Restaurant," was about an antiestablishment restaurant that he discovered, draft resistance, and a vision of peace and harmony. He sang the song at the Woodstock Festival in 1969, the same year the song served as the centerpiece of a film by the same title.

At the head of the class among folk musicians in the 1960s were Bob Dylan, Joan Baez, and the trio of Peter, Paul and Mary, all of whom took folk music once again into social activism, especially in support of the Civil Rights Movement and in opposition to the Vietnam War. Woody Guthrie was Dylan's hero and model. After arriving in New York in 1961 from his native Minnesota, Dylan began to visit Guthrie in his hospital and play the guitar and sing in Greenwich Village coffeehouses. His first album, *Bob Dylan* (1962), primarily a collection of traditional folk songs, included the Dylan-composed homage "Song to Woody." His 1964 album *The Times They Are a-Changin'*, with the song "With God on Our Side," continued to establish him as a leading protest singer. By the middle of the decade, Dylan had moved into folk rock, shocking the audience at the 1965 Newport Folk Festival by switching to an electric guitar. Folk purists strongly objected, but the change only increased Dylan's fame. Throughout the decade, Dylan was widely revered not only as a singer and musician but also as a poet. Many of his songs were sung by such luminaries as Joan Baez and Peter, Paul and Mary, the latter striking it big with "Blowin' in the Wind."

Joan Baez released twelve albums during the 1960s, emphasizing folk songs and songs of protest, among them the anthem of the Civil Rights Movement, "We Shall Overcome." Consistently taking stands on behalf of justice and peace, she spoke and sang at many demonstrations in southern cities, marched with Martin Luther King, Jr., in the March on Washington in 1963, refused to appear on the popular television show *Hootenanny* when the show banned Pete Seeger, established the Institute for the Study of Nonviolence in California in 1965, and withheld a portion of her income taxes to protest defense spending. When her husband, David Harris, was jailed for draft evasion, Baez recorded an album, *David's Album*, in 1969 as a tribute to him. Throughout the decade, Joan Baez's efforts as singer and social activist remained inseparable.

Peter Yarrow, Paul Stookey, and Mary Travers composed an enormously popular trio during the 1960s and throughout the rest of the century. Forming their group in 1961, the three played in folk clubs and at colleges while establishing themselves as major figures in the folk music revival of the 1960s. Yarrow and Stookey played acoustic guitars, and the trio excelled in lyrical renditions and pleasing harmonies. Like many other folk artists, they combined folk songs with protest themes, the latter often earning more lasting acclaim. Their 1962 hit recording of "If I Had a Hammer," composed by Pete Seeger and Lee Hays, called for justice, freedom, and love between brothers and sisters; the following year they had another hit with Bob Dylan's "Blowin' in the Wind," also a call for freedom. Still another of their top recordings was the Woody Guthrie creation "This Land Is Your Land." One of their most acclaimed children's songs was "Puff (the Magic Dragon)," which narrates a boy's loss of youthful imagination and capacity for fantasy as he grows into adulthood.

Other folk/protest singers included Tom Paxton and Phil Ochs, both accomplished songwriters as well. After serving in the army, Paxton turned to folk music and topical protest songs, becoming noted for his ballads ("Last Thing on My Mind," "Ramblin' Boy"), children's tunes ("The Marvelous Toy"), and antiwar songs ("Peace Will Come," "The Willing Conscript," the latter based on Paxton's revulsion at being taught how to disembowel an enemy with a bayonet). Ochs turned his academic background in journalism to musical use to become a "singing journalist." Inspired by Guthrie and Seeger, he moved to New York City in 1961 to embark on a career in folk music and, like so many of his contemporaries, political songs. *All the News That's Fit to Sing* (1964) and *Phil Ochs in Concert* (1966) were successful albums, and Ochs was viewed for a time as virtually equal to Bob Dylan as a folksinger. One of his most famous songs, "The Ballad of Medgar Evers," was a powerful commentary on the civil rights leader's murder. Unfortunately, his career did not continue to prosper and, severely depressed, Ochs took his own life in 1976.

Two very different venues for folk music demonstrated its importance during the 1960s—the television show *Hootenanny* and the series of Newport Folk Festivals in Newport, Rhode Island. Pete Seeger is usually credited with popularizing the concept of the hootenanny, which features performers playing and singing seemingly more for each other than for the audience, with considerable interaction among performers, but often also engaging the audience in active participation. The hootenanny therefore tended to be somewhat informal and quite personal. The hootenanny proved popular at festivals, clubs, and private parties. The television version was hosted

Mary Travers was part of the enormously popular folk trio Peter, Paul, and Mary. Source: Photofest, Inc.

by Jack Linkletter and was taped before live audiences at college campuses. Performers ranged from traditional folk singers such as the Carter Family (into which country singer Johnny Cash married) to modern groups, among them the Chad Mitchell Trio and the Limeliters. Unfortunately, the program blacklisted some performers because of their left-wing views, among them Seeger and the Weavers. That led many artists, including Joan Baez, the Kingston Trio, and Peter, Paul, and Mary, to boycott the program. Television's *Hootenanny*, despite its promising format, and partly because of the political controversy associated with it, lasted only from April 1963 to September 1964.

The Newport Folk Festival occurred nine times from 1959 to 1969, featuring a wide array of talented individuals and groups. George Wein, a Boston pianist, conceived the idea of the festival and co-produced the first one with Albert Grossman; however, Wein discontinued the festival after two years because it lost money despite its popularity. Pete Seeger then persuaded Wein to create a nonprofit organization, the Newport Folk Foundation, to sponsor the festival and use proceeds to support folk music research and scholarships. The nonprofit Newport Folk Festival began in 1963 and was held annually through the rest of the decade. In its first year, some forty thousand attended the three-day concert, listening to, among others, Joan Baez, Judy Collins, and Bob Dylan. The 1965 festival was especially noteworthy for being the venue at which Dylan switched from pure folk to folk rock. The switch in musical technique and lyrics (which lacked the social-activist content commonly associated with his early music) so surprised and upset his fans that they roundly booed his performance as a sellout of pure folk music and the fight for social justice.

As the decade progressed, rock music played an increasingly important role at the Newport festivals, and drugs became a serious problem. Under pressure from the Newport City Council, the Newport Folk Foundation canceled the 1970 festival, and the next year the city council withdrew the foundation's license.

Bob Dylan was one of the performers responsible for the merging of folk themes, including social and political protest, with big-beat music and electric sounds to produce folk rock. Dylan's album *Bringing It All Back Home* (1965) used a backup rock-and-roll band; combined with his performance at the 1965 Newport Folk Festival, the album placed him in the vanguard of the folk rock movement. Jim McGuinn teamed with songwriter Gene Clark to form The Byrds and reached Number One on the charts in 1965 with Dylan's "Mr. Tambourine Man." Especially important among The Byrds' albums in fusing folk with rock was *Sweetheart of the Rodeo* (1968). Paul Simon and Art Garfunkel teamed up to hit it big with "Scarborough Fair," "Sounds of Silence" (their first Number-One hit), and a string of other popular songs that often combined folk and rock. Their successful albums included *Parsley, Sage, Rosemary, and Thyme* (1966), *Bookends* (1968), and *Bridge Over Troubled Water* (1970). Simon and Garfunkel recorded the soundtrack for the film *The Graduate* (1967), with "Sounds of Silence" from the film reaching the top of the charts and the soundtrack winning three Grammy Awards. Overall, Simon and Garfunkel accumulated nine Grammys before going their separate ways in 1970.[1]

COUNTRY MUSIC

Traditionally southern, rural, and white, country music began to escape from its regionalism and even its racial limitations during the 1960s. There were at least three major reasons for the spread of country music: (1) a growing feeling of alienation by individuals swallowed up in large urban centers and a desire to return to their roots; (2) moderation of the nasal twang associated with country singers and replacement of the fiddle and steel guitar with a wider range of instruments; and (3) the rise of artists who were able to transcend the hillbilly and honky-tonk image to appeal to a wide audience.

Nashville, Tennessee, was the heart of country music, with performance at the Grand Ole Opry in Nashville the sure sign that a country music artist had arrived. By the end of the 1960s, about 300 country performers, 300 record labels, 400 publishers, and 900 songwriters were based or represented in or near Nashville.[2] If Nashville was the heart, however, the body was as large as the country. Market studies indicated that by the middle of the decade a large majority of country consumers were urban dwellers. In addition, Nashville had to share some of its influence with other locales. The so-called Nashville West was located in Bakersfield, California, where Merle Haggard and Buck Owens moved. Increasingly, recording and promoting of country music emanated from Bakersfield and Hollywood. Also during the 1960s, a country music center emerged in Austin, Texas. Known as the center of progressive country (a mixture of country and western), Austin hosted Willie Nelson among others.

During the 1960s, radio stations, primarily AM, brought country music to listeners throughout the United States, and American soldiers in Vietnam and elsewhere helped to spread country music around the globe. Strangely enough, given country music's virtually all-white past, one of the entertainers most responsible for the rapid diffusion of country music during the 1960s was an African American, the great rhythm and blues singer Ray Charles. Charles released *Modern Sounds in Country & Western* in 1962 and followed with *Modern Sounds in Country & Western, Volume 2* the next year. Among the songs in these important albums were "I Can't Stop Loving You" and Hank Williams' "Your Cheating Heart." As with Bob Dylan's transformation into a folk rock performer, Charles's movement into country excited considerable controversy among his fans. It would still be several years, however, before the color barrier in country music truly fell. Charley Pride was an important pioneer, singing ballads in a mellifluous voice that did not sound particularly country. He appeared at the Grand Ole Opry in 1967, the first African American ever to headline there.

The Queen of Country Music during the early 1960s was Patsy Cline. An individualist with a beautiful voice and great versatility as a singer, Cline influenced future generations of country singers and still remained enormously popular at the end of the century, almost forty years after her death in a 1963 airplane crash. Her hits included "I Fall to Pieces," "Crazy," "Walkin' After Midnight," and the posthumous "Sweet Dreams (of You)" and "Faded Love."

Patsy Cline's successor as most popular female country vocalist in the 1960s was Loretta Lynn. Born in Butcher Hollow (pronounced "Holler"), Kentucky, in 1936, Lynn was a true rags-to-riches story. Married at thirteen, pregnant at fourteen, and mother of four children by eighteen, she overcame her early poverty and managed to balance family responsibilities with professional drive to become one of the first female country singers to have wide appeal among women as well as men. Although not what anyone would likely label a typical feminist, she related to real problems women encountered with such stand-up-for-your-rights songs as "Don't Come Home A-Drinkin' (With Lovin' on Your Mind)," "Your Squaw Is on the Warpath," and "You Ain't Woman Enough (To Take My Man)."

Many listeners contrasted Loretta Lynn with Tammy Wynette, whom many unfairly saw as pushing a doormat philosophy of womanhood with her most famous song, "Stand by Your Man" (1968), which she co-wrote with her producer, Billy Sherrill. Three 1967 hits—"Your Good Girl's Gonna Be Bad," "I Don't Wanna Play House" (which won a Grammy), and "D-I-V-O-R-C-E"—reflect the wide range of ways in which Wynette's songs depict women. Often referred to as the First Lady of Country Music, Tammy Wynette became one of the most successful female country vocalist of all time. When she married male country star George Jones in 1969, the couple became known as Mr. and Mrs. Country Music.

Although folk music during the 1960s tended to be antiestablishment and antiwar, country music remained more politically conservative. Merle Haggard, a former San Quentin inmate, was inspired by a concert Johnny Cash performed at the prison to join the prison band. By 1960, Haggard was free and starting his singing career. The 1966 song "I'm a Lonesome Fugitive" hit Number One on the country charts, but the song that made him nationally famous (or infamous, depending on one's political beliefs) was "Okie from Muskogee" (1969), which venerated the nation's flag while attacking hippies and draft-card burners. The song made Haggard President Nixon's favorite country singer and helped Haggard win a pardon for his earlier burglary conviction from California Governor Ronald Reagan.

Before Haggard, Chet Atkins had become something of a presidential favorite himself, entertaining President Kennedy in 1961 at the Press Photographers' Ball and performing at the White House. A skilled guitarist who cut numerous records, Atkins also served as a talent scout, record producer, and a vice president for the RCA Corporation. Among the many future country stars that he at least partly discovered were Charley Pride, Bobby Bare, and Waylon Jennings.

Johnny Cash established himself as a country giant during the 1950s and 1960s. Growing up, Cash was fond of traditional hymns, ballads, and work songs. He especially identified with the down-and-out, including prison inmates. Two of his top albums in the decade were *Ring of Fire* (1963), with the title selection his signature song, and *Johnny Cash at Folsom* (1968). Cash also recorded a concert at San Quentin, *Johnny Cash at San Quentin* (1969). In 1968, he married June Carter, a member of the famous folk music family, the Carters, and the following year had his own television show from Nashville. *The Johnny Cash Show* ran until May 1971, helping to bring country music to a mass audience. Among the regulars were Mother Maybelle and the Carter Family, wife June, the Statler Brothers, and Carl Perkins.

Cash was not alone among country singers on television. Glen Campbell starred on *The Glen Campbell Goodtime Hour* from 1969 to 1972. The theme song was Campbell's hit "Gentle on My Mind," which won a Grammy in the country category in 1967, the same year that Campbell won in pop for "By the Time I Get to Phoenix." Other hit Campbell songs in the decade included the 1969 "Wichita Lineman" and "Galveston." Jeannie C. Riley's "Harper Valley P.T.A." (1968), about a mini-skirted protagonist getting the better of the stuffed shirts who found fault with her child-rearing, was such a hit that it spawned a short-lived television series (1981–82) with the same title starring Barbara Eden. The most popular country television show was *Hee Haw*, co-hosted by Buck Owens and Roy Clark. The show, a medley of country music, corny humor, and cameo appearances by guest stars, all done from a very fake cornfield, originated in 1969. CBS dropped the show in 1971, although it was in the top twenty, and *Hee Haw* went into first-run syndication until 1993, a hit for most of its long life.

Country music is often referred to as country and western, but during the 1960s the western element was not greatly in evidence. It is true that country performers were taking to western garb, especially cowboy hats, but the music tended to be country minus any especially western flavor. However, there were some exceptions. Johnny Cash released albums entitled *Bitter Tears (Ballads of the American Indian)* (1964) and *Johnny Cash Sings Ballads of the True West* (1965). The most western of the country singers, though, was Marty Robbins, who had cut *Gunfighter Ballads and Trail Songs* in 1959 and continued with western songs in the 1960s. His 1960s recordings included "Ballad of the Alamo," the theme song for the 1960 John Wayne film *The Alamo*.

POP AND ROCK

Rock had been shoving traditional pop music aside, since the 1950s, but pop never died out. A wide audience remained for the relatively easy listening, often romantic and nostalgic lyrics of singers with command of their lyrics, their phrasing, and their audience. Frank Sinatra was the master, known as the "Chairman of the Board" and "Ol' Blue Eyes." His hit singles in the 1960s included "It Was a Very Good Year," "Strangers in the Night," and "Cycles." His albums also did very well, among them *Sinatra's Sinatra* (1963), *September of My Years* (1965), *Strangers in the Night* (1966), and *My Way* (1969).

The 1960s actually produced many pop hits: Tony Bennett's "I Left My Heart in San Francisco" (1962) (not, of course, the Hippie San Francisco so much a part of rock music of the times), Connie Francis' "Everybody's Somebody's Fool" (1960) and "Where the Boys Are" (1961), Bobby Vinton's "Roses Are Red" (1962), Paul and Paula's "Hey Paula" (1963), Petula Clark's "I Know a Place" (1965), Peggy Lee's "Is that All There Is?" (1969), and many more.

Smooth crooners like Andy Williams, Perry Como, Johnny Mathis, and Nat "King" Cole remained popular. Williams had one of the top albums for 1963 with *Days of Wine and Roses*, including the title song from the powerful film of 1962 starring Jack Lemmon and Lee Remick as alcoholics. Also in 1963, Williams released the hit album *Moon River and Other Great Movie Themes*. Throughout most of the 1960s, Williams had a regular variety show on television, and in the interim did television specials. Perry Como reached gold with his 1963 and 1966 Christmas albums, *Season's Greetings from Perry Como* and *Perry Como Sings Merry Christmas Music*. Johnny Mathis registered a string of hit albums in the early 1960s, including *Heavenly* (1960) and *Faithfully* (1962). Nat "King" Cole's album *Unforgettable* reached gold in 1964, the year before the great singer died of lung cancer.

The two most successful composers of pop music in the decade were Henry Mancini and Burt Bacharach. Mancini achieved his first great success with "Moon River," from the film *Breakfast at Tiffany's* (1961). Mancini won two Academy Awards for his score for the film as well as a Grammy for "Moon River." Another Grammy Award and Oscar followed for "The Days of Wine and Roses" from the 1962 film of the same title. Burt Bacharach also created highly successful movie scores, earning Academy Award nominations for the songs "Alfie" (from *Alfie*, 1966) and "The Look of Love" (from *Casino Royale*, 1967) and winning in 1969 for "Raindrops Keep Fallin' on My Head" (from *Butch Cassidy and the Sundance Kid*).

The best bet to carry on the pop tradition of Frank Sinatra beyond the 1960s was Bobby Darin. Winner of two Grammy Awards in 1959, for Best New Artist of the Year and Best Vocal Performance, Male (for "Mack the Knife"), Darin was a gifted songwriter as well as singer. He also had a talent for business and established his own music publishing and recording

Frank Sinatra is joined by his daughter Nancy for a duet on his
television musical show, "Frank Sinatra: A Man and His Music—Part II,"
in 1966. Source: Photofest, Inc.

firm in 1963. He steadily moved away from the teenage market toward adult
audiences and focused more on albums than singles. His albums during the
decade included *It's You or No One* (1963), *You're the Reason I'm Living* (1963),
and *The Best of Bobby Darin* (1966). He also turned to acting, winning an
Oscar nomination for best supporting actor in *Captain Newman, M.D.* (1963).

Among women vocalists, the 1960s belonged to Barbra Streisand. Her first album, *The Barbra Streisand Album* (1963), went gold, as did her next six albums. She starred in the 1964 musical *Funny Girl*, based on the life of singer and comedienne Fanny Brice. Starting in 1965, Streisand turned to television with a series of popular specials, including a 1967 concert taped live in New York City's Central Park. Her first television special, *My Name Is Barbra* (1965), won five Emmy Awards. In 1968, she added to her long list of awards with an Oscar for a film reprise of her *Funny Girl* role.

As successful as these artists were, however, they were no longer in the mainstream of modern music. The pendulum that had started to swing from pop to rock in the 1950s continued in that direction, although with a minor slowdown at the beginning of the decade. The "payola" scandals of 1959–60 led to congressional investigations that revealed widespread pay-offs on the part of record companies and music publishers to induce disc jockeys to play their material. The fallout from the scandals drove the so-called father of rock and roll, Alan Freed, off the air and led to convictions of over 250 disc jockeys for accepting cash or gifts to play certain records.

An immediate impact of the payola incidents was a brief slowing down of the steamroller that had been rock and roll. Jazz, folk, and traditional pop had an opportunity to rebuild some strength in the musical world of the United States. That Elvis Presley had almost slipped off the musical radar screen due to his induction into the army also contributed to rock's problems. Elvis returned from the army in 1960 and resumed his recording career with considerable success. Although he largely abandoned live concerts for most of the 1960s, he continued to be hailed as the King of Rock and Roll until his death in 1977.

The teen audience in the 1960s was heavily influenced in its choice of favorites by Dick Clark, who followed Bob Horn as host of *Bandstand* on WFIL-TV in Philadelphia in 1956. By August 1957, Clark's renamed *American Bandstand* had gone national on ABC. The approach was simple but successful. Teens danced on a small dance floor to records and guest stars lip-synching their hit (or soon to be hit) records. The dance contests, spotlight dances, and rating of new songs by how easy they were to dance to became staples of the program and entranced teens across the country. Dick Clark helped to make a long line of stars, including Chubby Checker, Buddy Holly, Frankie Avalon, and the Everly Brothers. The heyday of the show ended by 1963, when the daily program was reduced to Saturday afternoons. Nonetheless, Dick Clark remained with *American Bandstand* until 1989, adapting endlessly to new music and becoming a music icon. Not least among his accomplishments were racially integrating the show, with white and black teenagers together on a national television program for the first time, and offering African American singers and musicians national exposure.

The Beach Boys were one of many groups to appear on *American Bandstand* in the early 1960s. Hailing from California, Brian, Dennis, and Carl

Wilson formed a band in 1961 with their cousin Mike Love and friend Al Jardine. They went through several names before settling on the Beach Boys, a happy complement to some of their early hits, such as "Surfin'" (1962), "Surfin' Safari" (1962), "Surfin' USA" (1963), "Surfer Girl" (1963), and "Fun, Fun, Fun" (1964). Three slightly later songs—"I Get Around" (1964), "Help Me, Rhonda" (1965), "Good Vibrations" (1966)—reached Number One on the charts. "California Girls" (1965) was another hit, helping to create the mystique of the California girl as the most beautiful in the world. The Beach Boys' close harmonies, coupled with dense musical layering, helped to create what came to be known as the California sound. Conveying an image of all-American youth with their clean-shaven, well-groomed appearance, the Beach Boys made fun at the beach seem like the most innocent of pursuits.

By the mid-1960s, conflicts with the Wilsons' manager-father Murray Wilson, health and drug problems, and a desire (especially on the part of Brian) to expand into more sophisticated lyrics were undermining the earlier success of the group. One of their greatest artistic accomplishments at this time was *Pet Sounds* (1966), usually credited with being the first concept album, a unified cycle of music intended to be heard from beginning to end. Artistically successful but commercially disappointing, the album was the model for the Beatles' later *Sgt. Pepper's Lonely Hearts Club Band* (1967).

The year 1964 was the year of the American counterrevolution, and music and American culture would never be the same again. John Lennon, Paul McCartney, George Harrison, and Ringo Starr, better known as the Beatles, arrived in the United States in February. Their appearance on *The Ed Sullivan Show* let loose the phenomenon known as Beatlemania. Huge crowds turned out for Beatles concerts at such places as the Coliseum in Washington, D.C., and New York's Carnegie Hall. Girls swooned, and boys grew their hairy long in the mop-top fashion sported by the musical group. The media as well as fans doted on the Beatles, exploring every detail of their lives. Undoing the original American Revolutionary War, the invasion made everything British (including music, hair, and clothes) good. Britannia ruled once more.

The hits followed fast and furious. "I Want to Hold Your Hand" sold more than a million copies within ten days of being released in the United States in 1964. Twelve Beatles records were among the one hundred best-selling records in April of that year. Five occupied the top five positions.[3] In that same magical year, singles "I Want to Hold Your Hand," "Can't Buy Me Love," "A Hard Day's Night," and "I Feel Fine," and albums *Meet the Beatles!, The Beatles' Second Album, Something New, Beatles '65*, and *The Beatles' Story* all went gold.

The Beatles also turned to films, with *A Hard Day's Night* (1964) and *Help!* (1965). As the group matured toward greater complexity in their music, they

The Beatles' appearance on *The Ed Sullivan Show* in 1964 excited the
nation and touched off the phenomenon known as "Beatlemania."
Source: Photofest, Inc.

withdrew from live performances. The Beatles experimented with Indian
mysticism and drugs, did additional films (*The Magical Mystery Tour*, 1967,
and the animated *Yellow Submarine*, 1968), released the concept album *Sgt.
Pepper's Lonely Hearts Club Band* (1967) and the double album known officially
as *The Beatles* (1968) and unofficially as the "White Album" after its cover.

The Beatles continued to experiment musically. Romantic themes began to yield to social consciousness in songs such as "Eleanor Rigby" and "Paperback Writer." In the *Sgt. Pepper's* collection and the "White Album," there was increasing intellectual subtlety in both lyrics and music, as well as greater attention to how songs fit together. The Beatles introduced new sounds with orchestral instruments, especially stringed instruments. Even album covers became part of the artistic effect for the Beatles. The *Sgt. Pepper's* cover, for example, combined psychedelic and pop art effects, with the lyrics to the songs printed on the back.

By the end of the 1960s, the Beatles had begun to think of themselves more as individuals and less as a group. John Lennon married the Japanese artist Yoko Ono, and Paul McCartney married photographer Linda Eastman. With career aspirations diverging and personal and legal tensions rising among the four, they split in 1970. For years, Beatles fans longed for a reunion. That dream died with the murder of John Lennon outside his New York City apartment in 1980.

The popularity of the Beatles triggered a deluge of British groups into the United States, including Herman's Hermits, Gerry and the Pacemakers, the Dave Clark Five, the Who, and the Rolling Stones. Most British groups, if not imitating the Beatles, at least tried to capitalize on their popularity. The Rolling Stones, though, were deliberately pitched as an anti-Beatles group. Featuring vocalist Mick Jagger and guitarist Keith Richards, the Rolling Stones also included bass player Bill Wyman and drummer Charlie Watts. In opposition to the relatively unthreatening image of the Beatles, they projected an image of sex, drugs, violence, and occultism. They originated from around London rather than the Liverpool of the Beatles, and their music, derived ultimately from the earthiest versions of rhythm and blues, also differed from the Beatles' Liverpool or Mersey sound, which evolved out of the rock music of Elvis Presley, Buddy Holly, and the Everly Brothers. Their hits included "(I Can't Get No) Satisfaction" (1965), "The Last Time" (1965), "Ruby Tuesday" (1967), and "Honky Tonk Woman" (1969). When the Rolling Stones performed "Let's Spend the Night Together" on *The Ed Sullivan Show* in 1967, they mumbled or altered the most objectionable lines. They also put out albums with titles like *Their Satanic Majesties Request* (1967) and *Let It Bleed* (1969).

Among the more bizarre imitations of the Beatles was a synthetic group named the Monkees. They were the brainchildren of Columbia Pictures, which decided to fashion a television show about a group of young men trying to make a go of a rock-and-roll band, in imitation of the Beatles' film *A Hard Day's Night* (1964). Four stars were chosen, three from the United States (Mickey Dolenz, Peter Tork, Mike Nesmith), one (David Jones) from England. Musical talent was less a requirement—the four actually had modest backgrounds and abilities—than the right mixture of personalities. One of the unsuccessful aspirants for a role was future mass murderer Charles Manson.

The television show, *The Monkees*, ran two seasons (1966–68) on NBC as the group released a number of hit songs, including "Last Train to Clarksville" (1966), "I'm a Believer" (1966), and "Daydream Believer" (1967). They also had several gold albums. Performing live, however, proved somewhat embarrassing, as audiences discovered that the Monkees had not played their instruments on their records. After a public rebellion by the Monkees demanding to play as well as sing on their records, they persuaded Screen Gems to go along. In the short term, the popularity of their recordings did not suffer any noticeable decline for this transition into authenticity. By the end of the decade, however, the Monkees' attempt to become a serious band had come to an end.

San Francisco became the center of flower power, hippie life, and psychedelic rock during the 1960s, although other places and people also played important roles in establishing links between music and drugs. The Beatles deserved much of the credit for popularizing the concept of psychedelic music with their *Sgt. Pepper's Lonely Hearts Club Band* (1967) and one of its tracks, "Lucy in the Sky with Diamonds." The song was widely interpreted as a tribute to LSD, even down to the initial letters of the three key words in the title. Another song in the album, "A Day in the Life," includes the lyrics "I get by with a little help from my friends, I get high with a little help from my friends."

A Swiss chemist, Albert Hofmann, invented a drug in 1938 that he named Lyserg-saure-diathylamid and abbreviated LSD-25. The drug distorted time, created a sense of the self melting into one's surroundings, and made objects appear fluid; in other words, the drug induced a sense of constant motion. By the 1950s, the term "psychedelic" (literally meaning to make the soul, or mind, visible) had been applied to these phenomena. Not until 1965 did the federal government ban the distribution of LSD, widely known as acid. Musical performers attempted to parallel the effects of LSD in their music by altering normal temporal dimensions of the songs, changing traditional ensemble patterns to create a less structured performance, increasing volume, and adding other sensory stimuli such as flashing lights.

One of the most famous San Francisco groups was the Grateful Dead, led by Jerry Garcia. The Grateful Dead actually played a mix of folk and blues in addition to psychedelic rock, but became firmly associated with drugs because of their advocacy for legalizing marijuana, the fact that they lived for a time on Ashbury Street in the Haight-Ashbury section of the city, and their performances (before adopting the "Grateful Dead" name) at Ken Kesey's acid tests, symposia sponsored by the writer at which participants took LSD to enhance their experiences. The Grateful Dead released popular albums such as *The Grateful Dead* (1967) and *Anthem of the Sun* (1968), but achieved more lasting fame for their enthusiastic live performances and remarkably faithful fans who called themselves Dead Heads and followed their idols from concert to concert.

The Jefferson Airplane debuted in San Francisco in 1965, and in the following year Grace Slick joined the group as lead vocalist. The group was unusual for having a female lead, and Slick's powerful voice proved their ticket to fame. The group lived together in Haight-Ashbury and tied themselves closely to the psychedelic rock-drug movement. The album *Surrealistic Pillow* was a hit in 1967, and two of its songs, "Somebody to Love" and "White Rabbit," made the top ten. The latter, loosely based on Lewis Carroll's *Alice's Adventures in Wonderland*, was an explicit call to use drugs: "feed your head," the song proposed. Grace Slick, who wrote "White Rabbit," really made the Jefferson Airplane take off. She combined considerable singing and songwriting talent with an outrageousness that varied from dressing like a nun to flashing her breasts. After Richard Nixon became president, she received an invitation from daughter Tricia to visit the White House. Slick appeared with antiwar activist Abbie Hoffman and a sizable quantity of LSD, which she planned to drop into the president's drink. Fortunately for Mr. Nixon, she and Hoffman were intercepted and removed from the premises.

Jimi Hendrix and Janis Joplin were two of the most talented and tragic figures of the San Francisco psychedelic scene. Hendrix, one of the most gifted guitarists of the decade, teamed with Noel Redding and Mitch Mitchell to form the Jimi Hendrix Experience. Their first album was *Are You Experienced* in 1967, including "Purple Haze," "Fire," "The Wind Cries Mary," and "Foxy Lady." Hendrix was especially skilled at creating striking effects with feedback from his guitar, and his music fused blues, rock, and jazz improvisations.

Hendrix's most memorable appearances included his performances at the Monterey International Pop Festival in 1967 and the Woodstock Music and Art Fair in 1969. At the former, his performance included simulated masturbation and actual burning of his guitar; the latter featured his unusual and controversial interpretation of "The Star-Spangled Banner." On September 18, 1970, Hendrix died from inhaling his own vomit after a drug overdose. He was not quite twenty-eight. The combination of extraordinary talent, drugs, and an early and tragic death made Hendrix for many people a symbol of the promises, confusions, and excesses of the 1960s.

Janis Joplin's life followed a parallel path of stardom to early death. Influenced by Billie Holiday and Bessie Smith, she helped to create "blue-eyed soul," blues sung by white artists. Her live performances, like Hendrix's, could be outrageous. She often drank whiskey while performing, engaged the audience in conversation, and mingled singing with running, jumping, and occasional screams. She performed as a member of the group Big Brother and the Holding Company in addition to appearances with her own backup group. Heavy drinking made her voice raspy, which with her haggard appearance caused her blues renditions to seem all the more genuine. Her albums included *Cheap Thrills* (1968) and the solo

Jimi Hendrix fused blues, rock, and jazz improvisations, and was especially skilled at creating striking effects with feedback from his guitar.
Source: Photofest, Inc.

I Got Dem Ol' Kozmic Blues Again Mama! (1969). After at least half a dozen overdoses, one finally caught up with Joplin at twenty-seven, three weeks after Jimi Hendrix's death. Her arm bore fresh puncture marks where she had injected the heroin. A 1979 film, *The Rose*, starring Bette Midler, was based on her life.

Janis Joplin updated the blues and often engaged in outrageously flamboyant onstage performances. Source: Photofest, Inc.

Many other groups and individual artists, of course, also left their mark on the 1960s, far too many to be discussed here. The Doors, for example, burst on the scene in the late 1960s to become a symbol of that decade's combination of enormous talent and tragic lack of self-discipline. Jim Morrison, a talented singer, poet, and musician who rejected his family's tradition of military service (his father was a naval officer) for rock music, founded the group. The Doors performed at the Whiskey-A-Go-Go club in Los Angeles in the mid-1960s but eventually were fired for their sexual comments on stage. At the time, the group was heavily into drugs, a preoccupation that Morrison would follow until his early death in 1971. The Doors signed with Elektra in 1966 and proved immediately successful with their first album, *Doors*, in early 1967. The single "Light My Fire" reached Number One in July. The Doors' music combined hard rock with broad images (fire, sun, sea) and psychological insights; some of the ideas, interestingly, were drawn from a favorite philosopher of Morrison's, Fredrich Nietzsche.

Things began to go seriously downhill for the group on March 1, 1969, when Morrison, late for a concert in Miami, Florida, arrived intoxicated and reportedly exposed himself on stage. Morrison was convicted of profanity and indecent exposure, resulting in canceled concerts and difficulty getting bookings and airtime for the Doors' records. The group rebounded in 1970, but then Morrison left for France to pursue his interest in poetry. In July 1971, Morrison was found dead in a bath tub, apparently of a heart attack perhaps precipitated at least in part by a respiratory condition. The groups' fame endured, with Morrison growing into something of a cult hero. Oliver Stone made a successful film about the group in 1991, *The Doors*, starring Val Kilmer as Morrison.

Another enormously successful but relatively short-lived group was the Mamas and the Papas, consisting of John Phillips, his wife Michelle, Ellen Naomi Cohen (known as Cass Elliott), and Dennis Doherty. Appreciated for their well-written lyrics, melodious harmonies, and versatility, the Mamas and the Papas released such hits as "California Dreamin'" (1966) and "Monday, Monday" (1966). They also had a string of top-ten albums, but by the end of the decade the Mamas and the Papas had decided to go their own ways. "Mama" Cass, unfortunately, had little time to pursue an individual career, as she died in a London hotel in 1974, according to contemporary media reports choking to death on a ham sandwich but in reality apparently dying of a heart attack. John and Michelle's daughter, Mackenzie Phillips, named for the parents' friend Scott McKenzie—who recorded the 1967 flower-child theme song "San Francisco (Be Sure to Wear Some Flowers in Your Hair)"—became a television star on *One Day at a Time* in the 1970s.

The 1960s live in people's memories in no small way for their pop and rock music festivals. The 1967 Monterey Pop Festival in June ushered in the so-called Summer of Love. Organizers of the festival included an all-star cast of performers, among them John Phillips of the Mamas and the Papas, Paul McCartney of the Beatles, Paul Simon, Smokey Robinson, and Brian Wilson of the Beach Boys. The three-day festival included Country Joe and the Fish, Janis Joplin, Jefferson Airplane, Otis Redding, and the Grateful Dead. Jim Hendrix introduced the Jimi Hendrix Experience to American audiences, lighting his guitar on fire and breaking it over an amplifier. The Monterey Pop Festival was enormously successful and generally trouble free, inspiring a number of other large-scale festivals during the closing years of the decade.

Among those events inspired by Monterey were the Woodstock and Altamont festivals. The Woodstock Music and Art Fair (as it was formally called) occurred in New York State from August 15 to 17, 1969. Organizers named it after the village of Woodstock, Bob Dylan's home, hoping unsuccessfully that the folk-rock star would participate. (The festival actually occurred near the town of Bethel.) However, many other stars did participate, including Jimi Hendrix, Joan Baez, the Who, Janis Joplin, the Grateful Dead, Jefferson Airplane, Creedence Clearwater Revival, and Ravi Shankar (an Indian sitarist). The highlight of the event was the controversial rendition of "The Star-Spangled Banner" by Jimi Hendrix. Woodstock (its more common name encountered more trouble than did the Monterey Festival, including overcrowding, a lot of rain and mud, inadequate restroom facilities, and demands by some performers to be paid in advance. The festival lost considerable money, partly because of bad planning, including not setting up ticket booths. Most of the rock stars, when not performing, remained far away, resting comfortably in hotels. The festival marked a new separation of rock stars from audiences, a distancing that would become standard practice. On the whole, however, the festival remained peaceful despite the many hardships endured by the audience of close to half a million.

Images of nudity, sexual freedom, and drug use at Woodstock struck Americans with horror or fascination, depending on their point of view or age. The festival earned a permanent place in American culture as one of the defining moments of the 1960s. It represented an open, classless society of music, sex, drugs, love, and peace, all the more so because the event remained largely free of violence and the tragic consequences one might expect from a gathering so large and so young. For many, it seemed to promise a new America.

The Altamont Music Festival, held at the Altamont Speedway in San Francisco on December 6, 1969, helped to dash the sense of innocence and optimism engendered at Monterey and Woodstock. Inadequate planning probably helped to lay the groundwork for disaster, as a weak sound system, a short stage just four feet high, and virtually no space between audience and performers led to a steady crush of audience members surging

The Woodstock Music and Art Fair (its formal name) held on August 15–17, 1969, near Bethel, New York, was a defining moment of the Sixties, representing an open, classless society of music, sex, drugs, peace, and love. Source: Photofest, Inc.

forward. The Rolling Stones were putting on the concert free as a type of thank-you conclusion to their 1969 tour of the United States. The Hell's Angels motorcycle gang was hired to provide security, reportedly for $500 worth of beer. A conflict developed near the stage between a male audience member, Meredith Hunter, and the Hell's Angels. Hunter apparently pulled a pistol and was stabbed several times. Hunter was one of four people who died during the festival. The violence at Altamont, coupled with increasing antiwar demonstrations, helped to transform the peace-and-love, flower-children movement into a widespread rebellion of America's youth spiced with considerable anger and distrust aimed at anything establishment.

By the end of the 1960s, rock had replaced folk music as the principal antiestablishment music. Rock music had come to epitomize revolution, in its often sexual lyrics, hard-driving power, associations with drugs, even in its tragedies, such as the early deaths of Jimi Hendrix and Janis Joplin. It represented a rejection of the culture of one's parents and a breakdown in the established order. The pelvic gyrations of Elvis Presley, which had helped to usher in rock and roll, much to the discomfort of adults, seemed quaint by then, a reminder of lost innocence. The world by the end of the 1960s seemed poised, in the words of the title to Barry McGuire's antiwar song, on the "Eve of Destruction."

SOUL

Soul emerged out of the testifying, call-and-response traditions of gospel music and the stylistic and thematic characteristics of rhythm and blues (R&B). The term "soul" had been used in relation to gospel music long before its adoption by rhythm and blues and later by "soul" performers. Ray Charles popularized the style with his synthesis of religious and R&B. The influential "What'd I Say" (1959) includes gospel-type calls and responses combined with moans and sexual allusions. In 1960, Charles had his first Number One hit, "Georgia on My Mind," a soulful rendition that fused with pop. Part of his genius was in taking a song, for example, "Take These Chains From My Heart" (1963), that had essentially nothing to do with soul traditions and giving it a soul treatment. The result was not only to increase his own popularity with the mass audience but also that of soul music.

The 1960s were a time conducive to soul music, which fit well with serious social movements, especially Civil Rights, and corollary developments like Black Power and the Black Is Beautiful theme. In addition, growing numbers of whites who wanted to express solidarity with African Americans, or merely wanted to be chic, sought out soul wherever they could find it, including in dress and food (subjects discussed in other chapters).

A large number of soul artists earned wide acclaim during the 1960s. Aretha Franklin was perhaps the finest of the female soul singers, releasing such hits as "I Never Loved a Man (The Way I Love You)" (1967), "Chain of Fools" (1967), "Since You've Been Gone" (1968), and "I Say a Little Prayer" (1968). In the latter year, she also released the album *Lady Soul*, the title only stating what audiences widely felt. And it was feeling that set Franklin apart. Drawing from such sources as singing with her minister father in Detroit, the sounds of Ray Charles, and personal tragedies (especially her mother's departure when Aretha was six and death four years later), she above all put emotion into her songs. Personal emotion is how she defined soul music, and she helped to make that an important ingredient of soul for both singers and audiences.

Otis Redding also helped to spread soul music around the globe and convert white audiences. A shy young man from Georgia, Redding was working as a chauffeur on a trip to Memphis, Tennessee, when he was invited to sing for Jim Stewart, who, although white, emphasized soul on the STAX label that he started with his sister, Estelle Axton (the name of the company derived from the first two letters of brother and sister's last names). Stewart heard something he liked and signed Redding up. By 1965, Redding's songs, such as "Mr. Pitiful" and "I've Been Loving You Too

Long," were being well received. He proved enormously popular while touring Europe and performed at the Monterey Pop Festival in 1967. Late in December 1967, he recorded the song that would become his greatest hit, "Dock of the Bay," a mournful soul tune about "sittin' on the dock of the bay, watchin' the tide roll in." Two and one-half weeks later, on December 10, the plane that he was riding in went down into a lake near Madison, Wisconsin. Redding's "Dock of the Bay" was released in January; it had sold four million records by the end of May.[4]

Among other soul performers, Wilson Pickett achieved stardom with "In the Midnight Hour" (1965), which reached Number One on the R&B Charts "Mustang Sally" (1966); and two more R&B number ones in 1966, "634-5789" and "Land of a Thousand Dances." Like Ray Charles, Joe Tex bridged country and soul. His *Soul Country* album (1968) included soulful versions of such country songs as "Green Green Grass of Home," "Ode to Billie Joe," and "By the Time I Get to Phoenix." Born Joseph Arrington, Jr., into a cotton-sharecropping family in Texas, he had his first hit in 1964 with "Hold on to What You've Got." The term "soul" became increasingly common within titles, for example, Sam and Dave's [Samuel Moore and Dave Prater] "Soul Man" (1967) and "Soul Limbo" (1968), and Isaac Hayes' *Hot Buttered Soul* album (1969).

The ultimate soul performer, though, was James Brown, the "Godfather of Soul." Also known as the "Hardest-Working Man in Show Business," Brown worked almost every night. So popular that he could fill large concert halls by himself, Brown recorded many hit songs during the 1960s, including "Think" (1960), "Prisoner of Love" (1963), "Don't Be a Drop Out" (1966), and "Cold Sweat" (1967). The song that most forcefully called out to the social and racial struggles of the decade was "Say It Loud, I'm Black and I'm Proud" (1968). Coming from a troubled background, Brown also devoted himself to pushing stay-in-school campaigns for youth, encouraging African American business efforts, and working for equal rights. He entertained the troops in Vietnam, and wherever he performed did so with extraordinary energy.

The largest black-owned company at the end of the 1960s was Motown, short for Motortown, that is, Detroit. Berry Gordy, Jr., a former Detroit autoworker, started Motown in 1959. Gordy knew a lot about assembly-line manufacturing and brought that concept to the production of records. He hired talented writers, musicians, producers, engineers, arrangers, and, of course, singers, and established a sort of assembly-line approach under strict controls. Gordy also made extensive use of modern recording technology, gaudy costumes, and carefully choreographed dance steps for his performers. He brought soul music closer to pop so his recordings would appeal to a wide audience, including white listeners. The Motown sound tended to be smoother than the sharp-edged soul coming from some other labels, but still often retained such traditional soul techniques as rhythmic repetitions and call-and-response patterns of phrasing. Among his greatest songwriters was the trio of Lamont Dozier and Brian and Eddie Holland. Gordy liked to sign young performers, often complete unknowns, and mold them into Motown artists. And he found a lot of future stars.

The list of Motown stars in the 1960s was enormously impressive. Many of the 1960s hits continued to occupy the airwaves into the next millennium: Marvin Gaye's "How Sweet It Is (To Be Loved By You)" (1964), "Your Precious Love," with Tammi Terrell (1967), and "I Heard It Through the Grapevine" (1968); Barrett Strong's "Money (That's What I Want)," Motown's first national hit (1960); Smokey Robinson and the Miracles' "Shop Around," the first Motown song to reach Number One (1960), "My Girl" (1964), and "The Tracks of My Tears" (1965). "Tracks," for example, opened with a line showing the effort people often make not to let others know how they really feel: "People say I'm the life of the party because I tell a joke or two." This ability to coin lyrics that connected deeply with listeners' fears, hopes, and anxieties was a hallmark of Motown, a direct result of the talented lyricists that Gordy employed.

There were still more: Jimmy Ruffin's "What Becomes of the Brokenhearted" (1966), with another of those memorable phrases that seemed aimed directly at each listener and to the times (a lament about "this land of broken dreams"); The Four Tops' "I Can't Help Myself (Sugar Pie, Honey Bunch)" (1965) and "Reach Out I'll Be There," with the connecting condition "If you feel you can't go on," for who has not felt that way at some time? (1966); the beautiful Mary Wells's "You Beat Me to the Punch" (1962) and "My Guy" (1964); and Gladys Knight and the Pips' "I Heard It Through the Grapevine" (1967), which was released prior to the Marvin Gaye version.

Motown was well known for its girls groups. The Marvelettes hit it big with "Please Mr. Postman" (1961), which reached Number One on both the pop and R&B charts. Martha [Reeves] and the Vandellas had "(Love Is Like a) Heat Wave" (1963), "Dancing in the Street" (1964), and "Jimmy Mack" (1967). In "Jimmy Mack," the singers wonder, "Jimmy Mack, when are you coming back?" The song was originally recorded in 1964, but by the time of its release the Vietnam War had heated up and the song seemed to be calling young American soldiers to return.

Phil Spector was another highly successful producer whose clients included famous all-girl groups during the 1960s. The Crystals recorded "Uptown," "'Da Doo Ron Ron," and "Then He Kissed Me." The Ronettes' hits included "Be My Baby," "Do I Love You?" and "Walking in the Rain." His other successes included hits by the Righteous Brothers (e.g., "You've Lost That Lovin' Feeling") and, in 1963, what many consider the finest Christmas album ever produced, *A Christmas Gift for You*, more commonly known as *Phil Spector's Christmas Album*.

The most successful of the girl groups was the Supremes, later Diana Ross and the Supremes. The original trio consisted of Detroit singers Diana

The Supremes, the most successful girl group of the Sixties, perform on *The Ed Sullivan Show* in 1966. Source: Photofest, Inc.

Ross, Florence Ballard, and Mary Wilson, who started their career as the Primettes before signing with Berry Gordy in 1961. Their first chart-topper was "Where Did Our Love Go" in 1964. Their most famous song was "Stop! In The Name of Love" (1965), the fourth of five consecutive Number Ones. Gordy choreographed the famous hand straight out in a stop gesture. "You Can't Hurry Love" (1966) included the "Mama said" refrain and began a run of four more consecutive tunes that topped the charts. In 1967, the name of the group was changed to give top billing to Diana Ross, and Florence

Ballard left, replaced by Cindy Birdsong. The final hit before Ross departed to pursue a solo career was "Someday We'll Be Together" (1969), chosen by Gordy as Ross's swan song with the group.

Even children were potential Motown performers, as Gordy continued his remarkable pursuit of talent. Little Stevie Wonder, blind like the great Ray Charles, was aptly named, for he was just a boy when he began with Motown. Signed by Gordy at twelve, Wonder quickly made his mark. The year 1963, as Wonder turned thirteen, witnessed several successful singles, most notably "Fingertips Part 2," and his first two albums, *The 12 Year Old Genius* and *Tribute to Uncle Ray*, the latter a homage to Ray Charles. Later 1960s hits included "Uptight (Everything's Alright)" (1965), with its effective use of hip slang ("Everything's alright. Uptight. Out of sight."), "Shoo-Be-Doo-Be-Doo-Da-Day" (1968), "For Once in My Life" (1968), and "Yester-Me, Yester-You, Yesterday" (1969).

CLASSICAL AND JAZZ

While rock, folk, and soul music earned most of the music headlines during the 1960s, classical music and jazz retained adherents, even gained new ones. Classical music accounted for between 5 and 10% of record sales during the 1960s, a significant chunk of the recording business.[5]

Aaron Copland and Leonard Bernstein were widely recognized as the foremost American composers of their time. Copland's 1960s compositions included *Nonet* (1960), composed for nine stringed instruments; and *Connotations for Orchestra* (1962), his first orchestral creation since 1948. His enduring fame (he would live until 1990, the same year Bernstein died) had been built on earlier compositions that musically portrayed a great cross section of America, both rural and urban. Copland also conducted the New York Philharmonic and in 1960 directed the Boston Symphony on a tour of the Far East.

Leonard Bernstein was a great showman and educator as well as composer and director. Enormously energetic on stage and in his work, he was a flamboyant popularizer of classical music and a prolific producer of music, books, and television specials. Bernstein directed the New York Philharmonic from 1959 to 1969 (conducting a special television concert in 1963 in honor of the assassinated John F. Kennedy), inaugurated the New York Lincoln Center for the Performing Arts in 1962, and in 1966 conducted the Vienna Philharmonic in a performance of Gustav Mahler's *Das Lied von der Erde*, a composer whom Bernstein forcefully promoted and whose music he introduced to millions. Granted a sabbatical from the New York Philharmonic for 1964–65, Bernstein composed the *Chichester Psalms* (1965), which he presented to the world with an acknowledgment of his essentially conservative tonal approach while many modern composers were gravitating toward atonality. That is, Bernstein continued to think of notes, keynotes, and the musical scale in traditional terms, while others were adopting a system in which each pitch was equal, keynotes gave way to openness, and new chord combinations were readily employed.

Yet there was nothing conservative about the way Bernstein tried to win adherents to classical music. The first television superstar of classical music, Bernstein conducted three nationally televised Young's People's Concerts (1964, 1965, 1966) in which he used Beatles songs to clarify aspects of classical music. He also wrote books in which he sought to make classical music more understandable and fun: *Leonard Bernstein's Young People's Concerts for Reading and Listening* (1961), *The Joy of Music* (1963), and *The Infinite Variety of Music* (1966).

As the 1960s progressed, Bernstein became increasingly political in his nonmusic hours. Among his concerns: civil rights (championing the Black Panthers), ending the Vietnam War, and supporting Israel.

In addition to Copland and Bernstein, much more was going on in classical music. Johann Sebastian Bach proved particularly popular among the giants of classical music. Ward Swingle arranged Bach compositions for voices, drums, and bass, producing *Bach's Greatest Hits* (1963) and *Going Baroque* (1964), the latter winning a Grammy. Walter Carlos (later Wendy Carlos after a sex-change operation) used his background in physics and music to produce electronic versions of classical pieces, most successfully *Switched-on-Bach* (1968), which won three Grammy Awards and became the first classical album to reach platinum.

The pianist Van Cliburn, who had won the Moscow Tchaikovsky Competition, became a big seller of albums on which he played Beethoven, Chopin, and Mozart. Beverly Sills reached operatic stardom in 1966 when she sang the role of Cleopatra in Handel's *Giulio Cesare* at the New York City Opera.

It also was a decade in which African Americans won widespread acceptance in classical music. Leontyne Price, inspired by Marian Anderson, who had been the first African American to sing at the New York Metropolitan Opera (1955), made her own appearance there in 1961. Her performance of Leonora's role in Verdi's *Il Trovatore* earned her a standing ovation that lasted more than forty minutes. Among her many accomplishments during the decade was her appearance in Samuel Barber's *Antony and Cleopatra* at the inauguration of the new Metropolitan Opera House. Other young African American operatic stars included Martina Arroyo and Grace Bumbry. African Americans also moved into important conducting positions: Henry Lewis as conductor of the New Jersey Symphony, Paul Freeman as associate conductor of the Dallas Symphony, George Byrd as assistant conductor of the American Ballet Theater.

While exciting events were happening in classical music, jazz was shimmering in the light of both old and new stars. Jazz enthusiasts during the 1960s could still enjoy the music and showmanship of perhaps the most important figure in the history of jazz, Louis Armstrong. Almost as an after-

Veteran Jazz trumpeter and singer Louis "Satchmo" Armstrong had hits with "Hello Dolly" in 1963 and "What a Wonderful World" in 1967. Source: Photofest, Inc.

thought, Armstrong recorded "Hello Dolly" for the stage show in 1964. Before long, it was the top song in America. Ill health, however, caught up with him by 1968, and he was unable to perform for several months. When Armstrong finally returned to the stage, he did so under doctors' orders not to play the trumpet. He passed away in 1971.

Duke Ellington, composer, pianist, and bandleader, was still on the road playing in venues from Europe to Africa to American proms. One of his gigs was at the White House in 1969, where he was honored on his seventieth birthday with the Presidential Medal of Freedom. He also listened to another, albeit amateur pianist, President Richard Nixon, play "Happy Birthday" to him.

Dizzy Gillespie was still playing his trumpet in the 1960s. Saxophonist Stan Getz won a Grammy Award in 1964 for "The Girl from Ipanema." Theolonious Monk, a composer and pianist noted for his individualism, determination to play only what he himself had composed, and stride-based keyboard style, returned from several years of self-imposed absence from public performances.

A white quartet headed by pianist Dave Brubeck had reached stardom in the 1950s and continued with its so-called progressive jazz in the 1960s, proving especially popular on college campuses. Brubeck's music was often labeled cool jazz, with its smooth phrasing and absence of any overt sense of the blues tradition, although Brubeck was daring in rhythm and improvisation. One of the quartet's most memorable albums, *Time Out*, was released in late 1959 and remained popular through the early 1960s. It included the top-forty hit "Take Five." Brubeck was especially popular on college campuses, and one of his most famous performances occurred at the New York World's Fair in 1964. Throughout the 1960s, though, jazz was largely dominated by African American artists.

At the most daring edge of jazz in the decade were three enormously talented musicians: John Coltrane, Ornette Coleman, and Miles Davis. In addition, jazz came to be associated with black nationalism. Hard bop, or funky jazz, was a reaction against cool jazz, an attempt to return jazz to its roots in black culture. Hard bop was strong, passionate, and heavily reliant on improvisation. One of the leaders of the movement was Miles Davis, a great jazz trumpeter. John Coltrane, who had worked for Davis, pushed the movement farther ahead. Coltrane had enormous range with his saxophone, seemingly seeking the hitherto unheard note. He incorporated African and Asian music into his work and achieved great nonharmonic complexity. Some of his greatest music is evident in *Live at the Village Vanguard* (1961), *Impressions* (1961–63), and *Ascension* (1965). Yet Coltrane did not identify himself as a black nationalist, and despite his deep concern with African music and civil rights refused to define jazz as a black art form. He saw jazz as a matter of music rather than skin color without losing his deep sensitivity toward those who were suffering. When four young African American girls were killed in the bombing of the Sixteenth Street Baptist Church in Birmingham in 1963, he composed and played an elegy for them that he called "Alabama." Unfortunately, Coltrane had only a few more years to live, dying of liver cancer in 1967 at the age of forty.

The next step from hard bop was free jazz, also called, quite simply, "the new thing." A series of 1964 concerts called "the October Revolution" at the Cellar Cafe in New York City contributed to the spread of the new type of jazz, which included clarinet squeals and saxophone shrieks, a strong sense of the blues, and even more improvisation than in hard bop. The result sometimes seemed more chaotic than musical. Free jazz varied with the performer, a condition required by the very freeness of the approach. It included considerable improvisation made possible by freedom from preset chord progressions, abandonment of regular patterns of rhythm, use of extremes in notes, and occasional silences. Free jazz was especially energetic, with drummers and other musicians feeling free to be as irregular as the spirit moved them. In some cases, each musician would essentially be playing a solo.

Free jazz mirrored the growing anger of black nationalists. It rejected the status quo rules and traditions and conveyed passionate feelings that paralleled blacks' passion for freedom from white domination. Seen as a primitive music, free jazz appeared to hearken back to African rhythms and the primitive roots of black consciousness. The poet LeRoi Jones, who changed his name to Imamu Amiri Baraka, saw the new-jazz musician as the poet of black nationalism, showing the way to a world in which black men and women can live their blackness.

Leading the free jazz movement was saxophonist Ornette Coleman, also a composer, who led the Ornette Coleman Quartet. Coleman even challenged the tradition of musicians specializing in one instrument; he himself played the violin and trumpet in addition to the saxophone. Another long-cherished standard to fall before his innovative spirit was the tradition of solo and accompaniment hierarchies. Coleman's *Free Jazz* (1960) was a milestone in the history of jazz, serving as inspiration to countless musicians and giving a name to the new style of jazz.

Toward the end of his career, John Coltrane also was influenced by Coleman and moved ever closer to the spirit and sound of the new thing. The free playing of Coltrane and the other musicians with whom he performed in his final few years sometimes sounded to an audience expecting the earlier Coltrane as merely chaos as the band members, including two drummers, improvised individually, sometimes drowning each other out. Miles Davis, who initially had not cared for free jazz and preferred what he called "controlled freedom," also began to change. His music grew more spontaneous, and he even paid his band members not to practice at home in order not to sound too polished. By 1969, Davis was combining jazz with rock, a mixture he called *Bitches Brew*; the album sold 400,000 copies during its first year.[6] As innovation continued in jazz, it remained clear that, whatever else jazz was about, whatever social, racial, or political ideas it represented, jazz was still very much about creating exciting music.

10
Performing Arts

The performing arts offered great richness in range and innovation during the 1960s. As in so many other areas of life at the time, these venues for expression followed, reinforced, and sometimes moved in the vanguard of changing societal ideas, attitudes, and values. What was happening in film, television, dance, and drama did not occur in isolation, but as part and parcel of the larger social, political, and aesthetic changes of the decade.

The most conservative of the four areas was television, which, rapidly becoming the country's foremost mass medium, sought to appeal to the large majority rather than smaller slices of American opinion. Yet even here change could not be ignored, as the growing importance of television journalism brought before the public in vivid images conflicts involving race, gender, and the Vietnam War.

In the 1960s the power of the media to shape culture was both growing rapidly and coming somewhat to be understood. Marshall McLuhan asserted that "the medium is the message,"[1] and that proved more true than false whether audiences were watching the Kennedy–Nixon debates in their living rooms or *The Graduate* in their favorite theaters. The image came to define reality rather than merely be a representation of reality.

In drama and dance, opposition to traditional modes of expression increasingly came to the fore, more ideologically on the stage with frank explorations of racial, sexual, gender, and political issues. But dance also demonstrated the power of newness. As the performing arts changed during the 1960s, so did audience expectations. Neither would ever be the same.

FILMS

Judging by the films that won Best Picture Awards from the Academy of Motion Picture Arts and Sciences during the 1960s, the film audience in the

1960s would seem to have been rather conservative: *The Apartment, West Side Story, Lawrence of Arabia, Tom Jones, My Fair Lady, The Sound of Music, A Man for All Seasons, In the Heat of the Night, Oliver!, Midnight Cowboy*. Four of these Oscar winners (*West Side Story, My Fair Lady, The Sound of Music, Oliver!*) were musicals in the last great heyday of the genre. *Lawrence of Arabia* was a historical epic, *A Man for All Seasons* a dramatic account of the life and death of Thomas More, and *Tom Jones* a comedy based on an eighteenth-century novel. *The Apartment* was a critically acclaimed satire on businessmen trying to get ahead by questionable means, a witty film starring Jack Lemmon in one of his best roles, but not particularly revolutionary. John Wayne won his first and only Oscar for his role as an aging, one-eyed lawman in *True Grit* (1969). Nonetheless, the list of Oscar winners included two films that defied industry conventions and aroused considerable controversy to be named best picture of the year: *In the Heat of the Night* (1967) and *Midnight Cowboy* (1969). In retrospect, it is clear that those two films, more than their fellow winners, represented the innovation and diversity that truly characterized moviemaking in the 1960s.

As the 1960s progressed, changes in society began to impact films in content and production values. Counterculture patterns, including drug use, greater sexual freedom, and a general straining against traditional mores, came up against the Motion Picture Production Code, established in 1930 by the Motion Picture Producers and Distributors of America (MPPDA), later known as the Motion Picture Association of America (MPAA). Increasingly, filmmakers found themselves unable to receive approval from the Production Code Administration (PCA), which administered the Code. In 1966, Jack Valenti, the new president of the MPAA, reexamined the Code in light of Supreme Court rulings on obscenity and changing attitudes toward censorship. The result was a new voluntary self-regulating rating system that made it easier for filmmakers to distribute their films and also enabled filmgoers, especially parents, to know what the films would contain in such areas as sex and violence. The ratings, which since the 1960s have undergone some revisions, included four categories: G for films suitable for a general audience; M for films suitable for a mature audience, with parental guidance suggested; R for films restricted to viewers at least sixteen years of age unless they were accompanied by a parent or adult guardian; and X for films to which only those sixteen years of age or older would be admitted. The criteria reflected in these categories were principally language, sex, and violence. Moderate profanity was allowed in R films, but certain sexual expletives were likely to earn the X rating. Nudity was usually X material, as was sexual behavior deemed abnormal by mainstream standards. Filmmakers could get away with more violence than sexual behavior and obscene language without losing an R rating.

With the new ratings system and revolutionary changes in society as context, films began to explore new frontiers in such areas as race, sex, drugs, violence, and the supernatural.

Two of the most important films to challenge racial prejudice were released in the same year (1967) and starred the same actor (Sidney Poitier): *Guess Who's Coming to Dinner* and the Oscar-winning *In the Heat of the Night*. In the former, African American Poitier comes to dinner, guest of his white fiancée, Katharine Houghton, to meet her parents, played by film immortals Spencer Tracy and Katharine Hepburn. The film uses humor, a gentle hand, and accomplished acting (with Hepburn winning the Oscar for best performance by an actress in a leading role) to make tolerance more palatable.

In the Heat of the Night stars Poitier as a homicide detective from Philadelphia, who is passing through a small Mississippi town called Sparta when he is arrested for murdering a prominent white man. Poitier is soon cleared but maneuvered into helping the bigoted sheriff, played by Rod Steiger (who won an Oscar as best actor for his performance), solve the crime. While doing so, Poitier encounters redneck and southern aristocrat types, both of whom would like him dead. Finally, the successful northern black detective and the southern white sheriff come to at least some glimmerings of respect for each other before Poitier catches his train for Philadelphia. The film vividly portrays southern racism, still sufficiently alive to cause the movie to be made in Illinois. The most dramatic moment in the film comes when Poitier's character slaps a wealthy white patrician after he had slapped Poitier for daring to question him. Although both films clearly broke important ground, they came under fire from more militant sectors of the Civil Rights Movement for relying on black characters (doctor, chief homicide detective) who represented only a small portion of the African American community.

Sex and drugs made their way into mainstream films as never before. *Midnight Cowboy*, which won Oscars in 1969 for best film and best director (John Schlesinger), introduced its audience to the world of male homosexuality in New York City. Joe Buck, played by Jon Voight, leaves Texas for New York to become a stud for wealthy women; instead, he turns to hustling tricks to support himself and his new friend, the dying Ratso Rizzo (Dustin Hoffman). The X rating the film received from the MPAA appeared not to hurt its standing with the public or with the Academy of Motion Picture Arts and Sciences. *Bob & Carol & Ted & Alice* (1969), starring Natalie Wood, Robert Culp, Dyan Cannon, and Elliott Gould, deals with wife-swapping and group therapy as the liberated couple (Wood and Culp) attempts to engage their friends in an equal sense of liberation. *Easy Rider* was the creation of Peter Fonda and Dennis Hopper, who starred in the movie (as Captain America and Billy, respectively), wrote the screenplay, and served as director (Hopper) and producer (Fonda). They are joined by Jack Nicholson on their motorcycle trip to find freedom and the real America, a trip financed by a cocaine deal. Nicholson is murdered along the way by rednecks, but Fonda and Hopper end up tripping through a psychedelic New Orleans where the sex is easy, especially in a cemetery. The two

The 1967 film *Easy Rider*, starring (left to right) Dennis Hopper, Peter Fonda, and Jack Nicholson, combined elements of the "road film" and the "buddy film" in a bleak portrayal of 1960s America. Source: Photofest, Inc.

heroes get murdered on the road after leaving the Big Easy, a lesson of sorts in a film that attempted to portray just about every aspect of counterculture possible, including communal living and free love in a desert.

Meanwhile, more traditional sex fantasies were conjured up by sex kittens like Raquel Welch in *One Million Years B.C.* (1966), in which she demonstrated that the first clothing ever invented was the bikini; Jane Fonda, who hid everything and nothing underneath a skintight black suit in *Barbarella* (1967); and the Swiss bombshell Ursula Andress in the first James Bond film, *Dr. No* (1962).

The most controversial erotic film for American viewers during the 1960s was a foreign film, *I Am Curious (Yellow)* (1967). The Swedish film includes male and female frontal nudity and simulated intercourse. After overcoming legal challenges, the film began playing in the United States by 1969. That year a theater showing it was set afire in Houston. Ultimately, it became the film that anyone who was anybody had to see. Even Jacqueline Kennedy Onassis went to a showing. On leaving the Manhattan theater, she met a crowd of photographers waiting outside, and a confrontation de-

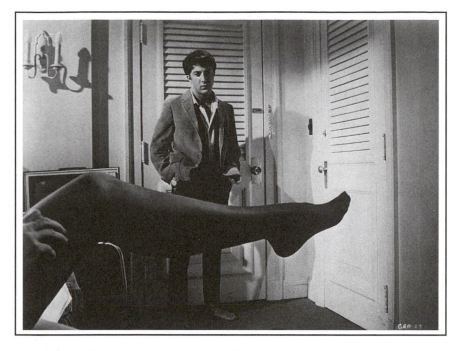

Dustin Hoffman tries unsuccessfully to resist being seduced by his girlfriend's mother (Anne Bancroft) in *The Graduate*. The film, directed by Mike Nichols, expressed a rejection of traditional American values. Source: Photofest, Inc.

veloped that brought Mrs. Onassis unwelcome attention but certainly sold more movie tickets.

Sex across the generations proved both shocking and popular on the big screen. Stanley Kubrick's *Lolita* (1962), based on a novel by Vladimir Nabokov, depicts a middle-aged man's obsession with a young teen. *The Graduate* (1967) stars Dustin Hoffman as a college graduate who becomes involved with his girlfriend's mother. One of the most successful films of the decade, *The Graduate* won its director, Mike Nichols, an Oscar while also depicting the alienation of the younger generation from the old. Mrs. Robinson, played by Anne Bancroft, became a symbol of the older generation's moral degeneration, and the film ends with the young lovers heading off for a life of love and truth apart from the corruption of their elders. The film also earned acclaim for its soundtrack, which won three Grammy awards for Simon and Garfunkel.

As with sex, mainstream films became much more graphic in depicting violence; they also increasingly glorified the outlaw. The most striking example was *Bonnie and Clyde* (1967), which featured Warren Beatty and Faye Dunaway as the Depression-era bank robbers and murderers turned anti-establishment heroes fighting an oppressive social and legal system, although they actually were viewed somewhat in that vein in their own time. In addition to romanticizing the gangsters, the film, directed by Arthur Penn, offers several especially violent scenes, including the extended riddling of Bonnie and Clyde with bullets when law officers ambush them in the film's final scene.

A similar ending occurs in *Butch Cassidy and the Sundance Kid* (1969), when the outlaws, played ingratiatingly by the irresistible Paul Newman and Robert Redford, are caught in a trap by Bolivian soldiers. The two die in a hail of bullets as they attempt a suicidal but heroic charge. Never have outlaws been so handsome, witty, and charming—and probably less based on reality. As in *Bonnie and Clyde*, the audience inevitably roots for the bad guys to outfox the forces of law and order. In 1967, Newman starred in another outlaw film, *Cool Hand Luke*. Imprisoned for breaking parking meters, Luke escapes three times before being shot down by "No-Eyes," a silent guard who, behind reflective sunglasses, longs to kill a prisoner. Luke becomes a hero of the struggle against an authority that relies only on its power for justification.

Characters such as those depicted by Beatty, Redford, and Newman reflect a growing interest in a different type of hero, often called the antihero. Antiheroes, rather than conveying the traditional characteristics associated with heroes, including bravery and a strong moral code of conduct, reflect values and patterns of behavior more often associated with villains, or at best with failures. The antihero tended to be portrayed, not as corrupt or ineffectual, but as in some way appealing and admirable, even if ultimately defeated. As American society increasingly turned away from inherited values in politics, sex, race relations, and many other areas of life, it proved ever more amenable to characters who similarly defied standard notions of heroism.

Even more violent but with less romanticizing than the Newman and Redford effort was *The Wild Bunch* (1969). One of the great Westerns of all time, *The Wild Bunch* was directed by Sam Peckinpah and starred William Holden as Pike Bishop, the leader of an outlaw gang. Although certainly wild, even vicious, the outlaws also prove capable of real friendship and loyalty. Ironically, these qualities finally do in the gang as most of the members are wiped out in a final apocalyptic shootout with Mexican General Mapache's forces in a futile attempt to rescue one of their own, the youthful Angel. The massive slaughter at the end is intricately choreographed in a grand ballet of death. It also brings the film full circle, as an early scene, an ambush of the gang by a group of railroad agents during a bank robbery, leaves a flood of dead bodies—outlaws, agents, and townspeople caught in the middle. That violence is part of the human condition rather than an aberration of a degenerate few is symbolized prior to the bank robbery by a group of children delighting in watching ants battle a scorpion.

Violence also came home to living rooms and marital relationships in films of the 1960s. Elizabeth Taylor and Richard Burton starred as husband

and wife Martha and George in the film version of Edward Albee's play *Who's Afraid of Virginia Woolf?* (1966), directed by Mike Nichols. Costarring were George Segal and Sandy Dennis as a young couple invited over to George and Martha's home after a faculty party. George, his college career having hit a dead end, and his frustrated wife prove less than gracious hosts. Martha quickly starts the psychological violence rolling with verbal attacks on George and attempts to seduce biology professor Nick. George responds by inducing the young wife, Honey, to acknowledge that George and Martha's son is dead, ending a fantasy that the childless couple had maintained to make their life more bearable. Taylor and Dennis won Oscars for their leading and supporting roles, and although most viewers recognized the success of the film, they also found it hard to take because of its unrelenting anger and mutual abuse.

Elizabeth Taylor began the decade by winning an Academy Award for her starring role as a prostitute in *Butterfield Eight* (1960). Later she played Cleopatra in the lavish film of that title (1963), costarring with Burton. The film was marred by a scandalous affair by the costars, who left their respective spouses, in the case of Taylor the actor Eddie Fisher, whose marriage to one of America's sweethearts, Debbie Reynolds, she had earlier helped to break up. Taylor and Burton married in 1964.

A film that led viewers into a more frightening supernatural terrain was *Rosemary's Baby* (1968). The film was directed by Roman Polanski (whose wife, Sharon Tate, would become one of Charles Manson's victims in 1969) and stars Mia Farrow as a young mother giving birth to a baby who supposedly is Satan's son, the result of an unusually graphic rape scene in which Satan assumes the form of her husband. There is no happy ending, as one of the Satanists proclaims "Here's to year one!" The forces of Satan, played, in keeping with the spirit of the times, by members of the older generation, triumph over the youthful hopes of the young mother.

Antiwar films drew large audiences, although the flood of successful commercial films about the Vietnam War was still a decade away. In the 1960s, antiwar films focused especially on the possibility of nuclear war as an outcome of the Cold War. The enemy sometimes is Russia; at other times the enemy is within, war-hungry American military leaders and corrupt or weak American politicians. Accidental war also proved good fodder for films. The most entertaining and outrageous of these films was *Dr. Strangelove: or, How I Learned to Stop Worrying and Love the Bomb* (1964), directed by Stanley Kubrick. General Jack D. Ripper, played by Sterling Hayden, isolates his air force base and launches World War III. The commies, Ripper is convinced, are literally polluting America to rob men of their sex drive. General Buck Turgidson, brilliantly overplayed by George C. Scott, supports the first strike, but is opposed by the otherwise ineffective president, one of three roles played by Peter Sellers. Sellers is also the British officer held prisoner by Ripper and the wheelchair-bound technical genius who becomes so excited by the prospect of war that he propels himself from his chair shouting "Mein Führer, I can walk!"—revealing himself as a secret Nazi born again in a new attempt to conquer, or destroy, the world. Ultimately, one bomber makes it through and drops its payload on Russia. The film, though enormously funny, also proved frightening in its satiric portrayal of what might go wrong with crazies running around loose with the technological means to destroy the world.

In *Seven Days in May* (1964), the offending general, played by Burt Lancaster, believes that the president (Fredric March) has concluded a nuclear arms treaty that so weakens the United States as to make it an easy prey to the communist menace. He accordingly leads a chiefs-of-staff plot to overthrow the president. Thanks to another military figure, played by Kirk Douglas, the plot eventually fails, but not until a great deal of intrigue and paranoia that appear just a bit too real for the audience's peace of mind. *Fail Safe* (1964), a Sydney Lumet-directed film, removes the human conspiracy and lunatic elements to make war a matter strictly of accident, of modern technology and communications gone awry. A "fail-safe" system designed to make it impossible for plotters to launch a nuclear first strike against the Soviet Union fails, making it impossible, in turn, for the president, played by Henry Fonda, to call back the threatening bomber. The president at first has trouble convincing his Soviet counterpart that he is on the level, and then the Soviets act too late. The only solution for avoiding an all-out nuclear war proves to be a trade-off, American cities for Soviet ones. Filmmakers found 1964 a particularly good year for scaring audiences with nuclear-war scenarios.

The major commercial film depicting the Vietnam War during the 1960s was a personal project of John Wayne's, *The Green Berets* (1968), based on Robin Moore's novel *The Green Berets* (1965) and capitalizing on Barry Sadler's "The Ballad of the Green Berets," which became a big hit in 1966. Ultimately, however, the film was a vehicle for Wayne to convey his views of the war and his definition of patriotism. Wayne directed the film and starred in it. David Janssen of television's *The Fugitive* costarred, playing a reporter skeptical of the war who comes around to Wayne's way of thinking after seeing Vietcong fiendishness and the suffering of innocent Vietnamese children. The film was not one of Wayne's best efforts; even geographical details are wrong, such as having the sun set in the East, into the South China Sea.

The variety of films during the 1960s was limitless. Genres that especially made a splash, in blood or water, included horror and gothic films at one extreme, and beach films at the other. *Rosemary's Baby* has been discussed in terms of stretching traditional boundaries of acceptability in films, but there were other successes in making people afraid of old houses, dark nights, and even shower stalls. *What Ever Happened to Baby Jane?* (1962) popularized a subgenre of the horror/gothic film known to movie insiders as the "menopausal murder story." Such films feature elderly women, often played by longtime leading actresses, who do horrible things in the darkness of their also aging homes. In this Robert Aldrich film, a reclusive Jane (Bette Davis), once upon a time a child vaudeville star known as Baby Jane, learning that her sister, Blanche (Joan Crawford), plans to have her committed to an asylum and sell off the old mansion, locks the wheelchair-bound Blanche in her room. An interesting touch in the film was the decision to use two actresses who in real life were bitter rivals.

Unfortunately, Crawford refused to team up again with Davis in the 1964 *Hush ... Hush Sweet Charlotte*, another Aldrich film. Here the partner-in-horror for Davis becomes by default Olivia de Havilland. Other veteran stars in the film include Agnes Moorehead, Joseph Cotton, and, in her last role, Mary Astor. Filmed in black and white, with creative use of shadows, camera angles, and intimations of violence rather than in-your-face graphic depictions, both films have become classics of the gothic genre.

The master of horror during the 1960s, though, remained the director Alfred Hitchcock. His *Psycho* (1960) included one of the most famous horror scenes of all time: Janet Leigh being stabbed to death while taking a shower in her motel room. The murderer is played by Anthony Perkins, who masquerades as his dead mother while running the Bates Motel. Another memorable Hitchcock horror film during the decade was *The Birds* (1963), in which birds go berserk and make war on humans, gulls and crows never having looked so menacing. Hitchcock also turned out espionage films during the decade and hosted his own television series, *Alfred Hitchcock Presents*.

Viewers more interested in water, sunshine, beaches, and pretty girls than blood and suspense had a tidal wave of beach films from which to choose. American-International Pictures brought out some of the most popular beach films, starring former lead Mousketeer of Walt Disney's *The Mickey Mouse Club*, Annette Funicello, and singer Frankie Avalon in such releases as *Beach Party* (1963), *Muscle Beach Party* (1964), *How to Stuff a Wild Bikini* (1965), and *Beach Blanket Bingo* (1965). Given Annette's image, carefully maintained by Disney, as young America's pretty and pure sweetheart, the films stayed away from the social turmoil and changing sexual mores flowing through American society. Annette, in fact, was not permitted to wear a bikini, and her relationship with love interest Frankie Avalon remained unceasingly chaste.

There was plenty of other escapist fare in the 1960s. Elvis Presley, back from the army, starred in twenty-seven films during the decade. The movies typically featured Elvis as a singing something (pilot, race car driver, ad infinitum), always sexy but invariably in a sort of all-American way. His costars were among the most beautiful actresses of the times: Juliet Prowse in *G.I. Blues* (1960), Ann-Margret in *Viva Las Vegas* (1964), and Julie Parrish in *Paradise, Hawaiian Style* (1966). The films did little to secure Elvis's long-term fame, which continues to depend on his music, but they did bring in the cash. One of the great social events of the decade was the King's marriage in 1967 to Priscilla Beaulieu, whom Elvis met when she was fourteen and he was stationed in Germany, as was Priscilla's father, a career military man. The approximately ten-year difference in their ages excited considerable attention in the media but did not seem seriously to harm Elvis's standing with his fans.

The James Bond films fed millions of men's fantasies during the 1960s, as they imagined themselves like Agent 007: handsome, suave, owner of high-powered cars and myriad other advanced gadgets, victorious over assorted villains, and always getting the beautiful and exotic girl. The original Bond, and for many still the ultimate, is the actor Sean Connery. The first Bond film was *Dr. No* (1962), followed by *From Russia with Love* (1963), *Goldfinger* (1964), *Thunderball* (1965), and *You Only Live Twice* (1967). The stories usually occurred in exotic locations and specialized in combating Cold War enemies of Great Britain and the Free World. Some of the title songs, such as Shirley Bassey's "Goldfinger" and Nancy Sinatra's "You Only Live Twice," became hits; and the Bond films helped their beautiful, foreign-born actresses achieve fame and fortune, among them Ursula Andress, Daniela Bianchi, Honor Blackman, and Shirley Eaton. The Bond women, especially in the later Connery films of the 1960s, helped to change the Western world's taste in beautiful women from busty, big-hipped sexpots like Marilyn Monroe and Jayne Mansfield to slender, youthful types who looked as if they would be as much at home riding a bike or climbing a mountain as inviting a handsome secret agent into their boudoir.

Finally, there were the alternative and underground films. Some of the films already discussed, such as *Easy Rider*, were clearly out of the mainstream in content and mode of production even while attempting to navigate the usual commercial waters of distribution. The so-called art film tended toward less narrative continuity than most commercial films and often shifted in unusual ways between realism and subjectivity. Individual style was especially important in the art films, and the content more explicitly represented social and sexual changes in American culture than did most commercial cinema. Consequently, films like *The Connection* (1961), filmed as if it were a documentary about junkies improvising jazz and talking street jive while waiting for their next fix; and *Putney Swope* (1969), which satirizes American society by having board members of a large business elect the lone black member chairman because each white member casts what he thinks is a token vote, assuming that no one else will vote the same way and not wanting the board to appear prejudiced, tended to attract fewer viewers and have more trouble finding theaters willing to exhibit them than mainstream films.

Andy Warhol especially stretched the boundaries of films—and sometimes the limits of viewers' patience—as he moved from minimal, avantgarde films to commercial productions. *Sleep* (1963), for example, simply has a camera trained on a person sleeping. *Chelsea Girls* (1966) includes a lot more action during its seven hours, coming across as a documentary made up of whatever the girls happened to be doing. The approach by Warhol was consciously imitative of wallpaper, the idea that a film is to be viewed as commonly (and with as much emotion or interest) as watching the wallpaper in one's room. For *Empire*, Warhol trained a camera on the Empire State Building from 1963 to 1964, thereby producing probably the longest film in history. His *Blue Movie* (1968) shows a couple meandering their way through sexual intercourse and a lot of talk.

Underground films usually emanated from New York City or San Francisco and, as the name indicates, represented subcultures and their sexual, aesthetic, drug, and political proclivities. Such films were usually little more than documentaries of these groups and proved even less commercially viable than art films. Sometimes, as with *Chelsea Girls*, the line between art and underground was difficult to draw. *Flaming Creatures* (1962) depicts underground pleasures of bizarre sorts, including orgies populated by drag queens and vampire lookalikes. *Inauguration of the Pleasure Dome* (1966) is one in the nine-part series of *The Anger Magick Lantern Cycle* films (1947–80) directed by Kenneth Anger. *Inauguration* includes a fancy party at which intoxicated guests violate a handsome boy, with the host growing stronger as he absorbs all that occurs.

TELEVISION

Television became the dominant communications medium in American society during the 1960s. At the beginning of the decade, over forty-five million households had at least one television, a figure that would rise to almost sixty million by the end of the 1960s, as the small screen became the primary distributor of entertainment and information.[2] Programming was dominated by the three major networks: the Columbia Broadcasting System (CBS), the National Broadcasting Company (NBC), and the American Broadcasting Company (ABC). A small amount of alternative programming was provided by the new Public Broadcasting Service (PBS), founded in 1969; and by cable television, available in about 7% of homes by the end of the decade.[3]

Television completed its transformation during the 1960s from a New York-based industry with single sponsors controlling shows to a Hollywood-based system with network control over shows and multiple sponsorship. Major film studios and independent companies produced the shows, which were licensed, distributed, and often owned by the networks. The A.C. Nielsen Corporation measured viewer attention, *TV Guide* magazine published television schedules, and the Federal Communications Commission (FCC) regulated the industry. The evening network news programs expanded in 1963 from fifteen to thirty minutes, ensuring that such news anchormen as Walter Cronkite on CBS and the team of Chet Huntley and David Brinkley on NBC became the primary dispensers of news to the masses. The movement to color programming by the mid-1960s further galvanized the viewing public.

These remarkable changes did not proceed without controversy. President Kennedy's FCC chairman, Newton Minow, blasted the television industry for its lack of quality programming, labeling the small screen a "vast wasteland" in 1961.[4] In the same year, Senator Thomas Dodd of Connecticut opened his Senate hearings on violence in television. The hearings finally ran out of gas in 1964, and Dodd was censured by the Senate in 1967 for using campaign contributions for personal expenses and double-billing the government for travel costs. His hearings, however, prompted a partial shift from action adventure shows to sitcoms and a spate of research projects exploring the effects of television violence on children.

The Untouchables (1959–63), starring Robert Stack as Prohibition-era crime fighter Eliot Ness, came in for special bludgeoning by Dodd. The attack was joined by Italian American groups objecting to the show's depiction of Italian Americans as gangsters. Proving quite touchable after all, the series toned down its violence, gave increased attention to the Italian American Untouchable, Nick Rossi, and provided more gangsters with non-Italian names.

Television, having become the most mass of the mass media, sought to avoid controversy as much as possible in its entertainment in order not to turn off its viewers. Throughout the decade, television, much more than theater films, stayed as far removed as possible from the changes going on in American society. Series continued to present the all-American families popular during the 1950s, as *Father Knows Best* (1954–63), starring Robert Young as the all-wise father, and *The Adventures of Ozzie and Harriet* (1952–66), with Ozzie and Hariet Nelson playing themselves along with their actual sons David and future rock star Ricky, continued their success into the 1960s. In the case of the former, Robert Young had tired of the show and left after the 1959–60 season, but the show continued in reruns on prime time for the next three years.

Wisdom and comedy combined in *The Andy Griffith Show* (1960–68). Griffith played Sheriff Andy Taylor of Mayberry, North Carolina, providing commonsense guidance to son Opie (Ron Howard) and bumbling Deputy Barney Fife (Don Knotts). Knotts won five Emmys from the Academy of Television Arts and Sciences as best supporting actor for his role.[5] The series, which also starred Frances Bavier as Aunt Bee and featured an endearing set of town characters (including Jim Nabors, who graduated to his own series, *Gomer Pyle, U.S.M.C.*), remained highly popular in reruns throughout the century.

A little less wisdom and more broad comedy characterized the families and friends on *The Dick Van Dyke Show* (1961–66) and *The Beverly Hillbillies*

The Untouchables starring Robert Stack, came under fire during Senator Thomas Dodd's hearings on violence in television. Source: Photofest, Inc.

(1962–71), two of television's all-time popular series. Van Dyke was joined by Mary Tyler Moore, who became one of the medium's most loved actresses, as his wife, and Rose Marie and Morey Amsterdam as co-comedy writers on the fictitious *Alan Brady Show*. Carl Reiner, writer and producer of the series, appeared occasionally as Alan Brady. A favorite with both viewers and critics, the series won a basket of Emmys, including four as top program in its field, three for Van Dyke, and two for Moore. *The Beverly*

Hillbillies, starring Buddy Ebsen as Jed Clampett, patriarch of an Ozarks family that struck it rich in oil and moved to Hollywood, was even more popular with viewers, finishing Number One in the Nielsen ratings for the 1962–63 and 1963–64 seasons.

Some families featured in comic series were even more unusual than Jed Clampett and his hillbilly clan, such as the mock-horror characters of *The Munsters* (1964–66) and *The Addams Family* (1964–66). Then there was the cartoon family that populated *The Flintstones* (1960–66). If the Munsters and Addams mocked traditional nuclear family stereotypes, Fred and Wilma Flintstone parodied suburban life in the 1960s. Somehow they enjoyed all the modern conveniences of life, prehistoric style, while maintaining traditional spousal stereotypes immortalized on television by Jackie Gleason and Audrey Meadows on *The Honeymooners* (1955–57), and earlier in skits on *The Jackie Gleason Show* (1952–55). The show introduced the nonsense phrase "Yabba Dabba Doo!" into the American lexicon.

The most consistent reflection of political issues in television entertainment occurred on crime and western series with good triumphing over bad in a moral struggle paralleling, albeit loosely, the Cold War antagonism between the United States and the Soviet Union. Crime-fighting took many forms in the 1960s, from J. Edgar Hoover's agents (led by Efrem Zimbalist, Jr.) tracking down spies, counterfeiters, and other unsavory types on *The F.B.I.* (1965–74) to the three youthful hippie cops of *The Mod Squad* (1968–73) to the interracial anti-espionage team of Robert Culp and Bill Cosby in *I Spy* (1965–68) to the James Bond spoof *Get Smart* starring Don Adams (1965–70). No one achieved more justice on television than Raymond Burr, first, on *Perry Mason* (1957–66), where he not only exonerated his clients but discovered the true evildoers; and later as a wounded chief of detectives confined to a wheelchair in *Ironside* (1967–71).

In one of the most remarkable series of the 1960s, David Janssen as Dr. Richard Kimble on *The Fugitive* (1963–67) searched the country for the one-armed murderer of his wife, both to gain justice for her and exonerate himself. Kimble was being taken by train to be executed for the murder when a derailment allowed him to escape from Lt. Philip Gerard. Throughout the series, viewers followed the dual pursuit, Gerard after Kimble, Kimble after the one-armed murderer. Along the way, Kimble, assuming a long line of new identities, and conveying a sense of brooding alienation combined with a strongly compassionate nature, solved countless problems for people suffering from their own problems. The series to some extent paralleled the real-life case of Dr. Sam Sheppard, who was convicted of murdering his wife but continued to claim that she had been killed by an intruder. During the years of the series, Dr. Sheppard was granted a new trial and found not guilty.

Most of the detectives fighting crime on television worked in the present, but on *The Untouchables*, previously mentioned, viewers were transported back to the Al Capone and Prohibition era of the 1930s. *Batman* (1966–68), on the other hand, was more futuristic with its gadgets, including the Batmobile. Batman (Adam West) and youthful sidekick Robin (Dick Grayson) battled a host of unusual earthly villains, such as the Penguin (Burgess Meredith) and the Riddler (Frank Gorshin), to preserve the peace and security of Gotham City.

Westerns during the decade responded to an increasingly complex society in a variety of ways—for example, emphasizing strong independent women, presenting a more balanced depiction of Native Americans, and deemphasizing violence when violence became a major issue on television during the early 1960s. The rise of the adult western in the 1950s had introduced greater complexity into motivation and behavior on the part of such heroes as Matt Dillon on *Gunsmoke* (1955–75) and Paladin on *Have Gun Will Travel* (1957–63). Yet the genre continued to appeal to a worldview that saw moral issues in stark good-versus-evil terms, with good triumphing. That attitude grew increasingly out of favor with the escalation of antiwar sentiment and civil strife over racial and generational issues in the second half of the 1960s, and with a growing realization that traditional ideas of right often were inadequate.

The "family" western emerged in the late 1950s and continued through the early 1960s, featuring a western family, usually minus the mother, such as *The Rifleman* (1958–63), starring former baseball and basketball player Chuck Connors as the widowed Lucas McCain rearing his son Mark (Johnny Crawford); *The Virginian* (1962–71), with Lee J. Cobb as ranch owner Judge Henry Garth until 1966, and James Drury as the Virginian; and *The High Chaparral* (1967–71), with Leif Erickson as Big John Cannon, owner of the ranch that supplied the title name of the series. *The Big Valley* (1965–69) was an unusual entry in this subgenre, as it was the widowed mother who headed up the family. Longtime film star Barbara Stanwyck played the strong, brave, and wise matriarch Victoria Barkley. Three sons and one daughter, played by Richard Long, Peter Breck, Lee Majors, and Linda Evans, supplied a lot of the action, but also some of the problems, in this usually exciting series.

The most popular of the family westerns, though, was *Bonanza* (1959–73), next to *Gunsmoke* the most popular television western of all time. Bonanza starred Lorne Greene as the father, Ben Cartwright, with Michael Landon, Dan Blocker, and Pernell Roberts as sons Little Joe, Hoss, and Adam. The series was the number one rated show on television for three consecutive seasons, 1964–67, and, resisting the overall drop in popularity of westerns, remained in the top ten for a decade, from 1961 to 1971. *Gunsmoke*, the longest running prime-time series with continuing characters in the history of television, also bucked the anti-western trend in the 1960s. Starring James Arness as Marshal Matt Dillon; Amanda Blake as Kitty Russell, owner of the Long Branch Saloon; and Milburn Stone as crusty Doc Adams;

Gunsmoke was the top-rated television show at the beginning
of the Sixties and continued on the air until 1975. Its twenty years on
television (1955–75) were the most ever by a prime-time series with
continuing characters. Source: Photofest, Inc.

and set in historic Dodge City, Kansas; the show also featured an excellent
supporting cast of townspeople. The cast included a young Burt Reynolds
as part-Indian blacksmith Quint Asper (1962–65); Dennis Weaver as Deputy
Chester Goode (1955–64); and Ken Curtis, formerly of the singing group
the Sons of the Pioneers and a son-in-law to famous director John Ford, as

Festus Haggen (1964–75), who spent about equal time arguing with Doc, helping Matt run down outlaws, and mangling the English language. *Gunsmoke* was the top-rated show during the four seasons of 1957 to 1961. After dropping out of the top ten (1963–67), it roared back in the 1967–68 season to fourth place, and continued in the top ten through 1972–73.

One of the most unusual westerns in the 1960s was *The Wild, Wild West* (1965–70), starring Robert Conrad and Ross Martin as Secret Service agents James T. West and Artemus Gordon. Working on behalf of President Ulysses S. Grant, the partners were James Bond types transported back in time. They operated out of a luxurious private railroad car, fought villains trying to destroy the world, got out of tight scrapes with technological gadgets as close as under a sleeve or inside a shoe sole, and interacted with an endless stream of beautiful, and sometimes villainous, women.

The 1960s began with westerns holding the top three spots in the ratings for the 1959–60, 1960–61, and 1961–62 seasons, thanks to *Gunsmoke, Wagon Train, Have Gun Will Travel,* and *Bonanza.* During 1959–60, eight additional westerns were in the top twenty-five. In 1969–70, *Gunsmoke* and *Bonanza* were second and third, respectively, but they stood alone as westerns in the top thirty. The demise of the western reflected not only the political changes in the United States during the 1960s but also the reality that with the western directed primarily toward an adult audience throughout the 1960s large numbers of children had come of age without connecting with the genre. By the end of the 1960s, the Old West was ancient history for most young adults, who preferred urban-centered shows. In addition, President Kennedy had proclaimed a "new frontier," that of space. Rather than looking westward across the plains and mountains, Americans were turning their attention upward, and television followed suit.

Among the space shows during the 1960s, *Star Trek* (1966–69) was the most memorable, carving out a following that endured throughout the rest of the century and beyond. That the producer of *Star Trek,* Gene Roddenberry, saw his series as something of a replacement for the traditional western is evident in his characterization of the series as a "Wagon Train to the stars," a reference to the *Wagon Train* series (1957–65), starring Ward Bond as wagonmaster, and, after his death, John McIntire.

Captain James Kirk (William Shatner), the unrelentingly logical Mr. Spock (Leonard Nimoy), Dr. McCoy (DeForest Kelley), and the rest of the crew of the starship *Enterprise* engaged various forms of alien life in battle on its interstellar journeys. Although not particularly popular during its original run, the series attracted loyal fans known as Trekkies who faithfully followed the show in reruns, staged *Star Trek* conventions, and in other ways demonstrated their unflagging enthusiasm for the show.

The 1960s witnessed considerable diversity in what the viewing public liked. Doctor shows were in, especially series that featured young, handsome doctors like Richard Chamberlain on *Dr. Kildare* (1961–66) and Vince

Edwards on *Ben Casey* (1961–66). Critics loved *The Twilight Zone* (1959–65), created and hosted by playwright Rod Serling, and featuring unusual, provocative stories, often with an ironic twist at the end. The show earned four Emmys and immortality but not a large viewing public, as the series never ranked in Nielsen's top thirty-five. Conversely, critics mocked *The Lawrence Welk Show* (1955–82) and Welk's at best modest musical talents, lamented that the show appealed to an aged audience, and did not take seriously the squeaky clean cast of Welk's musical family and their "champagne music." All the show did was run on network television for sixteen years and produce additional new episodes in syndication for more than another decade. In fact, it reached its peak of popularity during the second half of the 1960s as something of a counter-countercultural statement of traditional values.

Ed Sullivan came across as wooden and inarticulate, yet became a Sunday night fixture on television by hosting *The Ed Sullivan Show* (originally called *Toast of the Town*) from 1948 to 1971. Seemingly devoid of personal talent, Sullivan introduced viewers to a world of talent as various as trick-performing dogs, Senor Wences and his talking box, and two of history's greatest influences on music, Elvis Presley and the Beatles. Sullivan was a favorite of imitators, hugging himself with crossed arms and welcoming his audience to a "really big shew." Yet, despite his unappealing mannerisms, Sullivan changed popular culture in the United States. The performances by Elvis (shot from the waist up to hide his pelvic gyrations) in 1956 and the Beatles in 1964 introduced them to millions of American viewers for the first time and remain among the most important moments in television history. In addition, Sullivan integrated television by featuring a long list of African American performers, including Lena Horne and Pearl Bailey.

As viewers watched talent from all over the world on *The Ed Sullivan Show*, they could see regular people on *Candid Camera* (1960–67). Allen Funt started directing a hidden camera at normal people in the late 1940s, but had his steadiest run on television during the 1960s. The point was to film someone simply doing what he or she normally did to see the humor in the everyday, or set up an individual with a gag and see how the person reacted. Individuals would encounter vending machines that talked back and restaurants that served miniscule portions of food. Finally, the unsuspecting man or woman would hear the revealing words, "Smile, you're on *Candid Camera*."

Millions of Americans continued to retire for the night with *The Tonight Show* starring Jack Paar and, from 1962 on, Johnny Carson. Carson, with his opening monologue, comedy skits, and wide range of entertaining guests, proved a welcome, even comforting visitor in bedrooms across the country. His popularity was so great it was said that he depressed the birth rate, as viewers refused to turn their attention from his show.

Television only gingerly moved into social satire during the 1960s. *Rowan and Martin's Laugh-In* (1968–73) was acceptable because it emphasized humor and gentle mockery rather than serious social satire. Headed by Dan Rowan and Dick Martin and featuring a large and talented cast (Ruth Buzzi, Judy Carne, Goldie Hawn, Arte Johnson, Henry Gibson, Lily Tomlin *et al.*), the show made use of a fast-paced series of sketches, one-liners, and cameo performances by celebrities, including politicians. Expressions such as "You bet your bippy" and "Sock it to me" entered the nation's lexicon from *Laugh-In*. Even Richard Nixon appeared on the show, inviting the audience to "Sock it to me." The series was Number One in the Nielsen ratings during its first two seasons, but declined as many of its stars moved on to capitalize elsewhere on their newfound fame.

While *Laugh-In* offended few, *The Smothers Brothers Comedy Hour* (1967–69) offended too many people in high places within the industry. Tom and Dick Smothers started off inoffensively enough with folk songs, witty repartee, and enough mainstream guests such as George Burns, Jim Nabors, and Eva Gabor to offset their irreverent tone. Appealing to a youthful audience, the show included Leigh French as Goldie O'Keefe, a "hippie chick" who boasted of her drug experiences in terminology that older viewers did not sufficiently understand to get upset about. *The Smothers Brothers* moved steadily leftward in its second and shortened third seasons and ran into increasing trouble with CBS executives and censors over such performances as Pete Seeger's antiwar song "Waist Deep in the Big Muddy," Harry Belafonte's number about the 1968 Democratic convention in Chicago, "Don't Stop the Carnival," and an appearance by antiwar folksinger Joan Baez in which she talked about her husband, David Harris, who was sentenced to prison for resisting the military draft. CBS pulled the plug on the series on April 3, 1969, claiming that Tom Smothers had not provided an acceptable tape of the show's next broadcast in time for appropriate review by the Program Practices Department and local stations.

At the end of the 1960s, as *The Smothers Brothers Comedy Hour* was succumbing to controversy, a new show was revolutionizing children's television. Throughout the decade, social scientists, politicians, educators, and parents, among others, had been looking carefully, sometimes with considerable apprehension, at the effects of television programming on children. In 1969, *Sesame Street* began to offer preschool children both entertainment and education on PBS. An outstanding creative team and high production values made the show a welcome partner to parents and teachers. The heart of *Sesame Street* was a group of Muppets, the creative children of Jim Henson—Ernie and Bert, Big Bird, Oscar the Grouch, Cookie Monster, Kermit the Frog. The show was set on a city street to appeal to urban youth and included a serious commitment to ethnic diversity. Snappy tunes made learning the alphabet and much else a lot of fun. Some observers worried that the rapid pace of the show would depress children's attention span, but teachers quickly found youngsters starting school with much better knowledge of their numbers and letters. *Sesame Street* became a television fixture still doing its job at the beginning of the twenty-first century.

DANCE

The twist, the frug, the watusi, the jerk, the mashed potato, the funky chicken, the Freddie, the swim. No wonder many middle-aged Americans had trouble relating to what the young were doing in the 1960s. The names of these and other dances that proved popular, at least briefly during the decade, invite a shrug of disbelief, a raised eyebrow. But such dances, as short-lived as most of them were, make some important statements about the youth culture. They show a determination to manufacture new forms of entertainment sharply different from those of their parents. The dances convey enthusiasm and spontaneity, a sense of individualism, and a clear preference for the unconventional. Like changes in styles of dress, hair, and music, these dances were the property of a youth culture determined to create rather than inherit, a culture committed to being itself. What "itself" might be could vary considerably, but at least it was different from the older generation.

These dances certainly had some fairly standard movements, but nothing as firmly established as the steps of most ballroom dances. No one had to take lessons to participate, except for some older folks who wanted to share in the youth culture. There was a freedom with these dances that fit well the spirit of the 1960s—a freedom of movement, a freedom from the traditions of the older generation, a freedom to express oneself with spontaneous adjustments to the minimal patterns associated with the dances.

The origins of these dances were sometimes thoroughly spontaneous, even accidental. When Jacques Bostel tripped and fell at a French discotheque, other dancers followed suit by dropping to the floor. Thus was born La Bostella, named after its unwitting inventor. The Freddie was in imitation of Freddie Garrity of Freddie and the Dreamers, who hopped up and down while performing. Dancers did the same, with the realization that no two people hop precisely the same.

Pantomime played an important role in many of the popular dances of the decade. The swim involved dancers extending and retracting their arms as if they were swimming. Sometimes, the dancer would hold his or her nose with one hand while slowly sinking to the floor as if being submerging in a swimming pool. The mashed potato involved a mashing motion with the dancer's feet, as if potatoes rather than a dance floor were underneath. One was required to be able to jerk, as opposed to being a jerk, to enjoy the dance that went by that name. The jerk usually included holding one arm aloft while slowly sinking to the floor in a series of jerky movements that brought the entire body down, the arm following suit, then slowly jerking back upright with the other arm rising. The funky chicken usually accompanied soul music and included chickenlike movements such as flapping one's arms.

The dance that most symbolized the 1960s, and opened the dance floor to the dances mentioned earlier and countless others, was the twist. Unlike many popular dances of the time, the twist had a long history of cultural antecedents. It grew out of a twisting dance popular in African American settings in the nineteenth century that in turn yielded 1930s music by a gospel group, the Sensational Nightingales, who invited listeners to "do the twist." The 1960s version was the work of Hank Ballard, who recorded "The Twist" in the late 1950s. The song quickly spawned, in fact mandated, an accompanying dance. By July 1960, the song was a hit, and Dick Clark wanted to feature it on his *American Bandstand* show. Clark felt that Ballard, although an important rhythm and blues artist, was too associated with songs that included sexual allusions (like "Sexy Ways" and "Work with Me Annie") to fit the wholesome image that he wanted to project with his show. Clark therefore encouraged a young singer named Chubby Checker to record the song, which Checker tried out on *The Dick Clark Show* (an evening version of the daytime *American Bandstand*) in August 1960. Both the song and dance became even larger hits; Checker's version climbed to the top of the charts by September. In 1962, Checker's "The Twist" became the first record since Bing Crosby's "White Christmas" to make a return trip to first place after being off the charts.

"The Twist" precipitated some two dozen "Twist" songs, such as "Let's Twist Again" (Checker, 1961), "Twist and Shout" (The Isley Brothers, 1961), "Peppermint Twist" (Joey Dee and the Starlighters, 1961), and "Twistin' the Night Away" (Sam Cooke, 1962), with almost as many variations on the dance as people doing it. The dance also proved increasingly popular with older dancers because it was relatively easy to perform and did not require the bizarre gestures associated with some of the other youthful dances.

Where people danced depended somewhat on their age. Teenagers were primarily limited to private parties and school dances, including the "sock hops," so named because they often occurred in gyms with teens required to doff their shoes in order not to scuff the floor.

When teens were not dancing, they often were watching Dick Clark's *American Bandstand* (1956–89), a show that gave carefully selected teens an opportunity to perform the latest dances on national television to a combination of records (subsequently rated by the dancers) and live performers (more often than not lip-synching their songs). Clark also featured couples in spotlight dances. The show was enormously influential, helping to make stars of such performers as Chubby Checker, Frankie Avalon, Fabian, and the Everly Brothers. It also brought temporary fame to some of the dancers who became regulars on the show. Clark deserves credit for bringing white and black teenagers together in a social context on national television for the first time and for featuring a great many African American performers.

Chubby Checker demonstrates the twist in the film *Twist Around the Clock* (1961). Source: Photofest, Inc.

Young adults increasingly favored discotheques, which originated in France and featured records (disks) rather than live bands. The discotheques were most often found in cities, such as New York's Peppermint Lounge, which featured Joey Dee and the Starlighters and gave rise to the song "The Peppermint Twist." Some of the discos also highlighted attractive young women dancing on stages, in cages, or in otherwise prominent places. These "go-go dancers" typically wore skimpy attire and high boots, which came to be known as go-go boots.

Older adults who increasingly came to identify with the younger dancers could take their chances on the disco dance floors as well or try out their steps in private parties. A dance that went over well with the slightly older crowd was the limbo. The dance required a sense of humor and a bit of daring, as well as a stick held horizontally by two people. An individual dancer would dance up to the stick, perhaps to Chubby Checker's "Limbo Rock" (1962), and attempt to move underneath the stick, body bent back, without falling to the floor. The dance was sexually suggestive in a mild way, so even proper people could dance the limbo, just hinting at a touch of naughtiness.

The twist and related youthful dances certainly dominated popular dance in the 1960s, but ballet also won many headlines, not least for political reasons. The American Ballet Theatre in 1960 had become the first U.S. company to tour Russia. On June 16, 1961, the great Russian ballet dancer Rudolf Nureyev defected to the West while performing in Paris. He subsequently teamed with Dame Margot Fonteyn, performing with the Royal Ballet in London. Nureyev's defection was seen in the United States as another sign of Western superiority in the Cold War competition that featured the United States and Russia as primary antagonists.

In 1962, Nureyev debuted in the United States in *Don Quixote* for Ruth Page's Chicago Opera Ballet. Nureyev excited considerable attention, not only as a political statement, but also for his innovative and athletic dancing style and strong (some would say arrogant) personality. Throughout his performances, he demonstrated on stage aesthetic parallels to what the newspapers called his "leap to freedom" in Paris.

Throughout the 1960s, new venues for fine ballet kept opening up. William Christensen traveled from San Francisco to Salt Lake City to start Ballet West in 1963. In 1964, Virginia Williams created the Boston Ballet, Rebecca Harkness founded the Harkness Ballet in New York City, and the New York City Ballet, with $7 million from the Ford Foundation, opened in Lincoln Center's New York State Theater.

Yet despite the headlines, glamor, and inspiration emanating from Rudolf Nureyev, the most important creative force in presenting great ballet to American audiences in the 1960s was another Russian-born defector, George Balanchine. Born Georgi Balanchivadze in St. Petersburg in 1904, the ballet dancer, like Nureyev decades later, defected while performing in Europe, in 1924. Balanchine moved to the United States in 1933 to create the American Ballet Company. Viewed by many critics as the finest choreographer of the mid-twentieth century, Balanchine continued to produce exciting ballets throughout the decade for the New York City Ballet that in 1948 he had helped to create, including *A Midsummer Night's Dream* (1962), *Tarantella* (1964), *Don Quixote* (1965), and *Jewels* (1967). He also revived *Slaughter on Tenth Avenue* in 1968, which he had composed in 1936 for the musical *On Your Toes*.

Only a careful observer would have detected common denominators among the popular dances of the 1960s and the great ballets of Nureyev and Balanchine. Such an observer, though, would surely have spoken of such matters as enthusiasm, exuberance, a spirit of adventure, and artistic and political freedom, even rebellion.

DRAMA

The great masters of American drama at the beginning of the 1960s were Tennessee Williams and Arthur Miller. They had established themselves in the 1940s with such hits as *The Glass Menagerie* (1945) and *A Streetcar Named Desire* (1947) by Williams and *All My Sons* (1947) and *Death of a Salesman*

(1949) by Miller. Both playwrights followed these early plays with additional successes, but by the 1960s the critics judged the two writers to be in decline. That judgment was more accurate regarding Williams than Miller. Tennessee Williams created *The Night of the Iguana* (1961) about a group of people at a seedy coastal hotel in Mexico, with the iguana symbolizing the bondage afflicting the human participants. *The Night of the Iguana* earned Williams his fourth New York Drama Critics' Circle Award. Yet Williams's deteriorating health steadily impacted his writing for the rest of his life, until his death in 1983.

By the 1960s, Arthur Miller had become as well known to the general public for his marriage to actress Marilyn Monroe, previously married to baseball great Joe DiMaggio, as for his drama. They married in 1956, and Miller wrote the screenplay *The Misfits* for his wife. Released in 1960, *The Misfits* was the final film for both Monroe and Clark Gable. The following year, Miller and Monroe divorced, and Monroe committed suicide in 1962. Ironically, possibly his best play during the 1960s was *After the Fall* (1964), an autobiographical exploration of the playwright's life, including his wives. Marilyn Monroe is the inspiration for the character Maggie, who swallows pills with whiskey near the end of the play in order to commit suicide, avowing that she has been killed by a long line of people.

Musicals, long popular with American audiences, and viewed by many drama historians as a particularly American genre, continued to play well on Broadway with audiences that preferred traditional fare. The list of memorable musicals from the decade is long, including *The Sound of Music*, by Richard Rodgers and Oscar Hammerstein II, a Tony winner in 1960 as best musical; *Oliver!* (1963), by Lionel Bart; *Hello Dolly!*, starring Carol Channing, which set a record by winning ten Tonys, a mark not surpassed until 2001 when *The Producers* picked up twelve; Barbara Streisand's starring vehicle, *Funny Girl* (1964), by Jule Styne; and *Cabaret* (1966), by John Kander and Fred Ebb.

Camelot, another of the blockbuster musicals of the 1960s, occupies a special place in American culture. The show, by Frederick Loewe and Alan Jay Lerner, premiered on Broadway in 1960, starring Richard Burton as King Arthur, Julie Andrews as Queen Guenevere, and Robert Goulet as Lancelot. The story of a faraway time and place of great ideals ruled by a brave and honorable king was a favorite of President and Mrs. Kennedy. After the president's assassination, Mrs. Kennedy compared the Kennedy presidency to Arthur's legendary city, Camelot, establishing a lasting analogy between the abbreviated administration and a line from the musical referring to "one brief shining moment that was known as Camelot." The association became a lasting epithet (some would say myth) defining Kennedy's term in office and the country at that time.[6] Although musicals would continue to be produced, they never again would occupy such a powerful position on the Broadway stage.

As the 1960s progressed, new dramatists and types of drama began to alter the world of American theater. The brightest star among the young playwrights was Edward Albee. Among such accomplished plays of the 1960s as *A Delicate Balance*, which won the Pulitzer Prize for drama in 1967, *The Sandbox* (first produced in 1960), *The American Dream* (1961), and *Tiny Alice* (1964), *Who's Afraid of Virginia Woolf?* stands out. The play opened on Broadway in 1962 and won both the Drama Critics' Circle Award and a Tony for best play of the year. The Pulitzer Prize drama jury recommended the play to the administering board, but the board rejected the recommendation because of the strong language and violent verbal clashes between husband and wife in the play. Albee, influenced by absurdist drama, presents a couple whose lives have become largely meaningless, and whose attacks on each other include the husband's destruction of the imaginary purpose they had jointly created in imagining that they had once had a child. Albee helped to bring before the public a worldview that saw life as lacking the sorts of large, eternal truths that made life meaningful and bearable, substituting instead a world in which individuals must seek out their own meaning.

The new star of comedy was Neil Simon, who had honed his writing skills in early television on *Your Show of Shows* (1950–54), starring Sid Caesar and Imogene Coca. Simon was prolific during the 1960s, producing nine hit comedies in the decade, each examining a particular aspect of contemporary life. Finding comedy in discordant personalities, he created a pair of very different brothers in *Come Blow Your Horn* (1961), a spontaneous young bride and conservative husband in *Barefoot in the Park* (1963), and most famously the mismatched roommates, compulsively tidy Felix Unger and the slob Oscar Madison, in *The Odd Couple* (1965). *The Odd Couple* starred two of the great comic actors of the century in Art Carney and Walter Matthau, and translated on both the large and small screens into highly successful film (1967) and television (1970–75) versions, the former teaming Jack Lemmon with Matthau, the latter substituting Tony Randall and Jack Klugman. No Simon play better demonstrates his ability to build characters with whom, one or the other, almost everyone can identify. In his later plays of the 1960s, such as *Promises, Promises* (1968) and *The Last of the Red-Hot Lovers* (1969), Simon turned to the sexual revolution for comic situations. Although critics debated the quality of Simon's plays, few denied that, for better or worse, he had influenced the shape of American popular comedy.

Even greater change than one sees in the plays of Albee and Simon was on the way. Some of the great social issues of the day—racial justice, feminism, the antiwar movement, the continued rise of rock music, and sexual freedom—left their mark on American drama.

The two most important African American dramatists of the decade were Lorraine Hansberry and LeRoi Jones, who changed his name to Imamu Amiri Baraka in 1965. Hansberry became the first African American woman to have a play on Broadway when *A Raisin in the Sun* opened in 1959. The play chronicled, following Hansberry's own family plight, the difficulties of a black family trying to move from a Chicago apartment into a nice house in a white neighborhood. Critics applauded the play for its sophisticated depth and realism in tackling racial and gender issues, and for its excellent performances, especially by Sidney Poitier as Walter Lee Younger, a brother in the family. Some African Americans, however, took issue with the play, seeing it as championing an imitation of white middle-class values and noting its use of terms such as "Negro" and "colored" that were increasingly rejected by black activists during the 1960s as white-imposed designations.

A Raisin in the Sun also was turned into a successful film in 1961, with Poitier reprising his stage role. In 1973, a musical version, *Raisin*, appeared on Broadway. A second Hansberry play, *The Sign in Sidney Brustein's Window*, opened on Broadway in 1964. This play consisted mainly of white characters, including a homosexual, as Hansberry demonstrated her ability to explore not only racial and gender but also sexual and political issues. Unfortunately, this very talented playwright died in 1965 of cancer. The title of a compilation of her writings transformed into a 1969 off-Broadway hit summed up her great potential and the tragic loss: *To Be Young, Gifted, and Black.*

Baraka's decision to replace a name that he associated with slavery with one denoting black America's African roots was consistent with what he was portraying in his drama. Baraka served in the air force after college and later edited a literary magazine, publishing avant-garde white writers like Gregory Corso, Allen Ginsburg, and Jack Kerouac. He increasingly was coming to believe that writers must force change, a position that he argued in a 1965 essay, "The Revolutionary Theater." Baraka's *Dutchman* had foreshadowed this explicit call to revolution in 1964. *Dutchman* depicts the ultimately forbidden relationship in a racist society, between a black man and a white woman. Calling to mind the myth of the Flying Dutchman, who is condemned to wander the seas forever until he locates a woman who will remain faithful to him, the play inverts sexual and racial stereotypes. Lulu enters a subway car and proceeds to try to goad a black man into a sexual dance with her. Heavy in myth in a departure from the realism of most previous African American drama, the play shows Lulu eating an apple when she enters and announcing, "Eating apples is always the first step." The male character's name, "Clay," calls to mind the biblical Adam, created from clay. When Clay finally is roused to anger and threatens Lulu, she stabs him to death in a parodic inversion of the sex act, then turns her attention to another young African American who has entered the subway car. The cycle of destruction, the play implies, will continue.

Dutchman won an Obie for best new play of the year. Obie Awards, given to off-Broadway productions, often honor cutting-edge drama, and that was the case with Baraka's play. Other important productions by Baraka in the 1960s include three other provocative plays produced in 1964: *The Baptism*, featuring a minister and a homosexual in a Baptist church, and attacking religious and sexual hypocrisies; *The Toilet*, wherein a group of African American boys beat up a Puerto Rican who has made a sexual advance in a letter to one of them; and *The Slave*, with its lengthy argument between a black activist and a white liberal couple while explosions occur outside. Near the end of *The Slave*, Walker, once the wife's lover, kills her husband. An explosion destroys much of the house and fatally wounds the wife, who dies thinking that Walker has also killed her children. The play calls into question virtually every aspect of racial relations, including the "cause" and the efficacy of violent revolution.

Megan Terry was a major figure in the rise of feminist drama, through both her own writing and her leadership in supporting new venues for little known but talented playwrights. Terry helped to found the New York Open Theater and was its playwright-in-residence from 1963 to 1968. In the 1970s, she moved to Omaha, Nebraska, to join a feminist theater group, the Omaha Magic Theater. Terry's experimentation was largely responsible for development of the transformation play, which requires actors to engage in continuous improvisation, transforming the play in response to changing settings, incidents in the plot, and nuances in character development. Her transformation plays include *Calm Down Mother* (1965), *The Gloaming* (1965), *Keep Tightly Closed in a Cool Dry Place* (1965), and *Comings and Goings* (1966).

Terry also was an important pioneer in using drama to protest the Vietnam War. Her *Viet Rock: A Folk War Movie*, produced by the Open Theater in 1966, was the first significant play about the war. The play departs from traditional musicals in important ways, including its use of rock music and interaction between players and audience. In *Viet Rock*, the war machine is sexist and support for the war the product of the American genius for advertising. At the end of the play, all the performers drop to the ground amid giant explosions, with Americans and Vietnamese killed indiscriminately. A coda, however, offers hope for the future, with the actors rising and entering the audience, each actor touching a viewer's hand, face, or hair.

Some avant-garde groups, such as the San Francisco Mime Troupe and the Bread and Puppet Theater of New York, took their productions into the audience and onto the street to establish a unified voice with the protesters. The Bread and Puppet Theater used ten-foot high puppets that appeared in silent protest against the war in antiwar parades. The puppets were the work of the theater's leader, Peter Schumann, a sculptor and choreographer from Germany. One of the puppets, Uncle Fatso, a corpulent version of Uncle Sam, often appeared in parades wearing an "All the Way with LBJ" button and leading captive Jesus and the disciples (depicting the Vietnamese). In 1966, Bread and Puppet picketed at St. Patrick's Cathedral in New York to protest Cardinal Spellman's call for victory in the war. Participants wore black cowls, and a woman playing Mary attempted to place a bloody Jesus doll on the cathedral steps, only to be stopped by the police, who called her attempt littering.

Arthur Kopit combined reexamination of U.S. history in relation to Native Americans and myths of the Old West with opposition to the Vietnam War in *Indians*. The play, first produced on July 4, 1968, in London, attempts to debunk the supposed heroism of Buffalo Bill Cody and shed light on what the United States did to Native Americans. At the same time, past and present come together to draw parallels between government action against Native Americans at home and Vietnamese abroad.

As the antiwar demonstrations became theater themselves, dramatists tended to withdraw from the streets. Schumann's puppets, for example, increasingly became swallowed up in the huge crowds and frenetic activity and retreated back inside for indoor productions.

Opposition to the war in American society was part of a larger whole of antitraditionalism. Many of the young rejected the status quo and received authority across the board, including their parents' views on sexual morality. Changing attitudes toward sex are discussed elsewhere in this book, especially in Chapter 2, "The World of Youth." Those new attitudes also appeared on the stage, sometimes in conjunction with rock music.

Hair: The American Tribal Love-Rock Musical premiered at Joseph Papp's off-Broadway Public Theater in December 1967. In April of the following year, it opened on Broadway. The story line involves a young man, Claude, due to be inducted into the military. He decides instead to burn his draft card, but mistakenly burns his library card. Claude's friends stage a party with drugs, leading to a hallucinogenic trip about war's futility. The next day, they encounter Claude at the induction station, his hair already cut military style, and he becomes invisible to them.

Hair appears rather tame by later standards but was shocking at the time for its male and female nudity and references to a wide range of sexual relationships, including interracial, gay, bisexual, and nonmonogamous. It also seemed to condone drug use and was the first Broadway musical to use rock music. The musical combined innovation with considerable talent, including effective performances by unknown actors and a musical score that won a Grammy. Among the songs that earned lasting popularity are "Aquarius/Let the Sunshine In," "Good Morning Starshine," and "Hair." *Hair* proved both artistically and commercially successful, running on Broadway for 1,750 performances.

Oh, Calcutta!: An Entertainment with Music appeared on Broadway in 1969 after attracting considerable attention earlier in the year at the off-Broadway Eden Theater. Focused more explicitly on the sexual revolution than *Hair*, it included nudity and a series of sketches depicting sexual problems and situations. At the same time, it attempted to satirize people's preoccupation with sex. Kenneth Tynan created the play using scenes from other artists, including John Lennon and a promising playwright named Sam

Shepard, who would establish himself as a leading dramatist in the following decade.

Other plays that extended sexual freedom onstage included *Dionysus 69* and *Boys in the Band*. *Dionysus 69*, produced by the Performance Group in 1968, used improvisational techniques and group participation, including inviting a girl from the audience each night to be made love to on the stage. *The Boys in the Band*, written by Mart Crowley, opened in New York in 1968, the first successful production completely on the subject of homosexuality. The setting of the play is a birthday party hosted by Michael to honor a Jewish friend, Harold. All the attendees are gay, but a heterosexual, Alan, a college friend of Michael's, arrives uninvited. Alan is not aware of his former friend's sexual orientation and is blatantly hostile to gays.

The Boys in the Band, by presenting public discussion of homosexuality and a range of generally sympathetic gay characters, became part of the gay liberation movement that developed in the late 1960s, partly in response to the Stonewall Inn riot. The riot grew out of a police raid on a Greenwich Village gay bar, the Stonewall Inn, on Friday night, June 27, 1969. A policeman reportedly hit a patron on the head, and bystanders started throwing rocks and a burning garbage can into the building. Hundred of police arrived and beat gays with billy clubs, and a riot continued over the weekend. The incident is often credited with giving birth to the gay liberation movement.

So much experimentation was going on in American drama during the 1960s that new venues of production were required. Especially in Greenwich Village and on the Lower East Side of New York, Off Off-Broadway was being born. Plays typically by unknown playwrights pushing the envelope in both content and form were available to audiences that wanted to see something other than traditional imitative drama that either reflected or aspired to Broadway. These plays occurred in churches, coffeehouses, and any other places that offered some space. Among these new sources of theater were La Mama Experimental Theater Club, begun in a basement coffeehouse; and Caffe Cino, in Joe Cino's café. Soon similar efforts were underway in other cities across the country. Sam Shepard, Megan Terry, and many other new playwrights brought excitement to their audiences and to American drama in such settings. Off Off-Broadway was a sure sign that drama in the 1960s was a living art form at least as much concerned with the present and future as with the past.

11
Travel

The decade of the 1960s witnessed travel on a scope never before seen and only imperfectly imagined. Much that occurred in the decade had been the stuff of dreams and science fiction only a few years earlier, but in the 1960s humankind moved from an earthbound existence to explore the planets and, at the close of the decade, walk on the moon. Horizons were opened that would forever beckon men and women onward into explorations of the heavens.

At the same time, earthly travel also was changing. If the average man or woman was not yet able to fly into space, flight closer to Earth was becoming more common. The 1960s was a decade of great advances in air travel, reducing reliance on that earlier agent of national expansion, the train. Throughout the 1960s, railroad travel declined, squeezed by airplanes for long journeys and the automobile for shorter trips. With interstate highways increasingly available, families enjoyed new opportunities for vacations, now able to see more of the natural wonders of their country.

These advances in travel did not come without a price. A flash fire killed three of America's new astronaut heroes, delaying the first trip to the moon. Increasing demand for cars led to heavier traffic and sometimes to greater concern by manufacturers for style and profit than safety. An obscure agreement by oil-producing countries in 1960 had a profound effect on the United States in the following decade.

The space program, however, overcame the tragic accident to reach President John F. Kennedy's goal of a successful moon landing. Ralph Nader and other consumer advocates precipitated a national commitment to automobile safety, leading Congress to pass legislation to make the highways safer. Even environmental legislation became law before the end of the decade to protect the air that motorists and their fellow citizens breathed.

SPACE TRAVEL

The United States had come to think of itself as the most powerful nation in the world and the leader in all things important—as Henry Lee had spoken of George Washington on the first president's death, "first in war, first in peace." It was shocking, then, for U.S. citizens to recognize that their nation's primary Cold War rival, the Soviet Union, was first in the space race. That realization hit in 1957 when Russia launched its satellite, *Sputnik I*, into orbit. By 1961, the United States was still behind, as Russia became the first nation to put a man, Yuri Gagarin, into space on April 12, but the United States was coming up fast and would soon pull ahead.

President Kennedy, in the same year that saw Yuri Gagarin travel in space, declared, "I believe that this nation should commit itself to achieving the goal, before this decade is out, of landing a man on the moon and returning him safely to the earth."[1] The young president did not live to see his goal reached, nor had he initiated the American space program; however, he gave it a drive and focus essential to energize both the taxpaying public and the aerospace industry.

The National Aeronautics and Space Administration (NASA) was created in 1958, the year after *Sputnik I*. NASA's first major space program, called Mercury after the Greek messenger of the gods, began the same year with the goal of putting Americans into space. Seven astronauts were selected in 1959 to carry out the Mercury missions and instantly became America's new heroes: M. Scott Carpenter, L. Gordon Cooper, John Glenn, Virgil I. "Gus" Grissom, Walter M. Schirra, Alan B. Shepard, Jr., and Donald "Deke" Slayton. Their exploits were later chronicled in the book *We Seven* (1962). Other programs were developed to move the lunar project forward, including the Gemini and Apollo programs. Gemini consisted of two-person spacecraft designed to test systems and maneuvers necessary for space exploration, such as spacewalks and dockings with other spacecraft. The Apollo program would fulfill President Kennedy's lunar-landing goal.

Also in the 1960s, other space programs gathered important information about the moon and planets. Lunar Orbiter flights mapped the surface of the moon, and Surveyor craft landed on the surface to gather data concerning the lunar environment, both programs vital to later moon landings by humans. Mercury probes explored planets, principally Venus (the planet closest to Earth) and Mars (believed to have Earthlike characteristics such as seasonal changes and polar ice caps). Mariner flights would reach Mercury in the 1970s.

The United States began manned flights in 1961 with a series of Mercury launches. Less than a month after Gagarin's success, Alan Shepard became the first American to reach space, a fifteen-minute excursion aboard *Freedom 7*. Gus Grissom followed Shepard into space in July on *Liberty 7*, although the capsule sank on landing in the Atlantic Ocean. The first American to orbit the Earth was actually a chimpanzee named Enos, who made two revo-

John Glenn became the first American to orbit earth on February 20, 1962, averaging 17,400 miles per hour in the *Friendship 7* capsule.
Source: Photofest, Inc.

lutions around the planet on a three-hour twenty-one minute flight. The Russians retained their lead, as their second manned flight took Gherman Titov seventeen times around Earth.

The United States continued to chase Russia during the next few years, gradually inching ahead even while Russia scored public-relations victories.

Russia claimed the first dual flight in 1962 with two cosmonauts maneuvering their vehicles close together. The Russians later put the first woman into space (Valentina Tereshkova in 1963), launched the first multiperson flight (with three cosmonauts in 1964 aboard *Voskhod I*), and inaugurated floating in space (Alexei Leonov in 1965).

The first U.S. manned orbital flight, on February 20, 1962, launched John Glenn not only into space but later into the U.S. Senate. Glen orbited the Earth three times in the capsule he named *Friendship 7*, seeing four sunsets before he landed, and introducing the term "splashdown" into the English language. The flight made Glenn the first great American space hero. Later that year, Scott Carpenter made another three-orbit flight and Walter Schirra circled the Earth six times. Mariner II passed by Venus on August 27, the first successful interplanetary probe. Gordon Cooper made a thirty-four hour, twenty-two orbital flight in 1963.

The initial unmanned Gemini test flights occurred in 1964 and 1965 to test booster and spacecraft systems; Gemini III, in 1965, was the first U.S. two-man orbit, with Gus Grissom and John Young aboard. Meanwhile, Mariner IV sent back twenty-one pictures of Mars, showing Martian craters and indicating an atmosphere mainly of carbon dioxide. The first commercial satellite, *Early Bird*, was launched to transmit telephone and television signals. As the year progressed, four more successful Gemini flights occurred, with Edward White walking in space by means of a personal propulsion gun; Gordon and Pete Conrad demonstrating the feasibility of a moon mission by staying aloft eight days; and Gemini VIA, manned by Walter Schirra and Thomas Stafford, docking with Frank Borman and James Lovell's Gemini VII.

Both Russia and the United States managed soft lunar landings with unmanned spacecraft in 1966, but the year was primarily the story of several additional Gemini flights. Astronauts piled up valuable experience walking in space and docking with other craft, including unmanned vehicles. In addition, Lunar Orbiter I took the first pictures of Earth from the back side of the moon.

Then tragedy struck on January 27, 1967, as a three-man crew—Roger Chaffee, Gus Grissom, and Edward White—were engaging in preflight preparations for the Apollo I flight, which already had been hit with a number of engineering and training problems. As the three men engaged in a simulation exercise within the spacecraft, a fire broke out. The pure oxygen fire generated intense heat, and the three men died quickly of asphyxiation from toxic gasses before anyone could get the door to the craft open. Ironically, the Russians also lost one of their space explorers that year, as cosmonaut Komarov died on reentry. Some Americans questioned the advisability of continuing manned space flights. Even scientists argued for unmanned flights, not only for safety reasons but because, so the argument went, they could gather the necessary information and do so less expensively.

Other U.S. missions were more successful in 1967. Lunar Orbiter V pho-
tomapped the lunar surface, and Mariner V passed by Venus, measuring
the density of the planet's atmosphere.

The first manned Apollo flight did not take place until October 11, 1968,
when Walter Schirra, Donn Eisele, and Walter Cunningham on Apollo VII
carried out an eleven-day test of their command and service modules. They
conducted eight propulsion firings and sent back seven live television
broadcasts. Apollo VIII was launched on December 21, and Frank Borman,
James Lovell, and William Anders orbited the moon on Christmas Eve.
Apollo X, in May 1969, came close to the moon. Their mission was a pru-
dent step toward the first landing on the moon, but almost no one now
remembers their role, which was to separate the lunar module from the
command module and descend to within approximately nine miles of the
moon's surface. Eugene Cernan and Thomas Stafford in the lunar module
(with John Young back in the command module) must have longed to do
that final engine burn and land. Instead they set the stage for Neil Armstrong to be forever remembered as the first human being to walk on the
moon.

While preparations were under way for the first manned landing on the
moon, unmanned spacecraft continued to explore more distant regions of
the solar system. Mariner VI, launched February 24, 1969, flew by Mars on
July 31, transmitting seventy-five pictures of the planet. Mariner VII was
not far behind; launched on March 27, it photographed Mars on August 5,
recording 126 images of the Martian world.

The climactic space effort of the 1960s began on July 16 with the takeoff
of Apollo XI, carrying Neil Armstrong, Buzz Aldrin, and Michael Collins.
On July 20, Armstrong stepped onto the lunar surface, commenting for history that he was taking "one small step for man, one giant step for
mankind." Almost as memorable was Armstrong's earlier declaration
when the lunar module touched down: "The *Eagle* has landed." The landing spot bore the name Tranquillity Base on the Sea of Tranquillity, names
reflecting both the receptive terrain of that portion of the moon and the
hope for a future of peace and brotherhood among the nations of the world.

Armstrong was followed onto the moon by Aldrin; together they collected a treasure of lunar rocks and soil for analysis. As the two moon
walkers worked for about twenty-one and one-half hours on Earth's once
distant natural satellite, Michael Collins remained aboard the command
module, *Columbia*. Pictures of the moon landing filled television screens
throughout the world, as the era of science fiction transformed into a new
day of science fact.

The United States clearly had taken a major lead over the Russians in the
space race, but in a desperate attempt to cover some of the distance between them, Russia attempted an unmanned lunar landing at approximately the same time to gather samples from the surface. In fact, had the

Russians succeeded, scientists favoring unmanned projects would have had more evidence with which to argue their case that the same benefits could be gained without the risk and expense of sending humans into space. But that was not to be. The Russian craft, Luna 15, crashed onto the moon on July 21.

One more lunar landing would occur before the end of the 1960s. Apollo XII, despite being struck by lightning after takeoff, reached the moon in November. The flight, featuring astronauts Pete Conrad, Alan Bean, and Richard Gordon, was successful, and more moon samples ("moon rocks" they would be called by the media) returned to Earth with the crew.

The space programs in the 1960s reestablished America's supremacy in space even as its Earthbound might was being severely tested by the war in Vietnam. President Kennedy's call to conquer the moon had been answered affirmatively. The goal was reached, and the world would never again merely look upward and wonder. Now Americans could truly aspire to reach the heavens.

There also were many practical benefits to the space programs. Developments occasioned by Apollo research began to reach into offices, homes, and hospitals. Smaller computers required for space flights led to desktop computers; miniature cameras suitable for handling by astronauts yielded more compact and efficient handheld video cameras and miniature televisions; sensors to monitor astronauts' health found important applications in hospitals. Even the fastener Velcro soon began turning up on people's clothes until hardly a closet would lack its presence. If the Vietnam War looms as the United States' worst failure in the 1960s, the exploration of space stands as the nation's most extraordinary achievement in the areas of technology and the national spirit.

SPACE TRAVEL ON THE BIG AND SMALL SCREENS

Science fiction had long been a staple of the cinema. In the 1960s, with reality proving even more remarkable than fantasy, filmmakers turned to space in more profound ways. The ultimate space film of the decade would prove to be *2001: A Space Odyssey* (1968), directed by Stanley Kubrick. Minus the usual fare of science-fiction films, such as monsters from outer space, the transforming effects of radiation, or the impending destruction of Earth by approaching meteorites, and also without any romance or sex, the film seriously tackles the elusive concepts of time and space.

2001 also explores human origins and human nature, and does so in largely visual, nonverbal, and mythic ways. There is little dialogue, a major character is a computer named HAL, and plot is a somewhat amorphous ingredient. Although William Phillips has identified plotlines involving four groups—"man-apes, scientists, a computer and two astronauts, and the starchild"[2]—the tradition of plot as a logical sequence of events yields to a flow of time that seems unusually prescient for a film of the 1960s, perhaps because Kubrick did extensive consulting with scientists and aerospace organizations to make his film scientifically plausible.

The film moves from 4 million B.C.E. to a point transcending time. Kubrick's reliance on the visual ($6.5 million of the film's total budget of $10.5 million went for special effects)[3] contributed mightily to the mythic dimension of *2001*. The film asks vital questions about humankind through its images. An early scene, for example, is of a black monolith discovered by humanlike apes, the large black object representing the creation of imagination when the apes touch it. They then begin making tools. As an ape tosses a tool into the air, the object dissolves into a spacecraft. What, the film inquires, has humankind's creativity really wrought? Is humanity to be defined by creative tools or destructive weapons?

As the film proceeds, the one astronaut who has survived HAL's attempts at control tours the universe as past, present, and future merge. Old and young at the same time, the astronaut is reborn as a starchild. There no longer is a beginning, middle, and end, but an eternal process of death and rebirth.

Also in 1968 *Planet of the Apes*, directed by Franklin J. Schaffner, was released. Far more concrete and traditional than *2001*—with a clearly defined plot; battles; a love interest for the protagonist, astronaut George Taylor, played by Charlton Heston; and some humorous moments of self-conscious play with the simian makeup—*Planet of the Apes* nonetheless stakes out some serious social ground. The space travel here has misfired and it turns out that the astronauts have landed, not on a distant planet, but on Earth two thousand years in the future, but an Earth devastated by the technological failures of the human race. Space travel has inadvertently transformed into time travel.

On this future Earth, apes rule in a supposedly utopian society, with humans as mere animals without the power of speech. The ape society, though, proves far less than ideal. Apes periodically attempt to wipe out as many of the humans as possible, take others for scientific experiments, and enter into the old arena of conflict between science and religion as their leader hides scientific fact to maintain the political-religious ideology of ape supremacy.

Issues of racism, uses of technology, dangers of science (but also the importance of seeking the truth), and the nature of humanity permeate the film. Finally, adventure and fantasy probably cloud the more serious issues for all but the most socially conscious viewers.

Space travel also reached the small screen in the 1960s. Producer Gene Roddenberry created *Star Trek* as a futuristic version of the western television series *Wagon Train*, an approach thoroughly consistent with President Kennedy's theme of the New Frontier. The earlier series had run from 1957 to 1965, chronicling the journeys of American pioneers westward.

Roddenberry chose a young actor named William Shatner to fill the Ward Bond role as wagonmaster, or in this case, captain of the good ship *Enterprise*. Shatner replaced Jeffrey Hunter, who played the role in the show's pilot, and had co-starred with John Wayne in the classic western *The Searchers* (1956).

Leonard Nimoy's Mr. Spock, DeForest Kelley's Dr. "Bones" McCoy, and other interesting figures, male and female, helped Captain Kirk go "boldly where no man has gone before." Although the NBC series lasted just three seasons (1966–69) and never finished higher than fifty-second in the Nielsen ratings, it spawned a huge number of dedicated, lifelong fans (the Trekkies), sequels on television and film (the latter featuring several of the original cast), and eternal reruns. Governor Nelson Rockefeller of New York was an ardent fan, and President Gerald Ford named the nation's first reusable orbiting space shuttle after the *Enterprise*.

Star Trek was not the only television series to be inspired by the real space efforts of the country. *My Favorite Martian* on CBS featured Ray Walston as a visitor from Mars not much enamored of planet Earth. His earthly stay lasted three seasons (1963–66). Another CBS series, *Lost in Space*, appealed to the younger set with its story of a family parented by Guy Williams of Zorro fame and June Lockhart, who earlier had shared billing with television's Lassie. The family, off for a five-year jaunt to another star system, ran into vehicle trouble at the hands of a saboteur and became, as the title stated, lost in space. Their series of encounters with giant vegetables and other villains also lasted three seasons (1965–68). Space travel, well before the first moon landing, had clearly become not just a scientific endeavor but an important part of American popular culture.

THE AUTOMOBILE

Americans had been driving automobiles for more than half a century when the 1960s dawned, but as with several other modes of transportation the decade was a time of great change. The 1950s had featured the large and ornate in cars. High tail fins and a lot of ornamentation were popular, but under the influence of smaller foreign imports, including the German Volkswagen, consumers began to prefer simpler, sleeker, more compact cars. In addition, both the number of cars and drivers grew dramatically. Car registrations increased by 25 million during the decade, and urban passenger-car travel increased by almost two hundred million miles.[4] By 1969, more than 80% of U.S. families owned at least one car. The four largest U.S. automakers (General Motors, Ford, Chrysler, American Motors) increased their gross revenues from about $20 billion at the beginning of the decade to nearly $47 billion by the end.[5]

One of the first automotive superstars of the 1960s was the Ford Thunderbird. Originally introduced in 1955, the Thunderbird had grown so at-

The Ford Mustang was advertised as a "young people's car." Ford provided customers with custom-made cars, including notchback, fastback, and convertible models. Printed with permission of AP/Wide World Photos.

tractive by 1961 that President-elect Kennedy requested twenty-five for his inaugural parade. Having sold out of its stock, Ford was not able to oblige the young president. Another Ford to win considerable popularity in the 1960s was the Mustang, launched in 1964 and billed as a young people's car—with 418,000 sold in the first year.[6] Buyers included Frank Sinatra and actress Debbie Reynolds. Designed by Lee Iacocca, who later would save Chrysler from bankruptcy while chairman of that company, the Mustang came in notchback, fastback, and convertible styles with lots of options so that the customer could have almost an individually designed vehicle. Children could have their own toy Mustangs, available from dealers for $12.95.

The Studebaker Company produced an Avanti in 1962 (for the model year 1963) that turned many a head with its fiberglass, angular body, and cockpit-style overhead controls. Studebaker soon went out of business, but a private consortium took over the Avanti and still continues to produce it.

Another of the decade's most popular cars was the Chevrolet Corvette, long America's only sports car. Its luxurious interior, quick acceleration, and easy handling made it a long-lived favorite, especially after introduction of the Corvette Stingray. The 1963 original Stingray had a split rear window that was altered in later models. Today the 1963 Stingray is a leading collector's item.

The 1965 Oldsmobile Toronado introduced front-wheel drive to the American mass market and delivered on its promise to provide greater traction and easier handling. Other favorites in the 1960s were the Mercury Cougar, something of an upgraded version of the Mustang; the Chevrolet Camaro, 220,000 of which sold in its first year; and the Pontiac Firebird Trans Am with its distinctive sexy striping and a name borrowed from the Trans-American road race.

The most infamous car of the 1960s was the Chevrolet Corvair, first released in 1959 for the 1960 model year. The Corvair had a rear-mounted, air-cooled engine and a stylish exterior that appealed to consumers. When a convertible version appeared in 1962, the Corvair became even more popular. However, the car seemed to suffer an unusual number of accidents. Ralph Nader, then a young lawyer only a few years removed from Harvard Law School, was so concerned about its dangers that in response he published one of the most influential books of the decade, *Unsafe at Any Speed: The Designed-in Dangers of the American Automobile* (1965). The book strongly condemned the Corvair, claiming that the car's design caused it to oversteer and go out of control.

Nader, a squeaky-clean consumer advocate, readily survived investigation and harassment by General Motors, who hired a private investigator to get something on him. Nader's work led to abandonment of the Corvair by GM and the birth of serious congressional concern for automobile safety. Nader was asked to testify before Congress, which passed the National Traffic and Motor Vehicle Safety Act in 1966, asserting federal authority over automotive design. Nader, aided by legions of idealistic young Americans known as "Nader's Raiders," took on an array of safety issues in the decade, among them dangers in the meat, natural gas, and coal industries. In response, a large body of important safety legislation came out of Congress to help the American public stay healthy.

Environmental legislation also followed the increased driving, especially regarding automobile emissions: the Motor Vehicle Air Pollution Control Act of 1965 and, later, the Energy Policy and Conservation Act of 1975.

The growing popularity of the automobile had its origins in the efforts by President Dwight Eisenhower to create a new interstate highway system for both civilian and military use. The resulting Federal Aid Highway Act of 1956 authorized a National System of Interstate and Defense Highways networking for 42,500 miles across the United States. As construction proceeded in the 1960s, increasing numbers of families began to vacation at considerable distances from their homes. Greater ease of travel benefited national parks and other natural wonders throughout the nation. Motels, gasoline stations, and chain restaurants mushroomed along the highways

Ralph Nader's influential book *Unsafe at Any Speed* exposed the dangers of the Chevrolet Corvair and other automobiles caused by design flaws. Source: Photofest, Inc.

to accommodate the new tourists. Touring also became more aesthetically pleasing as the Highway Beautification Act of 1965, pushed by President Lyndon B. Johnson and his wife Lady Bird, encouraged states to keep billboards away from highways. Drivers found the language of the road enriched by such terms as "merging," "off ramp," and "exit."

A victim of the new interstate highway system was the old one—Route 66. Dedicated in 1926 though not completed until 1937, the highway traversed eight states (Illinois, Missouri, Kansas, Oklahoma, Texas, New Mexico, Arizona, and California) and some 2,400 miles. Route 66 led past some

Martin Milner and George Maharis starred on the television series
Route 66 from 1960 to 1964. Source: Photofest, Inc.

of the nation's most beautiful natural sites and stimulated both travel and
the imagination. Woody Guthrie and Pete Seeger sang of it during the Great
Depression, Jack Kerouac wrote of it in the 1950s, and the Columbia Broadcasting System filmed it. From 1960 until 1964, the television audience
could travel the highway on the series *Route 66* with Martin Milner and
George Maharis (in a red Corvette). As the highway declined and large seg-

ments closed, disappearing into dirt and grass, many fans of the romantic route sought with some success, through the U.S. Highway 66 Association and other groups, to keep Route 66 alive.

More people became "commuters" during the 1960s, driving longer distances to work. Automobile use steadily became both cause and effect of changing lifestyles, encouraging movement to ever expanding suburbs but also becoming more necessary as less of the family's life revolved around the immediate neighborhood. Businesses followed workers out of the city, and taxes followed both, creating serious economic problems for the inner cities of America. The financial problems for inner cities and neighborhood businesses accelerated as the suburban shopping mall became the place to go for every purchase from groceries to galoshes—as well as a favorite teen hangout. The car had transformed the life of the nation.

Still in the future were worries about gasoline shortages, but the first warning bell had rung, even if almost no one heard it. After oil companies lowered the prices they were paying for oil, five nations (Iran, Iraq, Kuwait, Saudi Arabia, and Venezuela) met in 1960 to address ways to restore prices and control production. They agreed to make their organization permanent. Not until the 1970s would many Americans focus on the Organization of Petroleum Exporting Countries. By then, OPEC had signed up still more countries and instituted an oil embargo against the United States in reaction to the 1973 Arab–Israeli war.

MOTORING IN THE MEDIA

Films and television reflected the growing popularity of automobiles during the 1960s and contributed to an image of cars (at least certain ones) as sexy and adventurous. As the red Corvette previously mentioned transported its two occupants from adventure to adventure along Route 66, plenty of other vehicles were journeying across the nation's screens.

Steve McQueen in *Bullitt* (1968) pursued murderers up and down the hills of San Francisco in a wild car chase that would influence later cinematic chases in *The French Connection* (1971) and beyond. Viewers were even taken inside McQueen's Mustang in camera shots outward through the windshield. Ultimately, the Mustang got the better of the criminals' Dodge Charger in the twelve-minute chase, much of the driving done by McQueen himself. McQueen did even more on-screen driving the next decade in *Le Mans* (1971).

Viewers of *The Graduate* (1967), especially students, envied Dustin Hoffman his graduation present, an Alfa Spider, the last car completely designed by the renowned Battista Pininfarina of Turin, Italy. James Bond not only regularly got the girl and the criminal but drove eye-catching automobiles heavily adorned with imaginative gadgets. The Aston Martin DB5 in *Goldfinger* (1964), a British sports car synonymous with aristocratic style, even had an ejector seat and radar. Perhaps most appealing were its machine guns, something many motorists have longed for when cut off by a rude driver. The James Bond film *You Only Live Twice* (1967, starring Sean Connery) featured a Toyota convertible 2000GT, a particularly beautiful product designed to improve Toyota's image; and the Agent 007 flick *On Her Majesty's Secret Service* (1969, with George Lazenby) showed its hero in an Aston DBS and a Mercury Cougar.

The car most associated with gadgets may be Batman's vehicle in the television series *Batman* that ran from 1966 to 1968 on ABC. Although the vehicle was equipped for speed and fighting Gotham City evildoers, the show, starring Adam West as Batman and Burt Ward as youthful sidekick Robin, received an award from the National Safety Council because the car's occupants always buckled up before taking off. The show during its brief run attained such a level of high camp that everybody who was anybody appeared on at least one of its episodes, including Liberace, Jerry Lewis, Sammy Davis, Jr., Edward G. Robinson, and former JFK press secretary Pierre Salinger.

At the opposite end from the stylistic vehicles usually seen on theater and home screens was the truck (at least it appeared to be a truck) loaded up with the earthly possessions of Jed Clampett (starring former dance and song man Buddy Ebsen) and family as they made their way from the Ozarks to Beverly Hills after striking oil in *The Beverly Hillbillies* (1962–71). The truck and family appeared in the lead-in to each episode, with the vehicle becoming a permanent image in television history. One of the most popular television shows of the 1960s, the CBS comedy skyrocketed to Number One in the ratings in its third week and stayed there for two years. Viewers loved the barely literate but wise Clampetts who inevitably knew better than their stuck-up neighbors and eternally confused bank manager, Milburn Drysdale (played by Raymond Bailey), who drooled over their money for nine seasons. Granny's possum-belly stew seemed just what the doctor ordered for the United States during the nation's psychological trauma following the assassination of President Kennedy and the social turmoil of a country struggling with civil rights and Vietnam. The eight most-watched half-hour television shows (as of 1998) were all *Beverly Hillbillies* episodes from early 1964.[7]

Traveling continued to be a popular television theme throughout the decade. *Green Acres* (1965–71 on CBS) was a reverse *Beverly Hillbillies*, this time a wealthy couple moving from the big city to an antiquated farm near Hooterville. The husband, a big-time lawyer played by Eddie Albert, and his voluptuous but scatterbrained wife (Eva Gabor), find they have a lot more to learn from than teach the Hooterville inhabitants, though the Eva Gabor character turns out to have a commonsense understanding that her loving but eternally confused hubby lacks.

No consideration of television travels in the 1960s could ignore the eternal popularity of *Gilligan's Island*. Perhaps the most illogical television show ever filmed, it nonetheless captivated the American audience, who tuned in from 1964 to 1967 on CBS to watch Bob Denver's Gilligan and the rest of the group struggle to escape from their South Pacific island on which they were marooned after a three-hour cruise and the wrecking of the *SS Minnow*. None of this, of course, made any sense. Nor did the show even attempt to explain the constant supply of Mary Ann's beautiful clothes and Thurston Howell III's alcoholic beverages. The clash of cultures, as with *Beverly Hillbillies* and *Green Acres*, provided much of the humor, as Thurston (Jim Backus) sought to maintain his upper-crust lifestyle, and wisdom steadily showed up in the strangest places, such as in Gilligan despite his weekly fumbling of attempts to escape the island. Symbolic of the essential illogic of the series was the popularity of Mary Ann, played by Dawn Wells, who had little to do on the show but look pretty yet received more fan letters than any of the other cast members. The show spawned three reunion telecasts from 1978 to 1981 and continues to be popular on reruns.

PLANES, TRAINS, AND TRUCKS

The airplane became a common mode of travel for Americans in the 1960s, both home and abroad, in the latter case largely eliminating ships as a means of crossing the oceans. What took days by ocean liner was reduced by air to hours.

The introduction of the jet plane at the end of the 1950s was crucial to expanded air travel. Amid general prosperity, vacationers as well as business travelers chose to fly. In 1960, airplane passengers numbered about 56 million; that number almost tripled by 1969, to over 158 million.[8]

Boeing dominated plane production with the 707 and 747, and along with Douglas Aircraft (later merging into McDonnell Douglas) and Lockheed had most of the world's business. Pan American announced in 1966 an order for twenty-five of the new 490-seat 747s, the first plane with two aisles. The 747—able to cruise faster than other jets (an average of 633 miles per hour) and fly farther (6,000 miles)—proved so reliable and popular that it continued in production beyond the end of the century.

France and England stirred the airways with their jointly developed supersonic *Concorde*, which flew from Seattle to New York on its first trans-U.S. flight in 1969. The *Concorde* appealed to the rich, but never proved sufficiently cost-effective to make a big dent in aviation travel or to induce the United States to produce an American version.

One of the negative effects of increased air travel was a burst of skyjackings. In 1968 alone, eighteen successful hijackings of U.S. planes occurred, and that number rose to thirty the following year.[9] Fortunately, improved security procedures at airports quickly reduced the threat, leaving the skies more crowded yet relatively safe. Plane crashes would continue to draw heavy attention from the media and public, like the 1960 collision of two airliners over Staten Island, but travelers statistically would be less likely to be injured or killed in a plane than in an automobile.

As automobile and plane travel increased, train travel declined. Although the number of train passengers did not decline dramatically, those passengers tended to take shorter trips, often business commutes between neighboring cities or between an outlying area and the downtown business section. Miles traveled by trains dropped about 50% from the approximately 200 million miles passenger trains covered at the beginning of the decade. Miles actually traveled by passengers went from 21 million to 12 million miles.[10] The number of railroad passenger cars dipped correspondingly through the decade, from almost 26,000 to approximately 11,000.[11]

Railroad work remained labor intensive, helping to account for serious financial problems. The railroads attempted to make up in freight what they lacked in passengers. Although freight revenues increased slightly during the decade, by 1969 the total was only about what it had been twenty years earlier.[12] Americans came increasingly to see trains as antiquated for tourism, lacking the speed of the jet plane and the comfort and flexibility of the automobile.

Nonetheless, there were efforts to stem the bleeding by railroads, including plans to develop a high-speed Northeast Corridor between New York City and Washington, D.C. Several companies tried with some success to speed up freight service and started to diversify what they carried, including trash and garbage. They also increased the practice of "piggyback" trailer service, hauling trailers on flat cars, a practice officially known as TOFC (Trailer on Flat Car).

There is no denying that the overall importance of the railroad was in decline throughout the 1960s. Where once Americans looked to the railroad as their primary means of traveling long distances and saw train travel as pragmatic, comfortable, and even romantic, they had come to see the railroad, usually when they were forced to stop their cars at railroad crossings, as at best a somewhat useful hauler of various products, but not a conveyance for people. Occasionally, of course, people did think fondly of railroads, but they increasingly did so nostalgically, as of something more suitable for a brief foray into the past than a steady diet for the present.

The meeting of the Union Pacific and Central Pacific railroads at Promontory Point near Ogden, Utah, on May 10, 1869, symbolized the fusion of parts into one united country. The final, golden spike radiated throughout the practical and imaginative lives of the United States. One hundred years later, if there were a golden spike, it had been transformed into an American flag on the moon. When Americans looked to the new frontier, they saw not railroads but spaceships. They imagined not just one country but worlds brought into harmony.

Not even in hauling freight could trains exert dominance, for the 1960s also was an era of increasing truck transports. The same highways that encouraged the passenger car called forth the truck, and families and truckers came increasingly to share, not always pleasantly, the highway.

Manufacturers of trucks had gained valuable experience constructing heavy trucks for use in World War II and applied their expertise to domestic vehicles in postwar years. Various technological advances in the 1950s and early 1960s also contributed to the popularity of trucks for hauling freight: power steering, especially important for large, heavy tractor-trailers; individual front suspension and variable rear suspension; the "Jake Brake" engine brake system; more powerful diesel engines; and air conditioning, tinted windows, and other advancements in providing for the comfort of the trucker on long hauls.

By 1964, sales of U.S. commercial vehicles had reached 1.5 million annually. The number of Americans making their livelihood from trucking had reached 8 million by the mid-1960s. Over 18 million commercial vehicles were in use by the end of the decade, up some 5 million from the early 1960s.[13]

Motorists on the steadily improving highways of the 1960s were passing, or being passed by, an almost unlimited array of goods transported by trucks, including logs, lumber, mail, livestock, gasoline, food stuffs (often refrigerated), alcoholic beverages, and other automobiles. Growing numbers of double trailers appeared on the better (and flatter) highways as haulers sought to maximize efficiency.

The variety in types of freight seemed almost equaled by variety in trucks. A name synonymous with truck is Mack, which produced its first vehicle in 1902 (actually a bus) and continued nonstop throughout the century. The Rapid Motor Vehicle Company brought out its first truck in the same year. Within the decade, Rapid Motor was part of the General Motors Truck Company. GMC continued to be a major player in the trucking industry during the 1960s and throughout the century. In 1960, GMC produced over 100,000 trucks. One of the most recognizable GMC rigs was the 1962 D series COE with its cube-shaped cab that gave the vehicle its "Crackerbox" nickname. At the end of the decade, the Kenworth K100 with a refrigerated trailer caused Kenworth's sales to quadruple in one year, from 1969 to 1970.

Certain trucking terms came into common usage by U.S. motorists and others: "rig" for the combination tractor (or cab) and trailer (sometimes dual trailers); "semitrailer" for the trailer pulled by the tractor, but usually shortened to "semi" and applied to the whole rig. As the 1960s began, a new type of enterprise arose in response to the new interstate highway system and increasing numbers of rigs on the road—the large truck stop catering especially to long-distance truckers. Tourists stopped in at the truck stops, too, when they were not flying to their destination. And the odds were good that both trucker and motorist would reach their destinations without having to stop even once at a railroad track to let a train pass.

12

Visual Arts

The decade of the 1960s was a time of tremendous variety, creativity, and aesthetic rebellion in visual art. Many painters, sculptors, photographers, and workers in mixed media not only pushed the aesthetic and conceptual envelope of art but ripped it apart. What was discovered within was troubling to some, especially traditionalists, but exciting and inspiring to many others. At the same time, the line between fine art and popular culture dissolved in the work of many of the new artists.

Despite the innovation, even revolution, in art, many older artists continued to work in traditional styles to considerable popular and/or critical acclaim. The old and the new shared, if not the same rooms in the house of visual art, at least the same house—an uneasy but nonetheless steady coexistence of traditional and revolutionary that proved much more difficult to maintain in many other realms (political, social, religious, etc.) of the 1960s.

So millions of Americans continued to love the realistic and emotional paintings of Andrew Wyeth, of the famous Wyeth family of painters that still attracts galleries of admirers in the early days of a new millennium. As the 1950s yielded to the 1960s, at a time when abstract expressionism still held sway before yielding to the even more revolutionary styles discussed later in this chapter, art historian John Canaday, writing in his book *Mainstreams of Modern Art*, praised Wyeth for "the most acute perceptions of personality, of the life in inanimate objects as ordinary as a weathered door."[1] Wyeth would soon disappear from critical examinations of art in the 1960s, but not from the approbation of the public.

Critics might visibly cringe at the mention of Norman Rockwell, but huge segments of the public loved his work throughout the 1960s, in fact, until and beyond his death in 1978. Rockwell's illustrations and paintings, most famously his covers for the *Saturday Evening Post*, captured the innocence of a small-town America that had only partly existed. Georgia O'Keefe visited New Mexico in 1929 and increasingly made that state her home, producing the paintings of bleached bones in the desert that may be her most famous works. She continued to paint throughout the 1960s until failing eyesight ended her painting career in the early 1970s. And, of course, Picasso lived throughout the decade, the most immortal of the painting immortals, extending his influence across all borders.

David Smith and the school of construction-sculpture, discussed later in this chapter, were firmly entrenched at the beginning of the 1960s, and that style never died out completely despite new directions in sculpture. The English sculptor Henry Moore, well established prior to World War II, lived on until 1986, his creations merging the curving lines of reclining figures with the imagined hills and valleys of the natural landscape, holes in the sculpture creating an interior as well as exterior reality. Alexander Calder, noted for his mobiles, lived until 1976. Louise Nevelson was born in Russia in 1899, grew up in Maine, and worked in a variety of media before finally receiving public recognition in her, and the century's, sixties, although she is almost never discussed in relation to 1960s sculpture. Her most recognizable works are large installation pieces in wood painted a dull black.

Photographers established prior to the 1960s continued to create artistic pictures and chronicle the important events of the world throughout the decade. Their names still live today: Ansel Adams, Edward Steichen, Man Ray, Harry Callahan, Minor White, Gordon Parks, William Eugene Smith, Walker Evans, Margaret Bourke-White.

Yet despite the fame and talent of these artists and others like them, they did not define the visual art of the 1960s. Their accomplishments still live, but they are not the focus of this chapter. The following sections instead explore the more unique developments of the 1960s, what, when we think back on the 1960s, we recognize as the visual embodiment of the spirit of the times.

ABSTRACT PAINTING

Abstract expressionism was the dominant style of painting from World War II to the 1960s. Focused in the so-called New York School, the movement included such important figures as Jackson Pollock, Franz Kline, and the Dutchborn Willem de Kooning. Abstract expressionism was the attempt to express powerful content through art as effectively as possible by removing all that is ephemeral and inessential and retaining what is intrinsic and essential. Cubists earlier in the century had sought to abstract out of familiar shapes and forms the essence of objects, analyze subject matter into its parts, and rearrange those elements. Abstract expressionists in the postwar years borrowed these techniques from their cubist predecessors.

By the 1960s, Pollock was dead following an automobile accident, but his influence continued. Pollock popularized the concept of "action painting," moving across a large canvas spread on the floor to drip, squirt, and fling paint onto the surface, using such simple instruments as housepainting brushes, syringes used for basting meat, and trowels. Despite the apparent randomness of Pollock's application, he maintained that he consistently remained in control of the painting process. Close examination of his paintings, such as *Autumn Rhythm* (1950), bears out that claim, with its complex lines and colors intertwining, as the title of the painting indicates, in visual rhythms.

Franz Kline, who died in 1962, was best known for his large black abstractions on white painted with the gestural strokes that supplied an alternate name for abstract expressionism—"gestural abstraction." Using housepainting brushes, Kline gestured with them as nonartists would with their hands, to express feeling and for emphasis. Critics have seen in Kline's figures echoes of constructions from the coal-mining area of Pennsylvania where he earlier lived, such as railway trestles and iron bridges. Kline's *Untitled* (1961) is representative with its black, rugged image reaching upward and to the left like vertical supports bending under the weight of a heavy bridge.

Willem de Kooning may have been the most influential of the abstract expressionists. De Kooning, who had moved to New York in the 1920s, saw himself within a long tradition of painting, a "painterly painter" to use a term more popular than abstract expressionism with some artists because it seemed a more neutral term regarding content and technique. Although highly abstract, with broad gestural strokes and multilayer painting, his pictures contained recognizable images as well as references to earlier paintings. Complex and metaphorical, they seemed created to express truths regarding the painter's environment and his own condition as an artist. De Kooning's *Detour* (1958) thus combines a focal shape evocative of a street sign with heavy brushwork and surrounding shapes and colors that imply improvisation; the totality of the effect prompts viewers to wonder about the personal message conveyed—just what, for example, the painting is calling the artist or viewer to detour around.

By the beginning of the 1960s, a reaction had set in against abstract expressionism, especially against its use of brushwork and cubist figures to imply three-dimensional space that supposedly denied the reality of flat paintings. Increasingly, regularity was preferred to the illusion of randomness, flat brushing or staining to heavy smearing, a depersonalized approach that emphasized color or the painting as object to the artist's individually expressed ideas and feelings. The impression sought by the new generation of abstractionists practicing what sometimes was referred to as "post-painterly painting" or "post-painterly abstraction" was a detachment that came to be labeled "cool." Because of the use of bright colors in the new acrylic and the absence of obvious brushwork, the style also was called "hard-edge painting."

Frank Stella has been called by art historian and critic Irving Sandler "the paradigmatic post-painterly painter."[2] Stella graduated from Princeton in 1958 and established his reputation in the 1960 exhibition at the Museum of Modern Art in New York entitled "Sixteen Americans." Stella's paintings were black canvases with parallel stripes about two and one-half inches wide. As the decade progressed, he moved to stripe paintings in a variety of colors and to paintings that featured bright colors and geometric shapes. Concerned with the painting as object, Stella helped to popularize serialism, a series of works that seek different solutions to a particular aesthetic problem.

Serialism was not a new approach to painting, having been practiced with great success by Monet in the nineteenth century in his series depicting the Old St. Lazare Railway Station in Paris, his garden at Giverny, haystacks, and the cathedral of Rouen. Josef Albers, who taught at Black Mountain College in North Carolina and Yale, created a series entitled *Homage to the Square* in the 1950s and 1960s. In Albers's paintings, squares float within other squares, varying in color, size, number, and placement (the squares usually were not centered). Stella took experimentation even further in such series as *Tuftonburo* and *Singerli*, questioning the shape of the canvas itself. *Singerli Variation IV* (1968), for example, is round, covered with curvilinear bands in a variety of colors; *Tuftonburo I* (1966) starts with a black rectangular background that breaks apart with a brightly colored triangle bursting beyond the canvas in the upper right corner.

Other early post-painterly artists were Morris Louis and Barnett Newman. Louis died of lung cancer in 1962, but his influence continued throughout the decade. His contributions to the new painting included using acrylic paint as a stain, pouring and spilling more than painting on cotton duck canvas so that the fabric and paint became one, more like dyed cloth than paint applied to canvas. Color thus became more important than shape or contrasts between light and dark, those elements so important to earlier artists. At the end of his life, Louis did return to some sense of drawing with a series called *Unfurleds* (1960–61), which included thin streams of colors applied diagonally at the edges of otherwise unpainted canvases; and a series of *Stripes* (1961–62), paintings featuring vertical ribbons of varied colors.

Newman saw his paintings as fields rather than compositions, with vertical bands (what he called zips) often cutting the surface into fields of color in bright oils. Like Pollock, Newman created extremely large paintings envisioned as "portable murals" or "environmental pictures" designed to stand alone, unlike most paintings that, given their relatively small size, are inevitably viewed near other paintings on the same wall. Newman's *Who's Afraid of Red, Yellow and Blue III* (1966–67), painted in red, is nearly twenty feet long.

Kenneth Noland, a friend of Morris Louis, adopted the staining technique and also painted in series. He is perhaps best remembered for his series of target paintings in the 1950s and 1960s depicting concentric rings, with circles of different colors and widths, the outer circle irregular at its edge, as in *Cantabile* (1962). He later turned to a chevron motif, as in *Grave Light* (1965), with the entire canvas painted in chevron-shaped bands. Still later the bands straightened out into horizontal stripes on canvases as long as thirty feet or more.

There were, of course, other talented artists working in the new post-painterly mode, among them Jules Olitski, whose paintings contrast the large size of the canvas with the minimal content, and are the result of staining, sometimes with a spray gun after the painting had been dragged through a trough of paint. In addition, Olitski sometimes would use a brush at an edge of the canvas. Among his most famous paintings are *Feast* (1965), a tall, thin work in red, and *High A Yellow* (1967), with a ragged strip of brushwork across the top and down the right side.

POP ART

Post-painterly abstraction was as much evolution as revolution. Not so pop art. Of all styles of art practiced during the 1960s, pop art remains the one most associated with the spirit of the times. It marked a radical departure from past practice, more in attitude even than technique. It also was a particularly American type of art, despite its British birth.

Pop art grew quickly out of various antecedents, including a group of British artists impressed with post–World War II U.S. culture, transitional neo-dada artists, the American democratic spirit, and the growth in American commercialism and technology in the 1950s and 1960s.

The United States, untouched directly by World War II, and with its economy booming, was a land growing steadily in many elements of what would soon be considered popular culture, including retail sales, advertising, print and screen media, and technology. England meanwhile was struggling to rebuild after the destruction of German bombing raids. The energy of the youthful and exuberant United States appealed to a group of young artists in England who called themselves the Independent Group in the early 1950s. In 1956, the Independent Group exhibited their art at the Whitechapel Art Gallery in London, an exhibition entitled "This Is Tomorrow."

A collage by Richard Hamilton, *Just What Is It That Makes Today's Homes So Different, So Appealing?*, served as the poster for the exhibition and introduced to the public important characteristics of pop art. It featured an assemblage of images taken from popular culture, among them the cover from a cartoon magazine entitled *Young Romance*, an advertisement for a vacuum cleaner, a canned ham, the Ford logo, a male modeling his physique, and a nude woman in a sexually provocative pose. The man holds a Tootsie Pop forward as a phallic symbol, with the picture one of the first to include the word "pop" in it. Another important British exhibition, "The Young Contemporaries," was held in 1961, showing work by several pop artists from the Royal College of Art, including the American R.B. Kitaj. As excited as British artists were about pop art, it remained principally American, in inspiration and in the most famous of pop artists. Nor could England claim sole credit for giving birth to pop art.

Dada had grown out of World War I disillusionment with both artistic traditions and modern society. The neo-dadaists shared their predecessors' rejection of traditional artistic styles and the notion of art as elitist but not their cynicism with society. Instead, despite occasional forays into irony, they tended to accept modern popular culture with its mass consumerism as, if not necessarily a good thing, at least the way life is. The line between art and life quickly began to disintegrate.

By the 1960s, perhaps the two most important neo-dadaists in the United States were Robert Rauschenberg and Jasper Johns. Rauschenberg, borrowing the collage technique of the cubists, had developed a style of "combine" or "assemblage" painting. This approach included using three-dimensional objects, such as in the early *Bed* (1955), which Rauschenberg created by pouring paint over his pillow and bedclothes. *Monogram* (1955–59) consists of a stuffed angora goat with a tire around its stomach. The goat stands on a canvas that includes painted wood, photographs, and cutout letters. During the 1960s, Rauschenberg turned to flat canvases with combinations of silk-screened images and painted additions. One of the most striking is *Buffalo II* (1964), which in the year after President Kennedy's assassination included repeated images of the president's gesturing right hand along with other media images.

Johns also helped to break down the distinction between paintings and sculptures. His best known works include *Flag* (1955), painted in oil on fabric-covered plywood, with a collage approach using bits of printed articles and advertisements within the red and white stripes; and *Painted Bronze II: Ale Cans* (1964), two bronze cans heavily painted as Ballantine ale cans. The latter supposedly grew out of a joke told about an art dealer who, according to Willem de Kooning, could sell even two beer cans as art.

The heyday of pop art featured many successful and talented artists, even if some critics and curators were slower than dealers and collectors to accept the style as genuine art rather than a put-on or denigration of serious art. Out of the crowd of artists, two figures rose above the rest, at least within popular consciousness—Roy Lichtenstein and Andy Warhol.

Lichtenstein's paintings are easy to recognize for their comic-strip approach. His subjects and techniques were borrowed from the comics, down even to the benday dots that characterized the printing process used in preparing comic books. Hiding his own self behind the paintings, Lichtenstein sought to offer the public only the paintings themselves, and they proved more than sufficient to get people's attention. *Whaam!* (1963), consisting of two panels, is over thirteen feet long and jumps into the middle of its "story" with an American jet destroying an enemy fighter. The usual balloon dialogue of comics appears in the painting: "I PRESSED THE FIRE CONTROL ... AND AHEAD OF ME ROCKETS BLAZED THROUGH THE SKY." The right panel, depicting the exploding enemy plane, has a typical comic strip sound effect: "WHAAM!"

We Rose up Slowly (1964) turns from war to love with two embracing lovers. In both this and the previous painting, Lichtenstein sought a cool detachment representative of pop art, so a viewer seeking antiwar or satirical intentions of any sort in his paintings faces a difficult quest. Instead, the point seems to be that one person's view of love or war is only one view among many. Aesthetically, Lichtenstein saw his painting as different from making comic strips. His objective was to create a unified whole rather than engage in an extended narrative. Even when he turned to a quasi-abstract approach, as in *Yellow and Red Brushstrokes* (1966), he continued with the comic-strip technique. Against the omnipresent dots, the two brushstrokes appear as if they might have been made, if by an abstract expressionist, with one sweep each of a brush.

Andy Warhol was a series of contradictions. He sought the type of cool distancing of self from his art as did other pop artists, yet he became even more famous as a personality than as an artist. He also claimed that to know his works of art was to know him. Some of his images, such as the *Big Campbell's Soup Can* (1962), became enormously recognizable, but none as much as his own image with his bleached blond hair. He contributed to his fame with many self-portraits, associations with the rich and famous, and flamboyant behavior. He claimed that everyone would be famous for fifteen minutes and far exceeded that dimension for himself.

The prophecy of brief fame involved a leveling that also occurred in Warhol's paintings, as he turned to such everyday objects as soup cans, stamps, dollar bills, bottles of coca cola, and, in his films, a man sleeping or getting a haircut. Yet he also chose as subjects such famous people as Marilyn Monroe, Jacqueline Kennedy, and Elvis Presley. He turned to the banal as subject matter in many of his creations, as did other pop artists, because, he felt, the banal constituted the essence of American life. Yet Warhol reassured his audience that he implied no criticism, that he merely painted what he knew best. Campbell's soup, for instance, he claimed to have eaten regularly for lunch.

Warhol's background did not portend artistic greatness. Born of working-class immigrants in Pittsburgh, he and his family struggled through the Great Depression. His father died when Andy was fourteen, but the father had set aside money for the son's schooling. Andy, who would later change his last name from Warhola to Warhol, attended the Carnegie Institute of Technology in Pittsburgh, preparing for a career as a commercial

Actresses Elizabeth Taylor and Marylin Monroe were two of the many
famous people whom Andy Warhol chose as subjects for his art.
Source: Photofest, Inc.

artist. Even then, he demonstrated a strong bias against the normative in
art, exhibiting a self-portrait with his finger in his nose that he called *The
Broad Gave Me My Face, but I Can Pick My Own Nose* (1949).

Warhol moved to New York City in 1949 and became a successful illus-
trator working for fashion magazines and department stores. By the early
1960s, he was turning to fine art, with comic-strip paintings of the fictional
detective Dick Tracy, highly realistic depictions of the commonplace subjects already mentioned, and portraits of celebrities. During the 1960s,
Warhol established his studio in a loft that he called the Factory and turned
from painting to a silk-screen process that involved photographic enlarge-
ments silk-screened onto a canvas, often in multiple images, with a layer
of coloring applied. Instead of one cola bottle, *Green Coca-Cola Bottles* (1962),
for example, included several rows of bottles much as they would be
stacked on shelves in a store. In some paintings, such as *Marilyn* (1967), different screens were used to apply different colors, in this case, yellow hair,
green eyelids, red lips, and a pink face against a green background.

At the same time, Warhol continued with commercial art and also started
making films, adopting the simple approach of turning a camera on such
commonplace subjects as the Empire State Building or, as mentioned earlier, a man sleeping. He explained that he saw his films as analogous to
wallpaper—in other words, something one might glance at from time to
time with a feeling of comfort but no requirement to keep paying attention.
Opposed to traditional concepts of plot and character development, Warhol
wanted the people in his films, even when he started to introduce more action, merely to be themselves as in the seven-hour *Chelsea Girls* (1966). He
also adopted a rock group called the Velvet Underground, producing their
first record in 1965 and filming them on stage.

In addition to the celebrity portraits, Warhol captured the decade of the 1960s in his often-called Disaster pictures. Done in his silk-screen technique, these pictures presented in multiple images such events as race riots, automobile accidents, firemen attempting a rescue, and a suicide leap. Andy Warhol's own life almost came to an end in 1968 when a radical feminist named Valerie Solanas, founder and the only member of S.C.U.M. (Society for Cutting Up Men), shot and wounded Warhol, whom she had been attempting to persuade to produce a play she had written.

Many other American artists played important roles within pop art, although none equaled Warhol in fame. James Rosenquist, a former billboard painter, utilized similar billboard techniques in his large, flat, collage paintings, such as *President Elect* (1960–61) with its large partial face of President Kennedy along with fingers holding a piece of cake and an automobile fender. Tom Wesselmann emphasized still lifes, for example, *Still-life No. 34* (1963) with its arrangement of a bottle of Coca-Cola, a package of Lucky Strikes, an ice cream soda, a pear, a vase with roses, and two walnuts; and assemblage paintings that combined photographic images and depersonalized, faceless female nudes, their erogenous zones emphasized by heavy paint, as in *Bathtub Nude Number 3* (1963). In this and similar paintings by Wesselmann, the dehumanized women seem less real than their everyday surroundings of tubs, doors, and towels. Claes Oldenburg, born in Sweden, combined sculpture with painting. *USA Flag* (1960) is an example, consisting of muslin in plaster over a wire frame, the whole painted with tempera. Working with his wife, Coosje van Bruggen, he turned later in the 1960s to soft sculptures, a sharp break with the hard, rigid tradition that had dominated the history of sculpture up to that time. His approach was to stuff vinyl or canvas with kapok, producing, among many works in that vein, *Shoestring Potatoes Spilling from a Bag* (1965–66), which was designed to hang from the ceiling, and *Soft Toilet* (1966), the figure collapsing forward as a toilet would if it suddenly went limp. Robert Indiana produced the most famous single image to come out of 1960s pop art—the word "LOVE" in stencil-like letters imitative of signs, with the "O" tilted (1966). Indiana both painted the message and sculpted it in aluminum. The image soon appeared virtually everywhere, on posters, on buttons, on almost any object that could contain the word, fitting well with such slogans as "Make love, not war" and with the general countercultural ambiance of hippies and flower children.

No discussion of pop art should ignore the pop art "happenings" of the 1960s. Warhol, Rauschenberg, Oldenburg, and Jim Dine were among the pop artists who sponsored these events. Typically (although no happening was truly typical of anything), a happening occurred in a specially created environment that might include theatrical sets, psychedelic colors, musicians, a radio or television blaring, a wind machine blowing confetti—anything that contributed to a mood of randomness and spontaneity. Participants improvised responses. The total experience shared more with the collage or assemblage approach to art than with theater, for little was plotted ahead of time. Dine's *Car Crash* and Oldenburg's *Store Days* were among the most famous happenings of the decade, the former intended to simulate the sensory experience of a real automobile crash, the latter held in a shop that Oldenburg rented in Manhattan and filled with plastic replicas of items sold in actual shops.

OP ART

Op art, or optical art, vied with pop art for attention during the 1960s. Op art, however, was very different from pop art, residing more in the abstract tradition than in the representational. And while pop art, even abroad, was thoroughly American in inspiration, op art reached greater heights in Europe than in the United States, perhaps because, as op art historian and analyst Cyril Barrett has suggested, America, unlike Europe, did not enjoy a tradition of geometrical abstraction.[3]

Influenced by the growth of science and technology, op art sought visual effects through such techniques as use of periodic structures (repeating the same value, or geometric figure, as a variable increases or decreases, like concentric circles that change in circumference and radius), the phi phenomenon (the impression that fixed images such as dots are moving), moiré patterns (superimposing one periodic structure on another to create a watery or shimmering effect), hard-edged designs to enhance contrast, and sharply contrasting colors. Op art is often allied with kinetic art, as the precise parameters of op art continue to invite disagreement. Some works of art create optical effects by moving (as in mobiles and other kinetic art forms), others by utilizing the impact of light on the work or even incorporating light sources into it, but the purest type of op art is sometimes seen as static and depending for its true completion on concentrated viewing, a certain amount of time being required for the viewer to register the illusion of movement. Many op art works are in black and white, which offer the ultimate color contrast and can create most of the optical effects that artists desire. However, many op artists also used color to good effect, employing new acrylic and emulsion paints to create glossy surfaces that enhanced the optical illusions.

Examination of op art in a more comprehensive study normally would begin with European artists, such as the Hungarian painter Victor Vasarely and British artist Bridget Riley, the latter possibly the best known op artist at the end of the twentieth century. Here, however, the focus is on Americans, and there were indeed some fine American op artists. Josef Albers, an American immigrant mentioned earlier in this chapter, played an important role in the history of op art in the United States. An educator as well as artist, Albers while at Yale taught Richard Anuszkiewicz, a prominent figure in the American op art world, and was a major reason American op art favored color contrasts rather than the black and white that dominated European op art. Although not primarily an op artist, Albers experimented with optical illusion, especially in his paintings of squares. Anuszkiewicz was part of "The Responsive Eye," an international exhibit of op art in 1965 at the Museum of Modern Art, favoring, as in *Radiant Green* (1965), interactions among colors.

SCULPTURE

As abstract expressionism was the dominant traditionalist style in painting at the beginning of the 1960s, before giving way to post-painterly abstraction and pop art, so construction-sculpture might be called the establishment sculpture at the beginning of the decade.

Construction-sculpture has been likened to drawing in space, with the lines and planes of the sculpture defining space and incorporating it into the work of art, unlike most earlier sculpture, where the solid mass of the object replaced space. Sometimes surfaces were painted, and those surfaces were more likely to be prefabricated, often industrial, materials than marble or bronze. Sculptors might choose used materials, such as pieces of scrap metal, or new items like I- and T-beams either bought off the shelf or fashioned to order, which they welded together.

The consensus master of construction-sculpture was David Smith, who began his artistic career as a painter. Turning to sculpture, he used steel for its durability and did not attempt to hide his indebtedness to modern industry. In the 1950s, Smith began to make large-scale sculptures, expressing an idea in a series of constructions, much like the serialists in painting. His progression also was toward increasing abstraction, as in the *Zig* (1961–64) and *Cubi* (1962–65) series. Smith was able, as in *Cubi XVII* (1964), to combine a variety of industrially shaped forms so that despite their mass they seem held together so tenuously that the slightest breeze might blow the construction apart.

Not yet sixty years of age, Smith died in 1965. Construction-sculpture, though, did not die with him, as a number of younger artists achieved critical and popular success. Mark di Suvero turned from wood to steel beams, with considerable use of moving parts. Not surprisingly, his sculptures, such as *Praise for Elohim Adonai* (1966) and *Are Years What? (For Marianne Moore)* (1967), had to be attached firmly to the ground to accommodate the considerable weight of both central core and moving parts. Anthony Caro welded metal together, not in high, monumental works, like di Suvero's, but in lower, more horizontal structures. His pieces, like *Rainfall* (1964), though rectilinear, achieve a sense of motion though different-sized elements tilted at varied angles.

As talented as the construction-sculptors were, they were generally seen as less innovative than the minimalists. As the term implies, minimal art was visually simple, using basic geometric forms in nonrepresentational ways. Only what the artist considered absolutely essential remained—no more, no less. Simplicity, of course, did not mean intellectually simple or a rejection of profound thought. In fact, the initial concept in minimal art is so much the essence of the work that minimalism is often considered closely related to conceptual art, the latter a natural development of the role of intellectual intention behind minimal art. (Conceptual art is discussed later in this section.)

Artists such as Frank Stella, Robert Rauschenberg, Ad Reinhardt, and many others created minimalist, or semiminimalist paintings during the 1960s, but the medium that produced the most distinguished body of minimal art was sculpture. Among the sculptors working in this style were Robert Morris, Donald Judd, Tony Smith, Dan Flavin, Carl Andre, and Larry Bell, plus practitioners of earth art, most prominently Robert Smithson and Michael Heizer.

Morris was deeply concerned with the process-product relationship, in a sense freezing the process and retaining it (as well as the past) permanently within the product (the present) in such sculptures as *Box with the Sound of Its Own Making* (1961), a walnut box enclosing a tape of the sounds of constructing the box. Morris also was interested in the art object's environment, which led to a set of four square boxes, *Untitled* (1965), each covered with mirrors to reflect their surroundings. The result is that the boxes largely melt into invisibility with the floor. Turning in the mid-1960s to single-object sculptures, his "unitary objects," Morris created works like the hollow circle two feet tall and almost one hundred inches in diameter (*Untitled*, 1965–66) that was slit at opposite points to permit light to escape from interior fluorescent tubes. The most startling effect of the circle was the perception of light where normally there would be shadows.

Donald Judd argued the superiority of sculpture to painting because real space consists of three dimensions, while paintings can convey no more than the illusion of real space. Judd's trademark sculpture in the 1960s was the series of boxes cantilevered vertically against a wall or suspended from a pipe. He progressed during the decade from wood that he painted to galvanized iron to a variety of media (stainless steel, copper, Plexiglas, etc.) sometimes sprayed with enamel and lacquer.

Tony Smith, a former apprentice of architect Frank Lloyd Wright, turned to sculpture because he considered sculptures more permanent than buildings. Not surprisingly, many of his creations are reminiscent of his architectural background, formed out of rectangles and sometimes tetrahedrons and octahedrons. The four- and eight-sided figures, Smith felt, gave him more flexibility, while most minimalists were working almost exclusively with cube forms. For example, Smith's *Cigarette* (1961), over fifteen feet high and twenty-five feet long, twists and turns to resemble something of a misshapen arch, or a giant cigarette bent while being snuffed out in an ashtray.

Flavin specialized in common fluorescent fixtures that he purchased at stores. Flavin apparently sensed a spiritual dimension to the lights, at least early in his career, and sometimes arranged the tubes in a series, as in *The Nominal Three (to William of Ockham)* (1964), which consisted of sets of one, two, and three tubes resting vertically against a common wall. Andre was especially noted for his use of rectangular plates resembling floor tiles to establish a place rather than a structure, as in *Lead Piece* (1969), 144 one-inch square plates laid down on a floor. He was unique among the minimalists in consistently avoiding hollow boxes in his art. Bell's favorite medium was glass, often cubes or sheets treated so that the glass both reflected and remained transparent. Bell's glass cube, *Untitled* (1967), thus almost disappears into the image reflected in it. Bell was one of the "Light and Space" sculptors of California, a group whose work had some parallels to California architecture during the 1960s in use of glass, light, and the surrounding environment.

Earth art often was essentially minimal sculpture, usually on a very large scale and, in its most notable examples, out of doors. Robert Smithson was perhaps more responsible than anyone for bringing earth art to public consciousness and critical acceptance. Smithson had created more "traditional" minimal art before turning to earth art, which he at first created for indoors, moving natural elements to what he called a "non-site" for exhibition, as with his *Non-Site (Palisades, Edgewater, N.J.)* (1968). Smithson would place the rocks or other materials in bins that permitted easy viewing and attach to the wall nearby a topographical map of the site from which the materials came.

Before long, Smithson was working at the sites themselves, making his own additions to nature. The most famous of these site sculptures was *Spiral Jetty*, which he began in 1969 and completed the following year. *Spiral Jetty* was a large spiral construction of stones and earth stretching out from the shore of the Great Salt Lake in Utah. The shape was suggestive of a number of parallels, demonstrating the relationship of earth art not only to minimal, but also to conceptual, art. Although a simple shape, *Spiral Jetty* resembled both the microorganisms living in the lake and spiral nebulae in space, linking the smallest of earthly life with cosmic forces. Although the tracks of the equipment used to construct the sculpture remained as part of the whole, the spiral shape also reminded people of primitive monuments, thus also linking humanity's early history with modern technology. The partial circles composing the spiral called to mind eternity, but the artist himself did not see his work as permanent. He took out only a twenty-year lease on the property, and the *Spiral Jetty* has long since been covered by lake water, continuing to exist only in such documentation as a film that Smithson made and photographs.

Michael Heizer displaced huge amounts of earth in some of his efforts. *Double Negative* (1969–70), located in Nevada, consisted of two trenches thirty feet wide and fifty feet deep separated by a canyon. Other artists deliberately created impermanent works that quickly disappeared as nature reverted to its previous state. Thus melting snow erased Dennis Oppenheim's *Annual Rings* (1968), which included a wide track cleared of snow on the Canadian–U.S. border at Clair, New Brunswick, and Fort Kent, Maine. The cleared area called to mind the trunk of a tree, while concentric circles in snow broken at the cleared area represented annual tree rings. The broken circles also reflected the one-hour difference in time on the two sides of the border, while the image of the tree represented a source of natural connection among the people and the land despite artificial barriers.

All art involves ideas, but conceptual art, even more than other styles, tries to make the idea the thing, eliminating as much as possible the normal physical dimensions of art and reliance on optical stimulation. Joseph Kosuth's *One and Three Chairs* (1965) includes little that would be considered traditional in art, consisting of an actual wooden chair, a photograph of the chair, and a dictionary definition of a chair. The question of reality is the essence of the work, which can be called sculpture only by applying the term rather broadly. Regardless of its medium, *One and Three Chairs* raises ideas that go back to Plato and Aristotle about whether reality lies in the universal or particular, in the object or its representation.

Because much conceptual art, like earth art, relied on documentation rather than the work of art itself for permanence, and because conceptual artists often rebelled against commercialism, many of them experimented with alternative methods of sharing their work, including printed exhibitions and documentation. Robert Barry thus published his concept in the book *One Billion Dots* (1968), each page filled with dots. Seth Siegelaub and John Wendler produced *The Xerox Book* (1968), with seven artists having twenty-five pages apiece to create a piece of conceptual art using Xerox technology.

Conceptual art usually tried to reduce the physical to a minimum, but some artists went to the opposite extreme whereby the work of art became their own physical selves. Nonetheless, the idea, at least in theory, remained primary, as when Bruce Nauman filmed himself in 1968 *Walking in an Exaggerated Manner Around the Perimeter of a Square*, or when Richard Serra in the same year filmed the act of catching in *Hand Catching Lead*. More reminiscent of traditional sculpture was the slightly later *Reading Position for Second Degree Burn* (1970), although rather than freezing the figure in marble, Dennis Oppenheim was fixed permanently only in two photographs. In the first, he lies on sand with a book open over his chest; in the second, he is without the book but with a sunburn. The type of art in these three creations is often called body art because the artists use their own bodies in creating their art. At the same time, body art uses basic, minimal actions, while inviting viewers to reflect on the idea behind the action. Sculpture at the beginning of the 1960s had sought to remove the artist from the work of art, substituting cool detachment in simple forms for individual expressiveness. By the end of the decade, some artists, while maintaining the minimal dimension, as well as the conceptual that had evolved out of minimal art, had gone full circle, making themselves the work of art.

PHOTOGRAPHY

The dominant style for art photography at the beginning of the 1960s was "straight photography," which emphasized content over form and presented realistic images in beautiful prints prepared with meticulous attention to light, shadow, framing, and perspective. Much of straight photography was aesthetically and spiritually uplifting, including magnificent scenes of both the small details and majestic grandeur of nature. Documentary photography of human subjects usually exhibited compassionate understanding and empathy. Operating along these traditional paths were such important photographers as Ansel Adams, Minor White, Paul Caponigro, and Wynn Bullock.

During the late 1950s and early 1960s, however, greater experimentation began to enter photography, with both theoretical statements and innovative practice inviting varied approaches. Two of the most important milestones along the road to photographic innovation were books, Robert Frank's *The Americans*, which first appeared in the United States in 1960, and John Szarkowski's *The Photographer's Eye*, published in 1966. Frank, who emigrated to the United States from Switzerland in 1947, took the photographs in this collection during the middle Fifties. He was concerned with subjects that other photographers certainly had explored—racism, poverty, religion—but he established a new style for the photographic documentary. Rather than praising his subject or indicting society, Frank brought a personal irony to bear on what he photographed. This attitude was evident in Frank's photographic techniques, as his pictures often were slightly out of focus or idiosyncratically framed, and in his approach to content, with people's gestures and expressions reflective more of a "candid camera" approach than deliberate posing.

John Szarkowski, by virtue of his position as director of the photography department at New York's Museum of Modern Art, was an influential figure in the world of art photography. That influence increased dramatically with publication of *The Photographer's Eye*. Szarkowski reexamined the history of photography in his book while focusing attention on photographic theory. He emphasized five elements crucial to a critical examination of photography: the thing being photographed, the detail, the frame, time, and vantage point.[4] With Szarkowski leading a critical and historical discussion of photography, and Frank leading through practice, the medium blossomed into a varied garden of flowers, some of them striking but far from beautiful in any conventional sense.

Paralleling pop art in painting, the new photographers turned increasingly to the commonplace, the banal, and the bizarre. Rather than objective representation heightened with considerable technical skill, these photographers looked to the art form as heavily subjective and at the same time clearly artifice. As pop art turned to the people and products of everyday, so did photographers, finding, along with subjects for their photographs, inspiration in the type of amateur snapshots available in drawers and photographic albums throughout the country. Thus was born the "snapshot aesthetic"—pictures exhibiting an amateurlike crudeness in lighting, focus, and arrangement.

Three of the most successful of the new photographers were Garry Winogrand, Lee Friedlander, and Diane Arbus, all three included in the important "New Documents" exhibition of 1966–67 at the Museum of Modern Art, curated by Szarkowski. Winogrand was an air force photographer and later photojournalist whose work appeared in such magazines as *Sports Illustrated*, *Look*, *Life*, and *Collier's*. His art photographs are especially notable for the busy, teeming numbers of people captured with wide-angle lenses. Humor, irony, even mockery appear in many of his pictures, including those published in *The Animals* (1969), taken at the New York City Zoo and the Coney Island Aquarium. The photographs include clever juxtapositions of humans and animals, the former more than the latter often coming off as subjects of Winogrand's humor.

Friedlander's photographs often appear like random snapshots of urban scenes, catching whatever happened to be there that moment. The result is a collage or assemblage effect similar to much 1960s painting. His pictures are notable not only for their detail but also for their metaphoric impact, like a church in the background behind traffic and pedestrians, and a trash can and stop sign in the foreground (*Santa Fe*, 1969). Yet, unlike Winogrand, Friedlander seldom appears anything but sympathetic to the humans he catches in his lenses.

Diane Arbus is the most disconcerting of the three. Whether because of, or despite, her early career as a fashion photographer, Arbus gravitated toward the bizarre, often photographing people she referred to as "freaks"—midgets, giants, transvestites, and other social outcasts. Other photographers followed in a similar direction. Danny Lyon, focusing on social commentary, was the official photographer for the Student Nonviolent Coordinating Committee, and later went so far as to join the Chicago Outlaw Motorcycle Club. The resulting photographs were published in *The Movement* (1964) and *The Bikeriders* (1968).

Somewhere between the traditional photographers such as Ansel Adams and the revolutionaries like Diane Arbus was Bruce Davidson. A photojournalist, Davidson's work incorporated the idealism and love of nature of an Adams while also looking closely at the people and objects that contained little of the grand and majestic. He saw in nature the same mountains and vast panoramas that Adams recorded, but in a photograph like *Yosemite* (1966) he also saw the automobile campers, folding chairs, and T-shirt-clad vacationers seemingly enjoying idle conversation more than the scenic wonders of their environment. Still, there is no condescension in Davidson's work, but a portrait of a world in which the same setting often provides both joy and sorrow, beauty and despair.

Finally, photojournalists, with a level of skill that blurred the line between photojournalism and art photography, captured many of the most important moments of the 1960s, and other moments that might easily have been missed had not a skilled man or woman with a camera been present. They helped shape both the public's vision of the decade and history's judgment of it. Unfortunately, many of these moments are shocking, disconcerting, even tragic: photographs by Robert Jackson of Jack Ruby shooting Lee Harvey Oswald, November 24, 1963; by Malcolm Browne recording the Buddhist monk Thick Quang Duc burn himself to death in Saigon on June 11, 1963; by Eddie Adams catching the instant when the bullet from South Vietnamese General Nguyen Ngoc Loan's gun entered the head of an assassinated Viet Cong prisoner, February 1, 1968; by Cecil Stoughton immortalizing the moment aboard *Air Force One* when the new president, Lyndon Johnson, with the new widow, Jacqueline Kennedy, by his side, took the oath of office on November 22, 1963. Many other photographs are equally memorable. In fact, photography itself, as a medium of dialectics—beauty and ugliness, joy and pain, hope and tragedy—through its dual function as art and social chronicler, is not only a part, but also a microcosm, of the 1960s.

Cost of Products
in the 1960s

FOOD

Hardee's cheeseburgers, $.20; French fries, $.10; milk shake, $.20; soft drink, $.20 (1961)

Round steak, $1.07 per pound (1964)

Sugar, $.59 per pound (1964)

Coffee, $.82 per pound (1964)

Bread, $.21 per pound loaf (1964)

Eggs, $.57 per dozen (1964)

Milk, $.48 per half gallon (1964)

Butter, $.76 per pound (1964)

Lettuce, $.25 per head (1964)

Arby's roast-beef sandwich, $.69¢ (1964)

Swift butterball turkey, $.45 per pound (1966)

Veal roast, $.79 per pound (1966)

McDonald's hamburger, $.15¢ French fries, $.15; milk shake, $.25; soft drink, $.10 or $.15 (1966)

McDonald's "Big Mac," $.45 (1968)

Chock Full O'Nuts coffee, $.15¢ hot dog, $.25; doughnut, $.10 (1968)

Hershey candy bar (3/4 oz.), $.5 (1968)

Hershey candy bar (11/2 oz.), $.10 (1969)

WOMEN'S CLOTHING

Bridal gown (Sears, long-length), $36.50 (1960)

Plaid skirt (Sears), $7.97 (1961)

Jumbo tote handbag (Sears), $5.99 (1962)

Reversible raincoat (Sears), $21.90 (1963)

Pillbox hat (Sears), $7.97 (1963)

Tiger-striped jumpsuit pajamas (Sears), $5.99 (1965)

Cotton denim jeans (Sears), $3.47 (1966)

Empire dress (Sears), $25 (1967)

T-shirt mini-shift (Sears), $7.99 (1968)

High leather boots (Sears), $20 (1969)

Fashion wig (Sears), $29.95, $49.95, $109.95 (1969)

Calvin Klein wool skirt, with slit, $165 (1969)

Diane von Furstenberg cotton midi dress, $100 (1969)

MEN'S CLOTHING

Seersucker suit (Sears), $19.97 (1961)

Wool sweater with elbow patches (Sears), $7.74 (1963)

Space Commander jump suit for boys (Sears), $3.99 (1964)

Corduroy sport coat (Sears), $18.95 (1969)

Hush Puppie shoes, $8.75–$9.95 (1963)

Brooks Brothers tweed sport jacket for boys, $30 (1964)

JEWELRY

Women's diamond ring (1/2 carat) and wedding band (Sears), $159 (1961)

Men's Timex watch, $13.15 (1961)

Men's 14K ring (Sears), $19.95 (1961)

Tiffany 14K cuff links, $35 (1962)

HOUSEHOLD ITEMS

Electric kitchen clock (Sears), $5.77 (1961)

Bedroom alarm clock (Sears), $6.97 (1961)

Stainless tableware (24 pieces, Sears), $3.87–$9.77 (1961)

Dishwasher-proof dinnerware (service for 8, Sears), $9.97 (1961)

Melmac dinnerware (service for 8, Sears), $16–$36 (1961)

Drip coffeepot (Sears), $3.47 (1961)

Desk set with ball point pens, calendar, pad (Sears), $4.87 (1961)

Toastmaster electric toaster, $34.95 (1960)

Interest on savings accounts, 5.25–5.75% (1966)

FURNITURE AND APPLIANCES

Maple cocktail table (Sears), $38 (1961)

Recliner chair (Sears), $60 (1961)

Early American tweed sofa (Sears), $130 (1961)

Steel bathtub (Sears), $57.95 (1961)

Plastic toilet seat (Sears), $2.77–$6.50 (1961)

Kitchen sink (Sears), $38–$55 (1961)

Gas oven (Sears), $199.95 (1961)

Electric oven (Sears), $189.95 (1961)

White refrigerator (Sears), $250 (1961)

Wringer washing machine (Sears), $93–$144 (1961)

Sunbeam canister vacuum cleaner, $49.95 (1968)

GARAGE AND YARD ITEMS

Push rotary power lawnmower (Sears), $77.88 (1961)

Volkswagen Beetle, $1,675 (1960)

Chevrolet Camaro (base price), $2,466 (1966)

RECREATION

Children's sidewalk skates (Sears), $1.64–$6.27 (1961)

Football (Sears), $3.84 (1961)

10-speed bicycle (Sears), $71.95 (1961)

Record player (with attached speakers, Sears), $127 (1961)

Hitachi tape recorder, $99 (1964)

Philco 17-inch portable television, $139.95 (1960)

23-inch black-and-white television, $260 (1961)

Zenith 20-inch color television, $399.95 (1968)

Fly rod, $49.95 (1961)

Broadway musical (best seats), $8.60 (1961)

Carnegie Hall Christmas Eve concert, 50¢ (1961)

New York Times (daily), 5¢ (1962)

New York Times (daily), 10¢ (1969)

Paperback edition of *The Catcher in the Rye*, 50¢ (1962)

Paperback edition of *Catch-22*, 95¢ (1969)

Look magazine, 25¢ (1964)

Boeing 747 (new), $21,000,000 (1966)

Notes

CHAPTER 1

1. George Thomas Kurian, *Datapedia of the United States, 1790–2000* (Lanham, MD: Bernan, 1994), 177.

2. Most of the financial figures in this section are drawn from Kurian's *Datapedia of the United States*.

3. United States, Bureau of the Census, vol. 2 of *Historical Statistics of the United States: Colonial Times to 1970*, Bicentennial ed. (Washington, DC: U.S. Dept. of Commerce, Bureau of the Census, 1975), 639.

4. U.S., vol. 2 of *Historical Statistics*, 1009.

5. Kurian, 80.

6. U.S., vol. 1 of *Historical Statistics*, 131.

7. Kurian, 144.

8. Kurian, 156.

9. The following figures relating to the Vietnam War are from Harry G. Summer, Jr., *Vietnam War Almanac* (New York: Facts on File, 1985).

CHAPTER 2

1. George Thomas Kurian, *Datapedia of the United States, 1790–2000* (Lanham, MD: Bernan, 1994), 8.

2. Kurian, 142.

3. For these integration statistics and a discussion of their significance, see Chapter 5, "Desegregating the South, 1955–1970," in J. Harvie Wilkinson III, *From Brown to Bakke: The Supreme Court and School Integration: 1954–1978* (New York: Oxford UP, 1979), 78–127.

4. Kurian, 38.

CHAPTER 3

1. George Thomas Kurian, *Datapedia of the United States, 1790–2000* (Lanham, MD: Bernan, 1994), 8.

2. Kurian, *Datapedia*, 299.

3. Ben H. Bagdikian, "Who Pays for the News?" in *The Commercial Connection: Advertising and the American Mass Media*, ed. John W. Wright (New York: Dell, 1979), 25–28.

4. Larry Dobrow, *When Advertising Tried Harder: The Sixties: The Golden Age of American Advertising* (New York: Friendly P, 1984), 22–24.

5. Dobrow, 28–30.

6. Thomas Frank, *The Conquest of Cool: Business Culture, Counterculture, and the Rise of Hip Consumerism* (Chicago: U of Chicago P, 1997), 109.

7. The figures relating to African-American demographics and purchasing, and to advertising directed at the African-American community, are from D. Parke Gibson's important study, *The $30 Billion Negro* (London: Macmillan, 1969).

8. William D. Wells, "Communicating with Children," in *The Commercial Connection*, 158–77.

CHAPTER 4

1. For these statements by Kahn, see Donald Leslie Johnson and Donald Langmead, *Makers of 20th Century Modern Architecture: A Bio-Critical Sourcebook* (Westport, CT: Greenwood, 1997), 169.

2. Robert Venturi, *Complexity and Contradiction in Architecture*, 2nd ed. (New York: Museum of Modern Art, 1977), 16.

3. Venturi, *Complexity and Contradiction*, 118.

4. Carole Rifkind, *A Field Guide to Contemporary American Architecture* (New York: Dutton, 1998), 81.

5. Rifkind, 153–77.

6. These details about the University of Notre Dame library are available online on the Notre Dame web site at <http://www.nd.edu/`ndlibs/aboutlib/history/hesb.shtml> and <http://www.nd.edu/~ndlibs/aboutlib/history/mosaic.shtml>.

7. *The Constitution on the Sacred Liturgy*, in *The Documents of Vatican II*, ed. Walter Abbott, trans. Joseph Gallagher (New York: Guild, America, Association Presses, 1966), sections 2, 14, 48.

8. Carter Wiseman, *Shaping a Nation: Twentieth-Century American Architecture and Its Makers* (New York: Norton, 1998), 232.

9. Jane Jacobs, *The Death and Life of Great American Cities* (New York: Random House, 1961), 187.

CHAPTER 5

1. George Thomas Kurian, *Datapedia of the United States, 1790–2000* (Lanham, MD: Bernan, 1994), 8, 177.

2. Sears prices given in this chapter are based on *Everyday Fashions of the Sixties: As Pictured in Sears Catalogs*, ed. JoAnne Olian (Mineola, NY: Dover, 1999).

3. Francois Baudot, *Fashion: The Twentieth Century* (New York: Universe, 1999), 210.

4. Frank W. Hoffman and William G. Bailey, *Fashion and Merchandising Fads* (New York: Haworth, 1994), 270.

5. Todd Gitlin, *The Sixties: Years of Hope, Days of Rage*, rev. ed. (New York: Bantam, 1993), 217.

CHAPTER 6

1. Much of the information, including recipes, in this section is from Sylvia Lovegren's *Fashionable Food: Seven Decades of Food Fads* (New York: Macmillan, 1995).

2. Lovegren, 285.

3. Tremendously informative regarding a wide range of developments in the food industry is James Trager, *The Food Chronology: A Food Lover's Compendium of Events and Anecdotes, from Prehistory to the Present* (1995; New York: Henry Holt, 1997). Most of the restaurant and food statistics in this section are from Trager.

4. Again in this section, I am indebted to Trager, especially for food production figures.

5. George Thomas Kurian, *Datapedia of the United States, 1790–2000* (Lanham, MD: Bernan, 1994), 177.

6. Alan L. Sorkin, "Agriculture," in *The Sixties in America*, ed. Carl Singleton, vol. 1 (Pasadena, CA: Salem, 1999), 14.

7. See Trager, 562–600.

8. Trager, 579–91.

9. These statistics, as well as the following figures relating to school lunches and substances endangering food and the environment, are from Trager.

CHAPTER 7

1. Charles Panati, *Panati's Parade of Fads, Follies, and Manias: The Origins of Our Most Cherished Obsessions* (New York: HarperCollins, 1991), 322.

2. Panati, 320–21.

3. The statistics given here for Barbie and G.I. Joe are from Frank W. Hoffman and William G. Bailey, *Fashion & Merchandising Fads* (New York: Haworth, 1994), 27–29 and 93–94.

4. Panati, 321.

5. Lois Gordon and Alan Gordon, *American Chronicle: Year by Year Through the Twentieth Century* (New Haven: Yale UP, 1999), 632.

6. David Maraniss, *When Pride Still Mattered: A Life of Vince Lombardi* (New York: Simon & Schuster, 1999).

7. Sam Chaiton and Terry Swinton, *Lazarus and the Hurricane: The Freeing of Rubin "Hurricane" Carter* (1991; New York: St. Martin's Griffin, 1999), 336.

CHAPTER 8

1. Robert J. Glessing, *The Underground Press in America* (Bloomington: Indiana UP, 1970).

CHAPTER 9

1. A useful listing of 1960s Grammy Awards as well as other important accomplishments, including Academy of Motion Pictures Arts and Sciences music awards and Recording Industry Association of America Gold and Platinum Record Awards, is available in Irwin Stambler, *The Encyclopedia of Pop, Rock and Soul*, rev. ed. (New York: St. Martin's, 1989). References to such awards in this chapter are based heavily on Stambler's book.

2. Ronald L. David, *The Modern Era, 1920–Present*, vol. 3 in *A History of Music in American Life* (Malabar, FL: Robert Krieger, 1981), 369.

3. David, 383–84.

4. Stambler, 559.

5. David Allen Duncan, "Music," vol. 2 of *The Sixties in America*, ed. Carl Singleton (Pasadena, CA: Salem, 1999), 506.

6. Geoffrey C. Ward and Ken Burns, *Jazz: A History of America's Music* (New York: Alfred A. Knopf, 2000), 446.

CHAPTER 10

1. Marshall McLuhan, *The Medium Is the Massage* (New York: Random House, 1967).

2. George Thomas Kurian, *Datapedia of the United States, 1790–2000* (Lanham, MD: Bernan, 1994), 299.

3. United States, Bureau of the Census, vol. 2 of *Historical Statistics of the United States: Colonial Times to 1970*, Bicentennial ed. (Washington DC: U.S. Department of Commerce, Bureau of the Census, 1975), 796.

4. Newton N. Minow made this comment in a speech to the nation's broadcasters in 1961. For a more recent examination of Minow's views on television, see his and Craig LaMay's *Abandoned in the Wasteland: Children, Television, and the First Amendment* (New York: Hill and Wang, 1995).

5. Much of the information in this chapter on Emmy awards, Nielsen ratings, and related matters is based on Tim Brooks and Earle Marsh's useful reference work, *The Complete Directory to Prime Time Network and Cable TV Shows, 1946–Present*, 25th anniversary ed. (New York: Ballantine, 1999).

6. Jackie Kennedy made the connection to Camelot in an interview with Kennedy biographer Theodore H. White on November 29, 1963. White then expanded on the comment in a piece that he wrote for *Life*, "For President Kennedy: An Epilogue," which appeared on December 6, 1963.

CHAPTER 11

1. John F. Kennedy, Special Message to the Congress, 25 May 1961, published in *To Turn the Tide*, ed. John W. Gardner (New York: Harper, 1962), 74–75.

2. William H. Phillips, *Film: An introduction* (New York: Bedford/St. Martin's, 1999), 291.

3. Louis Giannetti and Scott Eyman, *Flashback: A Brief History of Film*, 3rd ed. (Englewood Cliffs, NJ: Prentice-Hall, 1996), 347.

4. George Thomas Kurian, *Datapedia of the United States, 1790–2000* (Lanham, MD: Bernan, 1994), 267–68.

5. Peter B. Heller, "Automobiles and Auto Manufacturing," in *The Sixties in America*, ed. Carl Singleton, vol. 1 (Pasadena, CA: Salem, 1999), 52.

6. I am indebted for the statistics in this section relating to car sales and car manufacturing specifications to Martin Buckley and Chris Rees, *The World Encyclopedia of Cars: The Definitive Guide to Classic and Contemporary Cars*, rev. ed. (New York: Hermes House, 1999).

7. *Entertainment Weekly's The 100 Greatest TV Shows of All Time: Collector's Edition*, ed. Alison Gwinn (New York: Time, 1998), 143.

8. Kurian, 289.

9. Robert P. Ellis, "Travel," in *The Sixties in America*, vol. 3, 729.

10. Ellis, 727.

11. Kurian, 275.

12. Kurian, 276.

13. Statistics and manufacturing information on trucks in this section are from Niels Jansen, *Pictorial History of American Trucks* (Rijswijk, Holland: Elmar; Bideford, England: Bay View Bks., 1994).

CHAPTER 12

1. John Canaday, *Mainstreams of Modern Art* (New York: Simon and Schuster, 1962), 542.

2. Irving Sandler, *American Art of the 1960s* (New York: Harper & Row, 1988), 18.

3. Cyril Barrett, *Op Art* (New York: Viking, 1970).

4. See Robert Frank, *The Americans* (1960; Millerton, NY: Aperture, 1978); and John Szarkowski, *The Photographer's Eye* (New York: Museum of Modern Art, 1966).

Further Reading

Abbotson, Susan C.W. *Student Companion to Arthur Miller*. Westport, CT: Greenwood Press, 2000.

Abbott, Keith. *Downstream from Trout Fishing in America: A Memoir of Richard Brautigan*. Santa Barbara, CA: Capra, 1989.

Abbott, Walter M., ed. *The Documents of Vatican II*. Trans. Joseph Gallagher. New York: Guild, America, Association Presses, 1966.

Alexander, Paul. *Rough Magic: A Biography of Sylvia Plath*. New York: Viking, 1991.

Ali, Muhammad, with Richard Durham. *The Greatest: My Own Story*. New York: Random House, 1975.

Allen, Geoffrey Freeman. *Railways, Past, Present and Future*. New York: Morrow, 1982.

Allen, William Rodney. *Understanding Kurt Vonnegut*. Columbia: U of South Carolina P, 1991.

Allyn, David. *Make Love, Not War: The Sexual Revolution: An Unfettered History*. New York: Little, Brown, 2000.

Altieri, Charles. *Enlarging the Temple: New Directions in American Poetry During the 1960's*. Lewisburg, PA: Bucknell UP, 1979.

Amburn, Ellis. *Pearl: The Obsessions and Passions of Janis Joplin: A Biography*. New York: Warner, 1992.

Anderson, Patrick. *High in America: The True Story Behind NORML and the Politics of Marijuana*. New York: Viking, 1981.

Archer, Michael. *Art Since 1960*. New York: Thames and Hudson, 1997.

Armstrong, Neil. *First on the Moon: A Voyage with Neil Armstrong, Michael Collins* [and] *Edwin E. Aldrin, Jr*. Boston: Little, Brown, 1970.

Ashe, Arthur. *Days of Grace: A Memoir*. New York: Alfred A. Knopf, 1993.

Assayas, Michka. *The Beatles and the Sixties*. New York: Holt, 1996.

Atwan, Robert. *Edsels, Luckies and Frigidaires: Advertising the American Way*. New York: Dell, 1979.

Auerbach, Doris. *Sam Shepard, Arthur Kopit, and the Off Broadway Theater*. Boston: Twayne, 1982.

Baez, Joan. *Daybreak*. New York: Dial, 1968.

Baraka, Imamu Amiri. *The Autobiography of LeRoi Jones/Amiri Baraka*. New York: Freundlich Bks., 1984.

Barrett, Cyril. *Op Art*. New York: Viking, 1970.

Baudot, Francois. *Fashion: The Twentieth Century*. New York: Universe, 1999.

The Beatles Anthology. San Francisco: Chronicle Bks., 2000.

Bennett, David. *Skyscrapers: The World's Tallest Buildings and How They Work*. 1995; London: Greenwich Editions, 1998.

Bergreen, Laurence. *Louis Armstrong: An Extravagant Life*. New York: Broadway Bks., 1997.

Bernstein, Leonard. *The Infinite Variety of Music*. New York: Simon and Schuster, 1966.

Bertrand, Michael T. *Race, Rock, and Elvis*. Champaign, IL: U of Illinois P, 2000.

Beschloss, Michael R. *The Crisis Years: Kennedy and Krushchev, 1960–1963*. New York: Edward Burlingame, 1991.

Bianco, David. *Heat Wave: The Motown Fact Book*. Ann Arbor, MI: Pierian, 1988.

Bigsby, C.W.E. *Modern American Drama, 1945–1990*. New York: Cambridge UP, 1992.

The Blackwell Guide to Recorded Country Music. Cambridge, MA: Blackwell Reference, 1994.

Bloom, Alexander, ed. *Long Time Gone: Sixties America Then and Now*. New York: Oxford UP, 2001.

Booth, Stanley. *Dance with the Devil: The Rolling Stones and Their Times*. New York: Random House, 1984.

Bosworth, Patricia. *Diane Arbus: A Biography*. New York: Knopf, 1984.

Bowles, Jerry G. *A Thousand Sundays: The Story of* The Ed Sullivan Show. New York: Putnam, 1980.

Bracken, Peg. *Peg Bracken's Appendix* to The I Hate to Cook Book, *with over 140 Recipes and 323 Afterthoughts*. New York: Harcourt, 1966.

Brady, Frank. *Profile of a Prodigy: The Life and Games of Bobby Fischer*. Rev. ed. New York: McKay, 1973.

Branch, Taylor. *Parting the Waters: America in the King Years, 1954–1963*. New York: Simon and Schuster, 1988.

Brock, Ted, and Larry Eldridge, Jr. *Twenty-five Years: The NFL Since 1960*. New York: Simon and Schuster, 1985.

Brooks, Gwendolyn. *Report from Part One*. Detroit: Broadside, 1972.

Brooks, Tim, and Earle Marsh. *The Complete Directory to Prime Time Network and Cable TV Shows 1946–Present*. 7th ed. New York: Ballantine, 1999.

Brown, Dale, and Time-Life Editors. *American Cooking*. New York: Time-Life, 1968.

Bucher, Lloyd M., and Mark Rascovich. *Bucher: My Story*. Garden City, NY: Doubleday, 1970.

Buckley, Martin, and Chris Rees. *The World Encyclopedia of Cars: The Definitive Guide to Classic and Contemporary Cars from 1945 to the Present Day*. Rev. ed. New York: Hermes House, 1999.

Budds, Michael J. *Jazz in the Sixties: The Expansion of Musical Resources and Techniques*. Iowa City: U of Iowa P, 1978.

Bugliosi, Vincent. *Helter Skelter: The True Story of the Manson Murders*. New York: Norton, 1974.

Burne, Stewart. *Social Movements of the 1960s: Searching for Democracy*. Boston: Twayne, 1990.

Buscombe, Edward, ed. *The BFI Companion to the Western*. New York: Da Capo, 1988.

Cagin, Seth, and Philip Dray. *We Are Not Afraid: The Story of Goodman, Schwerner, and Chaney and the Civil Rights Campaign for Mississippi*. New York: Macmillan, 1988.

Campbell, Dorothy. *Poverty in the United States During the Sixties: A Bibliography*. Berkeley: U of California P, 1970.

Canaday, John. *Mainstreams of Modern Art*. New York: Simon and Schuster, 1962.

Cantwell, Robert. *When We Were Good: The Folk Revival*. Cambridge, MA: Harvard UP, 1996.

Carr, Ian. *Miles Davis: The Definitive Biography*. New York: Thunder's Mouth, 1998.

Carson, Clayborne. *In Struggle: SNCC and the Black Awakening of the 1960s*. Cambridge, MA: Harvard UP, 1981.

Carson, Rachel. *Silent Spring*. Boston: Houghton Mifflin, 1962.

Cash, Johnny. *Cash: The Autobiography*. San Francisco: HarperSanFrancisco, 1997.

Chaiton, Sam, and Terry Swinton. *Lazarus and the Hurricane: The Freeing of Rubin "Hurricane" Carter*. 1991. New York: St. Martin's Griffin, 1999.

Chamberlain, Wilt. *A View From Above*. New York: Villard, 1991.

Chapman, James. *License to Thrill: A Cultural History of the James Bond Films*. New York: Columbia UP, 2000.

Chenoune, Farid. *A History of Men's Fashions*. Paris, Flammarion, 1993.

Child, Julia. *The French Chef Cookbook*. New York: Knopf, 1968.

———, Simone Beck, and Louisette Bertholle. *Mastering the Art of French Cooking*. 2 vols. New York: Knopf, 1961–70.

Christy, Joe. *American Aviation: An illustrated History*. Blue Ridge Summit, PA: Tab Bks., 1987.

Clark, Dick. *Rock, Roll & Remember*. New York: Crowell, 1976.

Clarke, Gerald. *Capote: A Biography*. New York: Simon and Schuster, 1988.

Clemente, John. *Girl Groups: Fabulous Females that Rocked the World*. Iola, WI: Krause, 2000.

Cochrane, Willard W., and Mary E. Ryan. *American Farm Policy, 1948–1973*. Minneapolis: U of Minnesota P, 1976.

Connikie, Yvonne. *Fashions of a Decade: The 1960s*. New York: Facts on File, 1990.

Coplans, John. *Roy Lichtenstein*. New York: Praeger, 1972.

Cotton, Henry. *History of Golf Illustrated*. Philadelphia: Lippincott, 1975.

Curry, Jack. *Woodstock: The Summer of Our Lives*. New York: Weidenfeld & Nicholson, 1989.

Davis, Flora. *Moving the Mountain: The Women's Movement in America since 1960*. New York: Simon and Schuster, 1991.

Davis, Ronald L. *A History of Music in American Life*. 3 vols. Huntington, NY: R.E. Krieger, 1980–82.

Dawson, Jim. *The Twist: The Story of the Song that Changed the World*. Boston: Faber & Faber, 1995.

Dawson, John A., and J. Dennis Lords, eds. *Shopping Centre Development: Policies and Prospects*. New York: Nichols, 1985.

Densmore, John. *Riders on the Storm: My Life with Jim Morrison and the Doors*. New York: Delacorte, 1990.

Dickstein, Morris. *Gates of Eden: American Culture in the Sixties*. 1977; Cambridge, MA: Harvard UP, 1997.

Didion, Joan. *Joan Didion: Essays & Conversations*. Ed. Ellen G. Friedman. Princeton, NJ: Ontario Review, 1984.

Dieterich, Daniel, ed. *Teaching About Doublespeak*. Urbana, IL: National Council of Teachers of English, 1976.

Dobrow, Larry. *When Advertising Tried Harder: The Sixties: The Golden Age of American Advertising*. New York: Friendly, 1984.

Domina, Lynn. *Understanding* A Raisin in the Sun: *A Student Casebook to Issues, Sources, and Historical Documents*. Westport, CT: Greenwood Press, 1998.

Douglas, George H. *All Aboard: The Railroad in American Life*. New York: Paragon House, 1992.

———. *Skyscrapers: A Social History of the Very Tall Building in America*. Jefferson, NC: McFarland, 1996.

Draper, Hal. *Berkeley: The New Student Revolt*. New York: Grove, 1965.

Elderfield, John, ed. *American Art of the 1960s*. New York: Museum of Modern Art, 1991.

Ellington, Duke. *Music Is My Mistress*. Garden City, NY: Doubleday, 1973.

Ellwood, Robert S. *The Sixties Spiritual Awakening: American Religion Moving from Modern to Postmodern*. New Brunswick, NJ: Rutgers UP, 1994.

Engel, Joel. *Gene Roddenberry: The Myth and the Man Behind* Star Trek. New York: Hyperion, 1994.

Epstein, Dan. *Twentieth-Century Pop Culture*. London: Carlton, 1999.

Esslin, Martin. *The Theatre of the Absurd*. Rev. ed. Woodstock, NY: Overlook, 1973.

Farrell, James J. *The Spirit of the Sixties: Making Postwar Radicalism*. New York: Routledge, 1997.

Farrow, Mia. *What Falls Away: A Memoir*. New York: Nan A. Talese/Doubleday, 1997.

Fisch, Shalom M., and Rosemarie T. Truglio. *"G" Is for "Growing": Thirty Years of Research on Children and* Sesame Street. Mahwah, NJ: Lawrence Erlbaum, 2001.

Flink, Christopher. *The Car Culture*. Cambridge, MA: MIT, 1975.

Flowers, Ronald B. *Religion in Strange Times: The 1960s and 1970s*. Macon, GA: Mercer UP, 1984.

Floyd, Samuel A. *The Power of Black Music: Interpreting Its History from Africa to the United States*. New York: Oxford UP, 1995.

Frank, Elizabeth. *Jackson Pollock*. New York: Abbeville, 1983.

Frank, Thomas. *The Conquest of Cool: Business Culture, Counterculture, and the Rise of Hip Consumerism*. Chicago: U of Chicago P, 1997.

Franklin, H. Bruce. *Robert A. Heinlein: America as Science Fiction*. New York: Oxford UP, 1980.

Franklin, John Hope, and Alfred A. Moss. *From Slavery to Freedom: A History of African Americans*. 8th ed. New York: Knopf, 2000.

Friedan, Betty. *The Feminine Mystique*. New York: Norton, 1963.

Gaines, Steven S. *Heroes and Villains: The True Story of the Beach Boys*. New York: New American Library, 1986.

Garrow, David J. *Bearing the Cross: Martin Luther King, Jr., and the Southern Christian Leadership Conference, 1955–1968*. New York: W. Morrow, 1986.

Gelman, Morrie, and Gene Accas. *The Best in Television: 50 Years of Emmys*. Los Angeles: General Publishing Group, 1998.

George, Nelson. *Where Did Our Love Go?: The Rise and Fall of the Motown Sound*. New York: St. Martin's, 1986.

Gibson, D. Parke. *The $30 Billion Negro*. New York: Macmillan, 1969.

Ginsberg, Allen. *Journals: Early Fifties, Early Sixties*. New York: Grove, 1977.

Giovanni, Nikki. *Gemini: An Extended Autobiographical Statement of My First Twenty-Five Years of Being a Black Poet*. 1971. New York: Viking, 1973.

Gitlin, Todd. *The Sixties: Years of Hope, Days of Rage*. Rev. ed. New York: Bantam, 1993.

Gleason, Maureen, and Katharina J. Blackstead, eds., *What Is Written Remains: Historical Essays on the Libraries of Notre Dame*. Notre Dame: U of Notre Dame P, 1994.

Glessing, Robert J. *The Underground Press in America*. Bloomington: Indiana UP, 1970.

Godfrey, Tony. *Conceptual Art*. London: Phaidon, 1998.

Goodwin, Doris Kearns. *Lyndon Johnson and the American Dream*. New York: Harper & Row, 1976.

Gordon, Linda. *Woman's Body, Woman's Right: A Social History of Birth Control*. New York: Grossman, 1976.

Gordon, Lois, and Alan Gordon. *American Chronicle: Year by Year Through the Twentieth Century*. New Haven: Yale UP, 1999.

Graham, Hugh Davis. *The Civil Rights Era: Origins and Development of National Policy, 1960–1972*. New York: Oxford UP, 1990.

————. *The Uncertain Triumph: Federal Education Policy in the Kennedy and Johnson Years*. Chapel Hill: U of North Carolina P, 1984.

Green, Jonathan. *American Photography: A Critical History 1945 to the Present*. New York: Abrams, 1984.

Gregory, Hugh. *A Century of Pop*. Chicago: A Cappella Bks., 1998.

Griswold del Castillo, Richard, and Richard A. Garcia. *César Chávez: A Triumph of Spirit*. Norman: U of Oklahoma P, 1995.

Gruen, Victor. *Shopping Towns U.S.A.: The Planning of Shopping Centers*. New York: Van Nostrand Reinhold, 1960.

Gwinn, Alison, ed. *The 100 Greatest TV Shows of All Time: Collector's Edition. Entertainment Weekly*. New York: Entertainment Weekly Bks., 1998.

Hagan, Chet. *Grand Ole Opry*. New York: Holt, 1989.

Haggard, Merle. *Sing Me Back Home: My Story*. New York: Times Bks., 1981.

Hallin, Daniel C. *The "Uncensored War": The Media and Vietnam*. New York: Oxford UP, 1986.

Hamill, Pete. *Why Sinatra Matters*. Boston: Little, Brown, 1998.

Harrington, Michael. *The Other America: Poverty in the United States*. New York: Macmillan, 1962.

Harris, Kristina. *Vintage Fashions for Women: The 1950s and 60s*. Atglen, PA: Schiffer, 1997.

Haskell, Barbara. *Blam! The Explosion of Pop, Minimalism, and Performance (1958–1964)*. New York: Whitney Museum of American Art and Norton, 1984.

Hayman, Ronald. *Tennessee Williams: Everyone Else Is an Audience*. New Haven: Yale UP, 1993.

Helitzer, Melvin, and Carl Heyel. *The Youth Market: Its Dimensions, Influence and Opportunities for You*. New York: Media Bks., 1970.

Hicks, Michael. *Sixties Rock: Garage, Psychedelic, and Other Satisfactions*. Urbana: U of Illinois P, 1999.

Hoffman, Elizabeth Cobbs. *All You Need Is Love: The Peace Corps and the Spirit of the 1960s*. Cambridge, MA: Harvard UP, 1998.

Hoffman, Frank W. *Sports and Recreation Fads*. New York: Haworth, 1991.

———, and William G. Bailey. *Fashion and Merchandising Fads*. New York: Haworth, 1994.

Hollowell, John. *Fact & Fiction: The New Journalism and the Nonfiction Novel*. Chapel Hill: U of North Carolina P, 1977.

Ingles, Ian, ed. *The Beatles, Popular Music and Society: A Thousand Voices*. New York: St. Martin's, 2000.

Isaacs, Neil David. *All the Moves: A History of College Basketball*. Philadelphia: Lippincott, 1975.

Jackson, John A. American Bandstand: *Dick Clark and the Making of a Rock 'N' Roll Empire*. New York: Oxford UP, 1997.

Jacobs, Jane. *The Death and Life of Great American Cities*. New York: Random House, 1961.

Jacobus, John. *Twentieth-Century Architecture: The Middle Years 1940–65*. New York: Frederick A. Praeger, 1966.

Jakle, John A. *Fast Food: Roadside Restaurants in the Automobile Age*. Baltimore: Johns Hopkins UP, 1999.

James, David E. *Allegories of Cinema: American Film in the Sixties*. Princeton: Princeton UP, 1989.

James, Jamie. *Pop Art*. Ann Arbor, MI: Borders, 1996.

Jansen, Niels. *Pictorial History of American Trucks*. Rijswijk, Holland: Elmar; Bideford, England: Bay View Bks., 1994.

Jemie, Onwuchekwa. *Langston Hughes: An Introduction to the Poetry*. New York: Columbia UP, 1976.

Johnson, Claudia D. To Kill a Mockingbird: *Threatening Boundaries*. New York: Twayne, 1994.

Johnson, Donald Leslie, and Donald Langmead. *Makers of 20th Century Modern Architecture: A Bio-Critical Sourcebook*. Westport, CT: Greenwood Press, 1997.

Jones, Dylan. *Haircuts: Fifty Years of Styles and Cuts*. New York: Thames and Hudson, 1990.

Jones, Landon Y. *Great Expectations: America and the Baby Boom Generation*. New York: Coward, McCann & Geoghegan, 1980.

Jones, Margaret. *Patsy: The Life and Times of Patsy Cline*. New York: HarperCollins, 1994.

Kahanamoku, Duke. *World of Surfing*. New York: Grosset & Dunlap, 1968.

Kahn, Louis I. *Louis I. Kahn: Writings, Lectures, Interviews*. Ed. Alessandra Latour. New York: Rizzoli, 1991.

Kaiser, Charles. *1968 in America: Music, Politics, Chaos, Counterculture, and the Shaping of a Generation*. York: Grove, 1988.

Kaiser, Inez Yeargen. *The Original Soul Food Cookery*. Rev. ed. New York: Pitman, 1968.

Karnow, Stanley. *Vietnam: A History*. Rev. ed. New York: Penguin, 1991.

Kennedy, Robert F. *Thirteen Days: A Memoir of the Cuban Missile Crisis*. New York: Norton, 1969.

Kieran, John. *The Story of the Olympic Games, 776 B.C. to 1972*. Rev. ed. Philadelphia: Lippincott, 1973.

King, Billie Jean. *We Have Come a Long Way: The Story of Women's Tennis*. New York: McGraw-Hill, 1988.

Kirby, Michael. *Happenings*. New York: Dutton, 1965.

Klinkowitz, Jerome. *The American 1960's: Imaginative Acts in a Decade of Change*. Ames: Iowa State UP, 1980.

Kluger, Richard. *Simple Justice: The History of Brown v. Board of Education and Black America's Struggle for Equality*. 1975; New York: Knopf, 1976.

Knight, Janet M., ed. *Three Assassinations: The Deaths of John and Robert Kennedy and Martin Luther King*. New York: Facts on File, 1971.

Kofsky, Frank. *John Coltrane and the Jazz Revolution of the 1960s*. 2nd ed. New York: Pathfinder, 1998.

Kowinski, William S. *The Malling of America*. New York: Morrow, 1985.

Kroc, Ray, and Robert Anderson. *Grinding It Out: The Making of McDonald's*. Chicago: Contemporary Bks., 1977.

Lee, Martin A., and Bruce Shlain. *Acid Dreams: The Complete Social History of LSD: The CIA, the Sixties, and Beyond*. Rev. Evergreen ed. New York: Grove Weidenfeld, 1992.

Leeming, David Adams. *James Baldwin: A Biography*. New York: Knopf, 1994.

Leff, Leonard J., and Jerold L. Simmons. *The Dame in the Kimono: Hollywood, Censorship, and the Production Code from the 1920's to the 1960's*. New York: Grove Weidenfeld, 1990.

Levenson, Bob. *Bill Bernbach's Book: A History of the Advertising that Changed the History of Advertising*. New York: Villard Bks., 1987.

Levenstein, Harvey. *Paradox of Plenty: A Social History of Eating in Modern America*. New York: Oxford UP, 1992.

Levy, Peter B. *The New Left and Labor in the 1960s*. Urbana: U of Illinois P, 1994.

Lindenberger, Jan. *Clothing and Accessories from the '40s, '50s and '60s: A Handbook and Price Guide*. Atglen, PA: Schiffer, 1996.

Linden-Ward, Blanche, and Carol Hurd Green. *American Women in the 1960s: Changing the Future*. New York: Twayne, 1993.

Lipset, Seymour Martin, and Sheldon S. Wolin. *The Berkeley Student Revolt: Facts and Interpretations*. Garden City, NY: Anchor Bks., 1965.

Livingstone, Marco. *Pop Art: A Continuing History*. New York: Abrams, 1990.

Lloyd, Ann, ed. *Movies of the Sixties*. London: Orbis, 1983.

Lobenthal, Joel. *Radical Rags: Fashions of the Sixties*. New York: Abbeville, 1990.

Lois, George. *Covering the '60s: George Lois, the Esquire Era*. New York: Monacelli, 1996.

Longrigg, Roger. *The History of Horse Racing*. New York: Stein and Day, 1972.

Lopate, Phillip. *The Art of the Essay*. New York: Anchor Bks., 1999.

Lord, M.G. *Forever Barbie: The Unauthorized Biography of a Real Doll*. New York: Morrow, 1994.

Lovegren, Sylvia. *Fashionable Food: Seven Decades of Food Fads*. New York: Macmillan, 1995.

Lucie-Smith, Edward. *Movements in Art Since 1945: Issues and Concepts*. 3rd ed. 1995. London: Thames and Hudson, 1998.

Lydon, Michael. *Ray Charles: Man and Music*. New York: Riverhead, 1998.

Lynn, Loretta. *Loretta Lynn: Coal Miner's Daughter*. Chicago: Regnery, 1976.

MacDonald, J. Fred. *Black and White TV: African Americans in Television Since 1948*. 2nd ed. Chicago: Nelson-Hall, 1992.

———. *Who Shot the Sheriff?: The Rise and Fall of the Television Western*. New York: Praeger, 1987.

Mailer, Norman. *Pontifications: Interviews*. Ed. Michael Lennon. Boston: Little, Brown, 1982.

Malin, Irving. *Truman Capote's* In Cold Blood: *A Critical Handbook*. Belmont, CA: Wadsworth, 1968.

Marable, Manning. *Race, Reform, and Rebellion: The Second Reconstruction in Black America, 1945–1990*. 2nd ed. Jackson: UP of Mississippi, 1991.

Maraniss, David. *When Pride Still Mattered: A Life of Vince Lombardi*. New York: Simon and Schuster, 1999.

Marc, David. *Comic Visions: Television Comedy and American Culture*. 2nd ed. Malden, MA: Blackwell, 1997.

Marcus, Eric. *Making History: The Struggle for Gay and Lesbian Equal Rights, 1945–1990: An Oral History*. New York: HarperCollins, 1992.

Mariani, John F. *America Eats Out*. New York: Morrow, 1991.

Marqusee, Mike. *Muhammad Ali and the Spirit of the Sixties*. New York: Verso, 1999.

Marwick, Arthur. *The Sixties*. 1998. New York: Oxford UP, 1999.

Mary Quant's London. London: London Museum (exhibition catalogue), 1973.

May, Elaine Tyler. *Homeward Bound: American Families in the Cold War Era*. Rev. ed. New York: Basic Books, 1999.

McKeen, William. *Tom Wolfe*. New York: Twayne, 1995.

McKuen, Rod. *Finding My Father: One Man's Search for Identity*. Los Angeles: Cheval Bks., 1976.

Mead, Christopher, ed. *The Architecture of Robert Venturi*. Albuquerque: U of New Mexico P, 1989.

Mead, William B. *The Explosive Sixties: Baseball's Decade of Expansion*. New Berlin, WI: Redefinition, 1989.

Melody, William. *Children's TV: The Economics of Exploitation*. New Haven, CT: Yale UP, 1973.

Melton, J. Gordon. *Encyclopedia of American Religions*. 6th ed. Detroit: Gale Research, 1999.

Meyer, Ursula. *Conceptual Art*. New York: Dutton, 1972.

Miller, James. *Flowers in the Dustbin: The Rise of Rock and Roll, 1947–1977*. New York: Simon and Schuster, 1999.

Mills, Kay. *Something Better for My Children: The History and People of Head Start*. New York: Dutton, 1998.

Mitford, Jessica. *The Trial of Dr. Spock, the Rev. William Sloane Coffin, Jr., Michael Ferber, Mitchell Goodman, and Marcus Raskin*. New York: Knopf, 1969.

Monaghan, Thomas S., and Robert Anderson. *Pizza Tiger*. New York: Random House, 1986.

Morella, Joe. *Simon and Garfunkel: Old Friends, A Dual Biography*. New York: Carol, 1991.

Myers, Robert Julius. *Medicare*. Homewood, IL: For McCahan Foundation by R.D. Irwin, 1970.

Nader, Ralph. *Unsafe at Any Speed: The Designed-in Dangers of the American Automobile*. New York: Grossman, 1965.

Natalle, Elizabeth J. *Feminist Theatre: A Study in Persuasion*. Metuchen, NJ: Scarecrow, 1985.

Nelson, Cordner. *The Jim Ryun Story*. Los Altos, CA: Tafnews, 1967.

Nicklaus, Jack. *Jack Nicklaus: My Story*. New York: Simon and Schuster, 1997.

Norins, Hanley. *The Young & Rubicam Traveling Creative Workshop*. Englewood Cliffs, NJ: Prentice-Hall, 1990.

Norris, Floyd, and Christine Bockelmann. The New York Times *Century of Business*. New York: McGraw-Hill, 2000.

Nureyev, Rudolf. *Nureyev: An Autobiography*. New York: Dutton, 1963.

Ogilvy, David. *Blood, Brains and Beer: The Autobiography of David Ogilvy*. New York: Atheneum, 1977.

Ohls, James C., and Harold Beebout. *The Food Stamp Program: Design Tradeoffs, Policy, and Impacts: A Mathematical Policy Research Study*. Lanham, MD: UP of America, 1993.

Olian, JoAnne, ed. *Everyday Fashions of the Sixties: As Pictured in Sears Catalogs*. Mineola, NY: Dover, 1999.

O'Neill, William L. *Coming Apart: An Informal History of America in the 1960's*. Chicago: Quadrangle Bks., 1971.

Owens, Louis. *Other Destinies: Understanding the American Indian Novel*. Norman: U of Oklahoma P, 1992.

Palmer, Arnold. *A Golfer's Life*. New York: Ballantine, 1999.

Panati, Charles. *Panati's Parade of Fads, Follies, and Manias: The Origins of Our Most Cherished Obsessions*. New York: HarperCollins, 1991.

Pearson, Roberta E., and William Uricchio. *The Many Lives of the Batman: Critical Approaches to a Superhero and His Media*. New York: Routledge, 1991.

Peck, Abe. *Uncovering the Sixties: The Life and Times of the Underground Press*. New York: Pantheon, 1985.

Peterson, Theodore. *Magazines in the Twentieth Century*. 2nd ed. Urbana: U of Illinois P, 1964.

Phillips, Gene D. *Stanley Kubrick: A Film Odyssey*. New York: Popular Library, 1975.

Pichaske, David R. *A Generation in Motion: Popular Music and Culture in the Sixties*. New York: Schirmer Bks., 1979.

Pinsker, Sanford. *Jewish-American Fiction, 1917–1987*. New York: Twayne, 1992.

Pollack, Howard. *Aaron Copland: The Life and Work of an Uncommon Man*. New York: Henry Holt, 1999.

Polsky, Richard M. *Getting to Sesame Street: Origins of the Children's Television Workshop*. New York: Praeger, 1974.

Polykoff, Shirley. *Does She . . . or Doesn't She?: And How She Did It*. Garden City, NY: Doubleday, 1975.

Potts, Stephen W. *Catch-22: Antiheroic Antinovel*. Boston: Twayne, 1989.

Prince, Stephen. *Savage Cinema: Sam Peckinpah and the Rise of Ultraviolent Movies*. Austin: U of Texas P, 1998.

Pym, John, ed. *Time Out: Film Guide*. 8th ed. New York: Penguin, 1999.

Quant, Mary. *Quant by Quant*. London: Cassell, 1966.

Regan, Richard J. *Conflict and Consensus: Religious Freedom and the Second Vatican Council*. New York: Macmillan, 1967.

Richards, Stanley, ed. *Best Plays of the Sixties*. Garden City, NY: Doubleday, 1970.

Rielly, Edward J. *Baseball: An Encyclopedia of Popular Culture*. Santa Barbara, CA: ABC-CLIO, 2000.

Rifkind, Carole. *A Field Guide to Contemporary American Architecture*. New York: Dutton, 1998.

Riley, Clara, and Frances M. J. Epps. *Head Start in Action*. West Nyack, NY: Parker, 1967.

Ritzer, George. *The McDonaldization of Society*. Thousand Oaks, CA: Pine Forge, 2000.

Robert, Ron E. *The New Communes: Coming Together in America*. Englewood Cliffs, NJ: Prentice-Hall, 1971.

Roorbach, Bill, ed. *Contemporary Creative Nonfiction: The Art of Truth*. New York: Oxford UP, 2001.

Rudolph, Wilma. *Wilma*. New York: New American Library, 1977.

Rutenberg, Michael E. *Edward Albee: Playwright in Protest*. New York: DBS Publications, 1969.

Sander, Gordon F. *Serling: The Rise and Twilight of Television's Last Angry Man*. New York: Dutton, 1992.

Sandler, Irving. *American Art of the 1960s*. New York: Harper & Row, 1988.

Santelli, Robert, and Emily Davidson, eds. *Hard Travelin': The Life and Lagacy of Woody Guthrie*. Hanover, NH: UP of New England, 1999.

Sayre, Nora. *Sixties Going on Seventies*. Rev. ed. New Brunswick, NJ: Rutgers UP, 1996.

Scholes, Robert E. *Fabulation and Metafiction*. Urbana: U of Illinois P, 1979.

Schwienher, William K. *Lawrence Welk: An American Institution*. Chicago: Nelson-Hall, 1980.

Searles, George J., ed. *A Casebook on Ken Kesey's* One Flew Over the Cuckoo's Nest. Albuquerque: U of New Mexico P, 1992.

Segrave, Kerry. *Payola in the Music Industry: A History, 1880–1991*. Jefferson, NC: McFarland, 1994.

Shapiro, Gary. *Earthwards: Robert Smithson and Art After Babel*. Berkeley: U of California P, 1995.

Shapiro, Harry. *Jimi Hendrix: Electric Guitar*. 1990. New York: St. Martin's, 1991.

Sharp, Dennis. *Twentieth Century Architecture: A Visual History*. New York: Facts on File, 1991.

Shaughnessy, Dan. *Ever Green: The Boston Celtics: A History in the Words of their Players, Coaches, Fans, and Foes, from 1946 to the Present*. New York: St. Martin's, 1990.

Sheppard, Dick. *Elizabeth: The Life and Career of Elizabeth Taylor*. Garden City, NY: Doubleday, 1974.

Shippey, T.A. J.R.R. *Tolkien: Author of the Century*. Boston: Houghton Mifflin, 2001.

Simon, Neil. *The Play Goes On: A Memoir*. New York: Simon and Schuster, 1999.

Singleton, Carl, ed. *The Sixties in America*. 3 vols. Pasadena, CA: Salem, 1999.

Smith, Michael, ed. *The Best of Off Off-Broadway*. New York: Dutton, 1969.

Spada, James. *Barbra, The First Decade: The Films and Career of Barbra Streisand*. Secaucus, NJ: Citadel, 1974.

Spigel, Lynn, and Michael Curtin, eds. *The Revolution Wasn't Televised: Sixties Television and Social Conflict*. New York: Routledge, 1997.

Spitz, Bob. *Dylan: A Biography*. New York: McGraw-Hill, 1989.

Sports Illustrated *2000 Sports Almanac*. Kingston, NY: *Sports Illustrated*, 1999.

Stambler, Irwin. *The Encyclopedia of Pop, Rock and Soul*. Rev. ed. New York: St. Martin's, 1989.

———, and Grelun Landon. *Country Music: The Encyclopedia*. 3rd ed. New York: St. Martin's Griffin, 1997.

Stein, Harry. *Tiny Tim: An Unauthorized Biography*. Chicago: Playboy, 1976.

Stern, Jane, and Michael Stern. *Sixties People*. New York: Knopf, 1990.

Sterritt, David. *The Films of Alfred Hitchcock*. New York: Cambridge UP, 1993.

Stich, Sidra. *Made in the U.S.A.: An Americanization in Modern Art, the '50s amd '60s*. Berkeley: U of California P, 1987.

Stolley, Richard B., and Editors of Time-Life Books. *Turbulent Years: The 60s*. Alexandria, VA: Time-Life, 1998.

Stone, Albert E. *The Return of Nat Turner: History, Literature, and Cultural Politics in Sixties America*. Athens: U of Georgia P, 1992.

Sullivan, George. *How Do They Package It?* Philadelphia: Westminster, 1976.

Summers, Harry G. *Vietnam War Almanac*. New York: Facts on File, 1985.

Taper, Bernard. *Balanchine: A Biography*. New York: Times Bks., 1984.

Tischler, Barbara L., ed. *Sights on the Sixties*. New Brunswick, NJ: Rutgers UP, 1992.

Trager, James. *The Food Chronology: A Food Lover's Compendium of Events and Anecdotes, from Prehistory to the Present*. 1995. New York: Henry Holt, 1997.

United States Surgeon General's Scientific Advisory Committee on Television and Social Behavior. *Television and Growing Up: The Impact of Televised Violence*. Rockville, MD: National Institute for Mental Health, 1972.

Varnedoe, Kirk, and Adam Gopnik. *High and Low: Modern Art and Popular Culture* (exhibition catalog). New York: Museum of Modern Art, 1990. Distributed by Abrams.

Venturi, Robert. *Complexity and Contradiction in Architecture*. 2nd ed. New York: Museum of Modern Art, 1977.

———. *Learning from Las Vegas: The Forgotten Symbolism of Architectural Form*. Rev. ed. Cambridge, MA: MIT, 1977.

Vergine, Lea. *Body Art and Performance: The Body as Language*. New York: Abbeville, 2000.

Viorst, Milton. *Fire in the Streets: America in the 1960s*. New York: Simon and Schuster, 1979.

Waldman, Anne, ed. *The Beat Book: Poems and Fiction of the Beat Generation*. Boston: Shambhala, 1996.

Wallis, Michael. *Route 66: The Mother Road*. New York: St. Martin's, 1990.

Ward, Geoffrey C., and Ken Burns. *Baseball: An Illustrated History*. New York: Alfred A. Knopf, 1994.

———. *Jazz: A History of America's Music*. New York: Alfred A. Knopf, 2000.

Warhol, Andy. *The Andy Warhol Diaries*. Ed. Pat Hackett. New York: Warner, 1989.

———, and Pat Hackett. *POPism: The Warhol '60s*. New York: Harcourt, 1980.

Weiskopf, Herm. *The Perfect Game* @Bowling#. Englewood Cliffs, NJ: Prentice-Hall, 1978.

We Seven, by the Astronauts Themselves. New York: Simon and Schuster, 1962.

Williams, Juan. *Eyes on the Prize: America's Civil Rights Years, 1954–1965*. New York: Viking, 1987.

Williams, Tennessee. *Memoirs*. 1972. Garden City, NY: Doubleday, 1975.

Wilson, Brian. *Wouldn't It Be Nice: My Own Story*. New York: HarperCollins, 1991.

Wind, Herbert Warren. *Game, Set, and Match: The Tennis Boom of the 1960's and 70's.* New York: Dutton, 1979.

Winogrand, Garry. *The Animals*. New York: Museum of Modern Art, 1969.

Wolfe, Tom, and E. W. Johnson, eds. *The New Journalism*. New York: Harper & Row, 1973.

Wooden, John R. *They Call Me Coach*. Rev. ed. Chicago: Contemporary Bks., 1988.

Workman, Brooke. *Teaching the Sixties: An In-Depth, Interactive, Interdisciplinary Approach*. Urbana, IL: National Council of Teachers of English, 1992.

Wright, Gwendolyn, and Janet Parks, eds. *History of History in American Schools of Architecture, 1865–1975*. New York: Temple Hoyne Buell Center for the Study of American Architecture and Princeton Architectural P, 1990.

Wright, John W., ed. *The Commercial Connection: Advertising and the American Mass Media*. New York: Dell, 1979.

Yoggy, Gary A. *Riding the Video Range: The Rise and Fall of the Western on Television*. Jefferson, NC: McFarland, 1995.

Young, Al, ed. *African-American Literature: A Brief Introduction and Anthology*. New York: HarperCollins, 1996.

Index

About the Author

EDWARD J. RIELLY is Professor of English at St. Joseph's College of Maine.

RIDLEY TOWNSHIP PUBLIC LIBRARY
FOLSOM, PA 19033
610-583-0593